CONNECTING TO LEARN

CONNECTING TO LEARN

Educational and Assistive Technology for People With Disabilities

Marcia J. Scherer

American Psychological Association
Washington, DC

Published by
American Psychological Association
750 First Street, NE
Washington, DC 20002
www.apa.org

To order
APA Order Department
P.O. Box 92984
Washington, DC 20090-2984
Tel: (800) 374-2721;
Direct: (202) 336-5510
Fax: (202) 336-5502;
TDD/TTY: (202) 336-6123
Online: www.apa.org/books/
E-mail: order@apa.org

In the U.K., Europe, Africa, and the Middle East, copies may be ordered from
American Psychological Association
3 Henrietta Street
Covent Garden, London
WC2E 8LU England

Typeset in Goudy by World Composition Services, Inc., Sterling, VA

Printer: United Book Press, Inc., Baltimore, MD
Cover Designer: Aqueous Studio, Arlington, VA
Technical/Production Editor: Dan Brachtesende

The opinions and statements published are the responsibility of the authors, and such opinions and statements do not necessarily represent the policies of the American Psychological Association.

Library of Congress Cataloging-in-Publication Data

Scherer, Marcia J. (Marcia Joslyn), 1948–
    Connecting to learn : educational and assistive technology for people with disabilities / Marcia J. Scherer.—1st ed.
        p. cm.
    Includes bibliographical references and index.
    ISBN 1-55798-982-6
    1. People with disabilities—Education—United States. 2. People with disabilities—United States—Computer-assisted instruction. 3. Self-help devices for people with disabilities—United States. 4. Assistive listening systems—United States. I. Title.

LC4812.S34   2004
371.9'043—dc21   2003051877

British Library Cataloguing-in-Publication Data
A CIP record is available from the British Library.

Printed in the United States of America
First Edition

For the students and their educators of today and tomorrow.
In your hands lies the future of us all.

CONTENTS

vii

FOREWORD

LAWRENCE A. SCADDEN

This volume, *Connecting to Learn: Educational and Assistive Technology for People With Disabilities*, written by Dr. Marcia Scherer, is a rare resource that is written in a compelling style. Dr. Scherer's use of case histories, interviews, and personal observations enlivens the discussion of how technology affects the lives of people with auditory and visual disabilities. Quotes from and observations by others—teachers, parents, therapists, and researchers—provide an excellent and balanced perspective to the many topics discussed in this book.

The review of the technologies used by people with varying degrees of hearing and vision loss provides a good introduction to the tools that allow millions of people with sensory disabilities to adapt to their environments and to live full and productive lives. The evolution of educational approaches available to people with hearing and vision loss clearly illustrates the simultaneous evolution of societal attitudes toward disability and the important roles played by technology that have facilitated these changes.

Throughout the book, Dr. Scherer returns to the theme that people with sensory disabilities continue to have abilities that are augmented through the use of *appropriate* technologies. Even with the technological tools, however, self-actualization by people with sensory disabilities is significantly affected by the attitudes of others. The social context in which the technology is acquired and used cannot be overlooked. Technology on its own is not a panacea; it remains a potentially valuable tool that people can use to enhance existing abilities. The level to which these abilities can be used is tempered by relationships with others.

This book should be a highly valuable resource for anyone interested in improving the lives of people with sensory disabilities. Besides the compelling discussions of technology, the book contains good statistical data regarding the incidence of hearing and vision disabilities in the United States as well as many useful charts, tables, and figures. The enclosed resources should be of value to many professionals and nonprofessionals who seek to understand the magnitude of the problems and ways in which the lives of persons with sensory disabilities can be enhanced personally, socially, and educationally.

PREFACE

The subtitle of this book is "Educational and Assistive Technology for People With Disabilities." The reader will note that this book focuses on people with vision and hearing loss—those with sensory disabilities—and uses examples from childhood through adulthood. Educational technologies and assistive technologies are discussed throughout this text as well as a variety of learning environments. I believe that the recommendations and strategies for people with hearing or eyesight loss provided here have wide applicability, especially for those who have a learning disability. Thus, I hope that the reader will easily find applications to people with other disabilities (or no disabilities at all), to education in the broadest sense, and to life in general.

In 1993, I wrote the first edition of *Living in the State of Stuck: How Technology Impacts the Lives of People With Disabilities*. That book included examples of adults with cerebral palsy or spinal cord injury and their perspectives on the use of assistive technologies for mobility and communication in their daily routines, their quality of life, and the rehabilitation process. The book emerged from my doctoral dissertation (University of Rochester) and I wrote it while I was a research associate in educational research and development (and later, evaluation specialist in instructional design and evaluation), National Technical Institute for the Deaf (NTID), Rochester Institute of Technology in Rochester, New York. Also during this time I taught educational psychology at the Eastman School of Music, University of Rochester. Then, in 1994, a national symposium on technologies for people with either hearing or vision loss was sponsored by NTID and supported by the U.S. Department of Education. My role on the symposium organizing team and as symposium evaluator led to my increased interest in the topics of the symposium and the learners to whom it was addressed.

But it is my experiences in all these roles that formed my interest in and knowledge of the substantive content of this book. This book was truly a pleasure to write, and I hope you find it of merit and benefit as you work to enhance learning for people with all types of disabilities and at all levels of education.

ACKNOWLEDGMENTS

Much gratitude is due to the individuals who have encouraged and supported me as I wrote this book. First, to my husband John Scherer, an electrical engineer, many thanks for the forgone social life and all your help, including the wonderful diagrams you did for this book. As a *techie*, he observed years ago that not enough attention was being given to the users of technologies and their needs and preferences, which prompted him to say to me, "Maybe this is an area you could look into."

Second, my appreciation is extended to Drs. Larry Scadden, Larry Goldberg, and Anne Duryea Astmann for reviewing and insightfully commenting on drafts of the book chapters. Third, to Drs. Barbara McKee and Robert Frisina at the National Technical Institute for the Deaf/Rochester Institute of Technology for their help and friendship over so many years now. And fourth, to Dr. Gerald Craddock, for adapting and applying my work throughout the Republic of Ireland.

Development editor Ed Meidenbauer, assistant director Mary Lynn Skutley, acquisitions editor Susan Reynolds, marketing specialist Russ Bahorsky, production editor Dan Brachtesende, and all of APA Books receive my heartfelt appreciation for their support of this book and on-going guidance.

I greatly appreciate the photographs made available by Mark Benjamin at the National Technical Institute for the Deaf/Rochester Institute of Technology, the Rochester Hearing and Speech Center, and Dr. Deborah Gilden, Smith-Kettlewell Eye Research Institute. Thanks to you all, for otherwise it would be very difficult for readers to envision some of the available technology devices and systems.

Finally, tremendous gratitude is expressed to the students and educators, with or without hearing or eyesight loss, who shared their thoughts and experiences with me. Their frustrations and satisfactions, successes and failures, and hopes and dreams for what the future can be fueled me as I wrote and became the foundation on which this book was built.

I

INTRODUCTION

1

THE FUNDAMENTAL SENSE
OF CONNECTEDNESS

You have to make the choice between being connected and not
connected.

—A deaf woman

Life is going on all around me and I don't feel connected to any of it
. . . not to anyone or anything.

—A young adult with recent deafness

There is more than a verbal tie between the words common, community,
and communication.

—John Dewey, 1916

This is one person's description of what it is like when you cannot hear:

I felt different, socially different. I felt handicapped in not knowing
how to play the game. I felt that there were a lot of rules of conduct
out there that were not written rules of behavior. I did not know what
they were, so I would just violate some code of behavior. There were
times when that just ruined my self-confidence. I always felt I was on
the outside looking in. There was a glass window there, and I couldn't
get by it.

And another person describes hearing loss as follows:

I would get very irritable when I couldn't hear because it took so much
energy. I used to lie in bed in the morning and try my hearing aid.
And I could hear all kinds of things that I never heard in my life before,
and I thought, wow, this is really amazing. But I couldn't wear it . . .
the stigma . . . the embarrassment. And then as I got older and it was
such a help . . . I really felt as though it was a choice between being
connected and not being connected. My hearing aid was so beneficial,
that [stigma] was not really an issue anymore.

Hearing has been characterized as occurring on three psychological levels: (a) the *social or symbolic level,* which is the capability to receive and understand language (in other words, to communicate with others); (b) the *signal or warning level,* which enables people to respond to such cues as a baby's cry or a fire alarm; and (c) the *level of fundamental "connectedness,"* which gives people the sense of being in touch with the surrounding environment even though perhaps not consciously aware of such sounds as people moving around the house, traffic, and so on (Davis, 1997). It is the last level, the fundamental sense of connectedness, that gives quality to life and defines the world as being "alive." This quality to life, fundamental connectedness, is the main topic of this book. How it can be enhanced by today's technologies in light of current social priorities and educational practices is a key theme.

For people with vision loss, there also can be a loss of a sense of connectedness, a social isolation, and a feeling of being out of touch with what is occurring in the world. This is one person's description of what it is like when you cannot see:

> We had a meeting in New York and everything we did was the wrong thing to do and we ended up in the heart of Harlem. Me, a blind guy, and Tom, who can't see. Here we were, these two white guys and we were scared. We couldn't see to get help or even to know where to go to find a phone or anything. It was frightening to be so lost and, frankly, in that situation, helpless. It must be similar for people who do not speak English and who come here from another country, and have never been in such a big city before. But you know? People did, in fact, come up to us. But all they wanted to do was help.

Fear of the unknown, being unable to identify environmental cues so many of us take for granted, can result in anxiety for a person who is blind, but it can simultaneously bring out compassion in others for the nature of this situation. Another person says

> I think of all the different disabilities, there's an attitude about blindness that exists for no other disability. I can get anything I want from anybody I want. Actually, oversolicitousness is common. There's an attitude about blindness. I've never understood it, but I know it exists.

For a person who cannot see at all (who is blind), being able to get around independently is a big challenge. Specialized training in orienting oneself to environmental cues and assistance from a cane, guide dog, or another person are required. For both those who are blind and those with very low vision, reading and writing independently are also big challenges. There's a loss of privacy when you have to have a personal letter, bank statement, or whatever read to you by another person. Many persons with vision loss use audiotapes or take advantage of radio reading services, but these can't help with many forms of personal correspondence. And the act of listening is fatiguing. As one person said to me, "After a while I get tired of listening to tapes. My mind wanders and it's hard to concentrate. You can't listen forever."

INFORMATION IS THE
VITAL LINK TO CONNECTION

Hansell (1974) conceptualized seven essential attachments to the world in which we live, attachments consisting of a connection to other people, to a social role, and to the feeling one matters and that one's life is meaningful. Hansell's seven essential attachments necessary to achieve a high quality of life are the following:

1. supports necessary for existence (food, oxygen, information),
2. identity,
3. connection with other people,
4. connection to groups,
5. connection to a social role,
6. money and purchasing power, and
7. a system of meaning.

The seven essential attachments are interdependent, and all are necessary for a positive sense of self and a feeling of well-being. When there is a slight imbalance, readjustments can be made by, for example, getting hearing aids. But, as indicated by one of the quotes at the beginning of this chapter, such an attempt at readjustment can lead to new stressors, like feeling stigmatized. Throughout our lives, we are often in a process of rebalancing or reestablishing our sense of self and our subjective well-being.

Hansell's (1974) theory speaks well to the goals we have for students in today's varied education settings, from preschool through high school and college to continuing education in the workplace. It addresses particularly well the issues facing today's educational system as it confronts its mandate to connect individuals to other people, groups, and social roles; provide the knowledge necessary to be a productive member of society; and help individuals achieve a sense of identity, purpose, and meaning. Defining effective educational practices and qualified educators in a technology-rich society, however, is one of the largest challenges facing education in the 21st century.

Hansell's (1974) first, and key, attachment is one's dependency on the environment for life's basic needs: food, water, air, and information. Without information, an individual can experience social seclusion and is at risk for psychological distress. According to Hansell,

Abundantly flowing raw sensation provides a necessary engine for experience. Informative variety and pattern provide organization to the experiencer as well as body to the experience. When the flow of information is severely restricted [as with certain solitary styles of life or those resulting from isolation due to hearing or vision loss], the attachment to information often must be considered severed, or at risk of severance. (pp. 35–36)

Hansell believed that communication must be reciprocal. Just as we need certain information to thrive ("You need to see a doctor for that infection"), we also need to be able to send or feed back certain kinds of information ("I'm allergic to penicillin"). When we have reciprocity of communication, we have the ingredients for a positive communication interchange, which can lead to an enhanced sense of well-being.

Information and communication competence and involvement are keys to a successful life. Without them, people are typically left outside of the mainstream of society. For those who cannot hear the spoken word or cannot see text or visual images, it can truly be said that communication as well as sensory disabilities exist.

THE PREVALENCE AND INCIDENCE OF HEARING AND VISION LOSS IN THE UNITED STATES

A major obstacle individuals with severe hearing or vision loss must contend with is the fact that sensory disabilities are considered to be "low incidence." That is, they constitute a small proportion of the general population, and even among people with disabilities, they are a minority. Thus, it can be challenging to form relationships with age- and interest-related peers as well as with those sharing the same disability.

Focusing on those ages 6 to 21, the U.S. Department of Education (1998a) reported that during the 1996–1997 school year, 68,766 (or 1.3% of all students with disabilities) received special education services under the category of "hearing impairment." However, the number of children with hearing loss and deafness is undoubtedly higher, because many of these students may have other disabilities as well and may be served under other categories.

Statistical data related to disabilities are notoriously difficult to locate, can report discrepant figures, and are frequently out of date (e.g., LaPlante, 1995). Data from the National Health Interview Survey (1995) indicate that the prevalence of hearing impairments was 85.8 per 1,000 people (22,465,000). The Departments of Commerce and Labor provide a figure similar to that from the 1995 National Health Interview Survey, a count of approximately 22 million. The figure used by the National Institutes of

Health (NIH), however, is 28 million Americans with hearing loss. Strassler (1999), editor of the online publication DEAFDIGEST GOLD, noted these discrepant figures and commented,

> How many Americans have hearing loss? Ask NIH—they will tell you 28 million; ask the Departments of Commerce and Labor and they will tell you—in unison—that the count is 22 million. When government agencies feud over numbers then our missing 6 million may be factored into services that will not be available to us.

Definitions of hearing or vision loss vary from study to study. The above statistics may divide Americans into different age groupings, may or may not include noncivilian and noninstitutionalized individuals, and may rely on less reliable self-reports of hearing or eyesight loss as opposed to data obtained from audiometric or ophthalmic testing.

Although hearing loss can occur suddenly or over time at any point during an individual's life span, the incidence does rise sharply with age. Demographic data from the U.S. Census Bureau have consistently shown a rise in the absolute numbers and percentages of U.S. citizens over the age of 50 years. In 1985 there were 61.7 million people 50 years and older, a number that increased to over 76 million in the year 2000. This number exceeds the total number of Americans 100 years earlier in 1900.

Accommodation to a person's hearing loss must occur with every interaction, every communication. This requires extra effort by everyone involved, such as family members, friends, teachers, classmates, employers, and coworkers. Thus, for each person with a hearing loss there are probably at least three key people who are also affected in important ways. Using a compromise figure of 25 million people with hearing loss in the United States today, and multiplying that by four (the person with hearing loss and three significant others) yields a figure of approximately 100 million people across the nation, or 40% of the nation, who are directly affected by hearing loss.

As with hearing loss, severe vision loss in those age 18 and under is considered to be a "low incidence" disability. Their opportunities in the typical public school to interact with peers with the same disability and at the same age are minimal and as was found with data on hearing loss, data on vision loss from one source are not always consistent with those from other sources. Data from the 1995 U.S. National Health Interview Survey indicate that in that year, the prevalence of visual impairments in the general U.S. population was 32.5 per 1,000 persons (8,511,000). The prevalence of hearing impairments was 85.8 per 1,000 persons (22,465,000). If we consider just individuals age 18 and under, data from the National Information Center for Children and Youth With Disabilities (2001b) indicate that approximately 12 out of every 1,000 students (1.2%) have a "visual impairment." If we consider only students who are legally or totally blind, then there will only be approximately 1 out of every 2,000 students (0.05%).

There are 13 disability categories listed in the Individuals With Disabilities Education Act (IDEA) classification:

1. specific learning disabilities,
2. speech or language impairments,
3. mental retardation,
4. emotional disturbance,
5. multiple disabilities,
6. hearing impairments,
7. orthopedic impairments,
8. other health impairments,
9. visual impairments,
10. autism,
11. deafness,
12. deaf-blindness, and
13. traumatic brain injury.

However, more than 90% of the school-age students served under IDEA during 1996–1997 were classified in one of four disability categories: learning disabilities (51.1%), speech or language impairments (20.1%), mental retardation (11.4%), and emotional disturbance (8.6%). Only 1.3% were classified as having a hearing impairment and 0.5% with a visual impairment. Together, students with visual and hearing impairments represent not quite 2% of the total number of elementary and secondary students with disabilities (U.S. Department of Education, 1998a). For this reason, the President's Commission on Excellence in Special Education (2002) report, "A New Era: Revitalizing Special Education for Children and Their Families," recommends replacing the above 13 categories with the following 3 categories:

1. *sensory disabilities*, such as visual impairments, hearing impairments, deaf-blindness; identified on the basis of vision and hearing tests;
2. *physical and neurological disabilities*, such as orthopedic impairments, other health impairments, traumatic brain injury, multiple disabilities, autism; identified by parents and physicians through medical history and physical examinations;
3. *developmental disabilities*, such as specific learning disabilities, speech and language impairments, emotional disturbance, mild mental retardation, and developmental delay; closely linked with teacher referral and psychometric tests for identification; according to the report, "The disorder is always a matter of

TABLE 1.1

Children From Birth to Age 21 Who Were Served by Federally Supported Programs for Students With Disabilities, as a Percentage of Total Public K–12 Enrollment: 1976–1977 to 1995–1996

Type of disability	1976–1977	1980–1981	1990–1991	1995–1996
All disabilities	8.33	10.13	11.55	12.43
Hearing impairments	0.20	0.19	0.14	0.15
Visual impairments	0.09	0.08	0.06	0.06

Note. Based on the enrollment in public schools, kindergarten through 12th grade, including a relatively small number of prekindergarten students. From *Digest of Education Statistics,* by the National Center for Education Statistics, U.S. Department of Education, 1999, Table 52, p. 65. In the public domain.

degree on a dimension, not a disorder that you either have or do not have, and identification is ultimately a judgment based on the need for services."

These recommended changes in the identification process may be included in the reauthorized IDEA.

According to the U.S. Department of Education, Office of Special Education and Rehabilitative Services (2001), the number of school-age students (i.e., ages 6 through 21 years old) with disabilities served has increased at a higher rate than the general school enrollment over the past several years. Between 1977 and 1995, the number of students involved in federal programs for children with disabilities increased 47%, whereas total public school enrollment decreased by 2%. During the 1996–1997 school year, more than 5.2 million students ages 6 through 21 with disabilities were served under IDEA, a 3.1% increase over the previous year. Over the past 10 years, the number of students ages 6 to 11 with disabilities increased 25.3%, the number of students ages 12 to 17 with disabilities increased 30.7%, and the number of students ages 18 to 21 with disabilities increased 14.7%. Table 1.1 shows the increasing numbers of children with disabilities (from birth to age 21) served in public elementary and secondary schools from 1976 through 1996.

DEGREES OF HEARING LOSS AND USE OF ASSISTANCE: HEARING AIDS AND ASSISTIVE TECHNOLOGIES HELP PEOPLE TO CONNECT

An assistive technology, called AT for short, as defined by law is "any item, piece of equipment, or product system, whether acquired commercially off the shelf, modified, or customized, that is used to increase, maintain, or

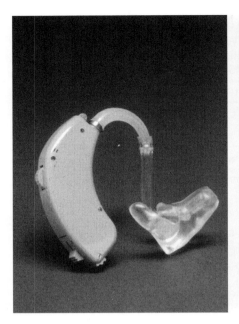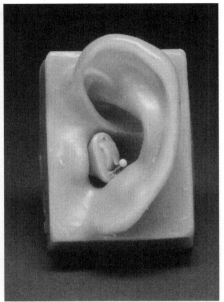

Figure 1.1. Examples of behind-the-ear and in-the-ear hearing aids. Courtesy of the National Technical Institute for the Deaf/Rochester Institute of Technology, Rochester, New York.

improve functional capabilities of individuals with disabilities" (Technology-Related Assistance of Individuals With Disabilities Act of 1988, Pub. L. 100-819, p. 3). An AT for a person with hearing loss can be the key to being connected to one's world. It may be something as simple as a vibro-tactile pager, flashing timer, strobe light alarm, and a dial on a telephone to amplify the sound being received. Hearing aids, which come in a variety of styles (two of which are shown in Figure 1.1), are one of the most common devices used by people with hearing loss. Cochlear implants benefit many people with severe hearing loss but will not be discussed here as a separate device. Assistive technologies for people with hearing loss fall into the following additional categories.

Alerting and Signaling Devices

These devices are designed to get the individual's attention through a flashing or strobe light or vibration and may be used in conjunction with a very loud sound. They include timers, alarms (fire, smoke, gas), pagers, alarm clocks, and signals that the doorbell or phone is ringing. Service animals are trained to alert individuals with hearing loss to a variety of environmental sounds, including ringing doorbells and telephones, alarms, and so on.

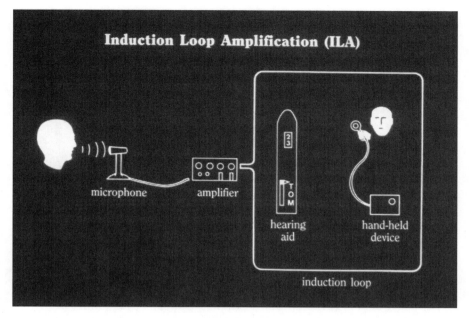

Figure 1.2. Diagram of an audio induction loop. Courtesy of the National Technical Institute for the Deaf/Rochester Institute of Technology, Rochester, New York.

Devices to Amplify Sound in Group Situations and Large Areas

To improve listening in large areas such as classrooms, theaters, large professional meetings, and so on, rooms may be equipped with wireless assistive listening systems. There are three major types: (a) FM systems use radio frequencies set aside by the Federal Communications Commission to allow for the transmission of sound from a microphone to a receiver (set to the same radio frequency) connected to earphones or hearing aids. FM systems are useful when the microphone can be placed close to the sound source. For example, speakers during a professional meeting may be asked to clip a transmitter on their belt and a microphone near their mouth so that their speech is directly inputted into the receiver. Other large areas may use (b) an audio induction loop (see the diagram in Figure 1.2) and (c) infrared systems that use infrared light to transmit sound. All systems require the person with hearing loss to have a receiver.

Telephone Devices

Amplifying the sound from a telephone can be accomplished through built-in volume controls, in-line amplifiers, and add-on portable amplifiers (good for traveling). For people with severe and profound hearing loss, a

Figure 1.3. A TTY or TT machine. Note that the cord in the upper right of the figure is connected to a cordless phone. Courtesy of the National Technical Institute for the Deaf/Rochester Institute of Technology, Rochester, New York.

text telephone (TT) or TTY may be required to converse with another person. A TTY or TT allows the use of a standard phone. It works like this:

> TTYs are made up of a typewriter-like display. The visual display may be in the form of printed characters on paper, an alphanumeric display, or both. The telephone handset is placed on a coupler and the message is typed. Pressing letters on the keyboard generates different tones for each character. Tones that form the typed message are sent over the telephone lines to the telephone on the other end of the line. This telephone also must be linked to a TTY so that the message can be decoded and displayed. The latest models of TTYs have a voice carry-over (VCO) mode so that the hard of hearing person can speak the message but receive the answer on the TTY. (Dugan, 1997, p. 54)

There are conventional abbreviations for TTY conversations that have evolved over time. For example, in Figure 1.3, the message ends with GA, which is short for "go ahead." Cagle and Cagle (1991) have developed a book of TTY etiquette and abbreviations that should be read by any new TTY or TT user. If a TTY user wishes to speak to someone without a TTY, relay services can be used. Since 1993, relay services have become available in each state. A person with hearing loss calls the service via a TTY and a hearing operator receives the message over a TTY. The operator then telephones the other party and relays in voice the message of the TTY user. The TTY operator then types the voice response into the TTY. It is important when using a relay service to talk to the operator just as you would to the person with whom you are conversing. Then the relay operator will type or voice verbatim messages and responses.

Other resources for communicating over distances include digital wireless phones, two-way messaging, and electronic mail.

Telecommunications Devices and Accommodations to Telecommunication Technologies

Devices in this category apply to such media as radio, television, and CD/stereo systems. For people with mild to moderate hearing loss, these devices can be connected to hearing aids through an induction loop system or earphones. For people with severe and profound hearing loss, closed and open captioning will display what is said in text that flows along the screen and can be read. It is important to note that the Decoder Circuitry Act requires that all TV sets 13 inches and larger manufactured after July 1, 1993 have circuitry included that would decode captions. Newer products include personal captioning systems that pick up text provided by a captioned transmission system and display it through a pair of eyeglasses with Clip-On Captioning Display attached. The captions seem to float in front of the eye.

As can be seen in Table 1.2, people with more severe hearing loss will need a combination of sophisticated technologies. Many require a tolerance for fidgeting with gadgets, asserting one's needs for assistive listening devices, and becoming accustomed to being inconvenienced in exchange for being connected.

DEGREES OF VISION LOSS AND USE OF TECHNOLOGIES AND OTHER FORMS OF ASSISTANCE

Vision loss can result from a variety of causes, such as lack of oxygen at birth, trauma to the eye, and diseases such as diabetes. These can lead to varying degrees of vision loss from total blindness to affected eyesight in one eye only. According to the National Information Center for Children and Youth With Disabilities (2001b), the terms *partially sighted, low vision, legally blind,* and *totally blind* are used in the educational context to describe students with visual impairments. They are defined as follows:

- *Partially sighted* indicates some type of visual problem has resulted in a need for special education.
- *Low vision* generally refers to a severe visual impairment, not necessarily limited to distance vision. Low vision applies to all

TABLE 1.2
Options for Being Connected According to Degree of Hearing Loss

Degree of loss	Alerting	Group and large area	Telephone	Telecommuni- cations
0–25 dB (normal hearing)	None	None	None	None
26–40 dB (mild loss; hard of hearing)	None	Large area listening systems	Telephone amplifier	TV/radio amplifying head sets, amplified telephone
41–70 dB (moderate/ severe loss; hard of hearing)	Flashing lights for ringing doorbell, phone; flashing lights on fire, smoke, gas alarms	Personal amplifier, large area listening systems	Telephone amplifier	Television listening devices (FM, infrared, audio loop)
71+ dB (severe; deaf)	Flashing lights for ringing doorbell, phone; flashing lights on fire, smoke, gas alarms, vibrating alarm clock	Personal amplifier, large area listening systems, sign language interpreting services, real-time captioning	Text telephone (TT) or relay services	Closed captioning (useful for all degrees of loss, but essential for severe loss)

Note. From *Keys to Living With Hearing Loss,* by M. B. Dugan, 1997, Hauppauge, NY: Barron's Educational Series. Copyright 1997 by Barron's Educational Series. Adapted with permission. From *Hear Better Now: Participants Handbook* (pp. 44–46), by Rochester Hearing and Speech Center, 2001. Copyright 2001 by Rochester Hearing and Speech Center. Adapted with permission.

individuals with sight who are unable to read the newspaper at a normal viewing distance, even with the aid of eyeglasses or contact lenses. They use a combination of vision and other senses to learn, although they may require adaptations in lighting or the size of print, and, sometimes, braille.

- *Legally blind* indicates that a person has less than 20/200 vision in the better eye or a very limited field of vision (20° at its widest point).
- *Totally blind* refers to those students who will learn via braille or other nonvisual media.

Table 1.3 provides examples of technologies appropriate for individuals in these four categories. It is important to note that as the vision loss becomes more complete, the individual typically needs to use more assistance

TABLE 1.3

Examples of Technologies According to Degree of Vision Loss

Degree of vision loss	Reading/Writing	Mobility
Partially sighted/ low vision	Simple to complex magnification devices; yellow acetate placed over a printed page to heighten contrast, magnification of computer text	None to long cane, guide dog
Legally blind	Closed circuit television (CCTV) or video magnifier; alternative means of computer input, output, and navigation	Guide dog, long cane, sonic guides, global positioning system (GPS)-based locators
Totally blind	Braille and braille technologies (e.g., portable notetakers); optical character recognition (OCR) software; alternative means of computer input, output, and navigation	Guide dog, long cane, sonic guides, GPS-based locators

Note. From "Assistive Devices for People Who Are Blind or Have a Visual Impairment," by J. D. Leventhal, in *Evaluating, Selecting and Using Appropriate Assistive Technology* (pp. 125–143), by J. Galvin and M. Scherer (Eds.), Gaithersburg, MD: Aspen. Copyright 1996 by Aspen. Adapted with permission.

as well as high-tech and complex technologies for reading, writing, and mobility.

ASSISTIVE TECHNOLOGIES CAN ALSO HAVE NEGATIVE ASPECTS AND BRING FRUSTRATION

In most areas of life, technology has brought both promises and pitfalls. Although there are many benefits to be gained by using assistive technologies, they have the potential to limit and isolate as well as enable, liberate, and connect their users. As paradoxical as it sounds, some ATs, particularly the very high-tech ones, can sometimes work against connectedness as they highlight a person's differences and set AT users apart as looking "different." While many individuals have grown to be grateful for their ATs (such as indicated in the second example at the beginning of this chapter of someone with hearing loss), they have often felt stigmatized by them and even resented the need to use them. One hearing-impaired student I interviewed felt personally stigmatized by a peer wearing a body hearing aid. In other words, without even wearing a hearing aid herself, she perceived the stigma of the AT as spreading to her because of having a hearing loss similar to that of the hearing aid user. She describes this as follows:

When I was growing up, another boy in school was hearing-impaired. He could hear a little better than me . . . he used to wear one of those hearing aids that you attach to your body. I could never tolerate that kind of thing. People look at you. And being a girl with those little bumps right there. . . . He was the only other hearing-impaired person, and we avoided each other.

EDUCATIONAL IMPLICATIONS OF HEARING AND VISION LOSS

The National Information Center for Children and Youth With Disabilities (2001b) listed the following implications for the education of children with vision loss:

> The effect of visual problems on a child's development depends on the severity, type of loss, age at which the condition appears, and overall functioning level of the child. Many children who have multiple disabilities may also have visual impairments resulting in motor, cognitive, and/or social developmental delays. A young child with visual impairments has little reason to explore interesting objects in the environment and, thus, may miss opportunities to have experiences and to learn. This lack of exploration may continue until learning becomes motivating or until intervention begins.
>
> Because the child cannot see parents or peers, he or she may be unable to imitate social behavior or understand nonverbal cues. Visual handicaps can create obstacles to a growing child's independence. Students with visual impairments may need additional help with special equipment and modifications in the regular curriculum to emphasize listening skills, communication, orientation and mobility, vocation/career options, and daily living skills. Students with low vision or those who are legally blind may need help in using their residual vision more efficiently and in working with special aids and materials. Students who have visual impairments combined with other types of disabilities have a greater need for an interdisciplinary approach and may require greater emphasis on self care and daily living skills.
>
> Children with visual impairments should be assessed early to benefit from early intervention programs, when applicable. Technology in the form of computers and low-vision optical and video aids enable many partially sighted, low vision and blind children to participate in regular class activities. Large print materials, books on tape, and braille books are available. (Fact Sheet No. 13)

According to the National Information Center for Children and Youth With Disabilities (2001a), children with hearing loss can have difficulty in learning vocabulary, grammar, word order, idiomatic expressions, and other aspects of verbal communication. By age 4 or 5, most children who are deaf are enrolled in school on a full-day basis and do special work on communication and language development. Students with hearing loss

> use oral or manual means of communication or a combination of the two. Oral communication includes speech, speechreading and the use of residual hearing (this may include use of hearing aids and/or assistive listening devices). Manual communication involves signs and finger-spelling (and requires the presence of a sign language interpreter to facilitate communication between hearing and non-hearing persons). Total Communication, as a method of instruction, is a combination of the oral method plus signs and fingerspelling. (National Information Center for Children and Youth With Disabilities, 2001a, Fact Sheet No. 3)

Learners with hearing and vision loss are becoming increasingly dependent on technologies. In fact, the majority of the information they receive is now technology-based and delivered via telecommunications or computer-based technologies. This makes literacy all the more important. For people who are deaf, captioning or speech-to-text systems are commonplace; for people with vision loss, they can choose among speech output, electronic magnification, optical character recognition (OCR) technologies, and Braille technology. Yet, their specialized needs and preferences regarding technologies continue to be understudied in all levels of their education. Other areas in need of research are (a) an analysis of the influences on successful and unsuccessful outcomes from these technologies and (b) the identification of strategies and tools that result in the most appropriate match of person and technology, training in its use, and optimal use of the technology.

STRUCTURE OF THIS BOOK

While technologies have had a significant impact on the number and quality of educational opportunities available to people with vision and hearing loss, there is tremendous potential for many more opportunities to occur. There also exists a need to monitor new developments for possible limitations or barriers they may create for individuals with hearing or vision loss. It is also crucial that opportunities be made available to people throughout their life span and educational careers, including school readiness and adult literacy.

An important aspect of this book is that it focuses on the parameters and steps that must be taken to ensure a good match of person and technology. I subscribe to a comprehensive and life span perspective to such matching.

For a match to be good and enhance learning, many factors need to be taken into account. These include the following.

Learner Characteristics and Preferences

Technology should not be a mere "gee whiz" and possible distraction to learning but must be used to unlock and enhance individuals' abilities. Sometimes technologies create as many barriers as they remove. Equal emphasis needs to be on the people aspects of learning.

Environments for Learning

Despite legislative support for widening the quality and amount of educational opportunities available to people with disabilities, most attention has focused on the classroom environment. Lifelong learning requires equal attention to laboratory settings, libraries and other repositories of information, community-based centers for learning, and the home. Distance learning needs to be developed to enable people to access education in more environments.

Technologies for Access to Information and for Instructional Delivery

Learners with or without disabilities, regardless of age, share the goal of having complete access to information. For people with vision loss, however, print and graphic/pictorial information present a tremendous challenge; for people with hearing loss, their challenge is sound and auditory information. Many barriers remain to the utilization of technologies by people with disabilities due in part to their lack of knowledge of available technologies and training in their use.

There are many needs, learning styles, and different ways of presenting information. More information on the implications of choosing particular technologies and delivery systems for students with disabilities needs to be available. Educators need an active introduction to and practice in using technologies.

Matching Learners With the Most Appropriate Technologies and Strategies for Their Use

The key to teaching and learning is making sure that information is linked with meaning, and for students who have disabilities the key to making this link possible is often technology. Each individual has specific strengths, learning styles, and needs. Finding the right match between technology and student requires being aware of all of these factors.

This book is organized in four sections around these general topics. The state of the art regarding technologies for people with hearing or vision loss is discussed, but in light of educational and social practices needed to make those technologies work to the advantage of an individual's learning, social participation, and quality of life or sense of well-being. Rather than a text devoted exclusively to technological and pedagogical theorizing, which can often seem to be devoid of real-world relevance, narrative case examples are used liberally to highlight and bring to life everyday examples of good, workable practices "from the trenches." Thus, this book relies heavily on the actual words and experiences of those who are struggling to discover innovative and successful ways to learn and succeed (in the case of individuals themselves with hearing or vision loss) and to educate (in the case of those who teach and help those with hearing and vision loss) in the face of communication and sensory disabilities. To achieve a book rich with take-home and practical applications, I spent many hours interviewing and observing people in their natural environments and asking them to describe their successful experiences, the problems they encountered and what they tried to do about them, the results of these efforts, and their recommendations for change or improvement. For individuals with hearing or vision loss, a technique I frequently used was the *lifeline interview* (e.g., Rubin, Rahhal, & Poon, 1998). It is very simple, but it never fails to help people recall important incidents and see connections among events. I begin by drawing a line representing their full life span on a sheet of paper and asking the people I am interviewing to mark the spot on the line indicating today. This gives me an immediate idea of the length of the future they see for themselves. Then I ask them to mark on the line the day they were born. From that mark on, I ask them to indicate key events in their lives. By seeing things in a sequence, they often come to remember things they had not thought about in years and see how certain key events played an important role in shaping subsequent ones. I have observed many "aha" and "lightbulb going off" experiences with this technique. It also serves to have them project into the future, articulating their expectations and goals.

A fundamental sense of connectedness, a sense of well-being, is usually derived from the quality of interactions experienced over time. People need to feel connected with their environments and the persons and information they value. How this can be achieved for people with hearing and vision loss is explored in the chapters that follow. Assistive and educational technologies have already done much to eliminate the challenges and barriers posed by disabilities, and they will be even more crucial to the educational and vocational success of this population from the boardroom to the classroom, in the community, and in the home. As such, this book is appropriate for a wide range of readers: developmental, educational, health, rehabilitation, and school psychologists; special educators; parents and individuals with disabilities; adult educators; faculty training the aforementioned in university-based courses; rehabilitative therapists; and people specializing in services and education for persons with vision or hearing loss. This book will be of great interest to people with hearing and vision loss as their self-advocacy efforts on behalf of enhanced opportunities for interaction and learning will occur throughout their life spans—lives bettered by both technology and education and filled with a rich sense of connectedness.

A list of key people discussed in this book with their identifying information follows:

Betty, a teacher at the New York State School for the Blind

Frank Bowe, professor at Hofstra University who became deaf at the age of three

Philip Bravin, former President and Chief Executive Officer of the National Captioning Institute, Inc.

Norm Coombs, Rochester Institute of Technology, who is blind and who taught distance learning courses in history to deaf students

Dave, an engineer with a major corporation who has a severe hearing loss

Ellen, a blind kindergarten student who also has cerebral palsy

Jamie, student at the New York State School for the Blind who is deaf, blind, and autistic

Janet, has a PhD in electrical engineering and works for a Fortune-500 company and is very hard of hearing

Jeffrey, a college freshman who has low vision

Kate, very hard of hearing, describes the difficult college years

Larry Scadden, former senior program director at the National Science Foundation Program for Persons with Disabilities, who became blind at the age of four

Stephen, fifth-grade math student with low vision in a public school

II

LEARNER
CHARACTERISTICS
AND PREFERENCES

2

THE EFFECTS OF LOSS OF HEARING OR VISION ON THE LEARNER AND LEARNING

Abundantly flowing raw sensation provides a necessary engine for experience. Informative variety and pattern provide organization to the experiencer as well as body to the experience. When the flow of information is severely restricted, the attachment to information often must be considered severed, or at risk of severance.

—Norris Hansell (1974, pp. 35–36)

Learners have varying characteristics and preferences. To maximize each learner's educational success, ideally, instruction and learning environments would be individualized to allow learners to select from an array of options the ones that best suit their unique characteristics and goals. Philip Bravin, former president and chief executive officer of the National Captioning Institute and a 25-year veteran employee of IBM Corporation, addressed this from his perspective:

> Normally we have five senses—smell, touch, vision, hearing and taste. But I want to focus on just two of them—hearing and vision. . . . All of these senses are receptors, not expressors of anything. We name our five senses in the five ways we receive information.
>
> What we receive is data or information. Data from computers comes in three basic forms—text, graphics and sound. I want to differentiate between data and information. As I give you numbers, a string of numbers, they don't mean anything to you. If I put parentheses, 9-1-4 and then 738 and a dash and then four more numbers, what is that? Obviously it's a telephone number. The data is meaningless. It becomes information when meaning is added to it.
>
> A person receives data through the sense of vision or hearing, which allows them then to process the data into information. If we don't think

of it that way, then we can't individualize the learning environment. The input is modified to suit the needs and the wishes of the individual, to maximize his or her effectiveness of learning. (Bravin, 1994)

The loss of hearing or vision does, indeed, affect the ways individuals can take in data. And without data, meaningful information cannot be obtained or understood completely. This chapter presents the more physical experience of hearing or vision loss as well as technologies and other strategies used to take in data; the next chapter discusses the personal meaning of hearing and vision loss in the words of a sample of individuals who articulate both the obstacles they have encountered and the successes they have achieved.

UNDERSTANDING HEARING LOSS

There are many good resources on the causes and consequences of hearing loss (e.g., Dugan, 1997; McFadyen, 1996; Mencher, Gerber, & McCombe, 1997; Myers, 2000; Scheetz, 2001) and the discussion in this section is a distillation of information from these materials. At a very fundamental level, hearing loss can occur in only one ear or in both ears and can occur as a result of damage to any part of the ear: outer, middle, or inner ear. When the damage or obstruction is in the outer or middle ear, the person experiences a *conductive* hearing loss. Ear wax buildup or infection of the auditory canal in the outer ear can lead to conductive loss. This typically results in a loss of hearing in the low-frequency ranges (the lower pitched, deep sounds) that provide volume but are less important for speech understanding. Middle ear problems include perforation of the eardrum and infection. With conductive hearing loss, "sounds seem soft but speech is clear as long as it is loud enough" (Dugan, 1997, p. 17). Conductive hearing losses usually do not result in severe losses, and a person with this type of hearing loss can usually use a hearing aid well. Also, conductive losses can often be helped medically or surgically.

Sensorineural hearing losses commonly result from damage to the sensory apparatus (hair cells of the inner ear or the nerves that supply it) or to the auditory centers of the central nervous system by disease (e.g., due to high fever and reactions to medications), trauma (including noise), and, most commonly, age-related losses in sensorineural sensitivity. Damage to the inner ear results in *sensorineural* loss, and the person will likely experience difficulty with high-frequency, high-pitched sounds such as with soft consonants like *s*, *f*, and *sh*. These hearing losses can range from mild to profound, and even with amplification to increase the sound level, a person with a sensorineural hearing loss may perceive distorted sounds. The ability to clearly understand speech is diminished because parts of words and sentences are missed. There will also be a reduced ability to enjoy television and radio. Sometimes successful use of a hearing aid is not possible.

A combination of both conductive and sensorineural losses means that a problem occurs in both the outer or middle and the inner ear. This results in *mixed* hearing loss. The fourth type of hearing loss is *central* hearing loss, which results from damage or impairment to the nerves or nuclei of the central nervous system, either in the pathways to the brain or in the brain itself.

Hearing loss is generally described as mild, moderate, severe, or profound, depending on how well a person can hear the intensities or frequencies most associated with speech. The most common means by which hearing loss is evaluated is through audiometric tests, which use pure tone or speech stimuli. Audiometers are calibrated according to established standards; variance from these norms are then considered to represent hearing loss. Sound is measured both by its loudness or intensity (measured in units called decibels, dB) and its frequency or pitch (measured in units called hertz, Hz).

> The threshold of "normal" hearing is denoted as an intensity of 0 dB. Each 3-dB increase represents a doubling of the sound intensity. Hearing loss is also measured in dB. A person with a 25-dB hearing loss would not hear a sound below 25 dB in intensity. (McFadyen, 1996, p. 145)

Nonauditory factors, such as personal and social experiences, combine with hearing loss and result in a highly unique perception of the meaning of that loss to the individual. Because the influence of such nonauditory factors is difficult to measure, audiologic recommendations can sometimes seem to miss the desired mark.

HEARING LOSS IN CHILDREN

The Individuals With Disabilities Education Act (IDEA) is legislation designed to ensure that children with disabilities receive the best education possible and that they are provided with the essential accommodations and devices for this to occur. IDEA is discussed in more depth in chapters 4 and 6, thus the focus here is just on hearing impairment and deafness as two of the categories under which children with disabilities may be eligible for special education and related service programming under IDEA.

Although the term *hearing impairment* is often used generically to describe a wide range of hearing losses, including deafness, the regulations for IDEA define hearing impairment and deafness separately. *Hearing impairment* is defined by IDEA as "an impairment in hearing, whether permanent or fluctuating, that adversely affects a child's educational performance." A child with a hearing impairment can generally respond to auditory stimuli, including speech. *Deafness*, on the other hand, is defined by IDEA as "a hearing impairment that is so severe that the child is prevented from receiving sound in all or most of its forms and is impaired in processing linguistic information through hearing, with or without amplification." Generally, only children whose hearing loss is greater than 90 dB are considered deaf for the purposes of educational placement, although this can vary according to the state in which the child lives. Table 2.1 lists ranges of hearing loss in dB with associated listening difficulties.

Whereas hearing loss in itself does not affect a person's intellectual capacity or ability to learn, children who are either hard of hearing or deaf generally require some form of special education services to receive an adequate education.

TECHNOLOGIES AND ACCOMMODATIONS

Assistance available to children with hearing loss under IDEA includes language and auditory training, amplification systems, the services of an interpreter for those students who use manual communication, favorable seating in the classroom to facilitate speech reading, captioned films/videos, the assistance of a notetaker (who takes notes for the student so the student can focus on the teacher and instructional material displayed to the class), instruction for the teacher and peers in alternative communication methods (such as sign language), and counseling for personal development. The physical aspects of hearing loss result in a range of hearing capability and strategies to help individuals take in data that can be processed as information. Within any given range of hearing loss, strategies to enhance the inputting of data for both adults and children are quite similar. Table 2.2 below lists recommended strategies for both children and adults across five different situations of communication difficulty.

Various forms and causes of vision loss were discussed in chapter 1. Therefore, the remainder of this chapter focuses on children and the effects of vision loss on their learning as well as the kinds of technologies typically used to assist them in taking in data.

VISION LOSS IN CHILDREN

According to the American Foundation for the Blind (2002a), approximately 93,600 children, from birth through age 21, are blind or visually

TABLE 2.1
Range and Description of Hearing Loss Effects in Adults and Children

Degree of loss	Description	Children	Adults
0–25 dB	Normal	None	None
26–40 dB Speech area (consonants)	Mild "Hard-of-hearing"	Difficulty in groups and with soft, distant speech. May have language delay. Environmental accommodations may be sufficient.	Difficulty in background noise and in group situations. Environmental accommodations may be sufficient.
41–55 dB Speech area (vowels)	Moderate "Hard-of-hearing"	Difficulty in groups, and conversation must be loud to be heard. Difficulty with language and learning. In addition to environmental accommodations, hearing aids and assistive listening devices may be beneficial. May benefit from special education placement, counseling.	Conversation must be loud to be understood and increasingly will depend on visual cues. In addition to environmental accommodations, a hearing aid and assistive listening devices may be beneficial.
56–70 dB Baby crying	Moderate/severe	Difficulty understanding conversations in many situations. Will benefit from a hearing aid(s), assistive listening devices, and special education placement.	Increasing difficulty in conversations and hearing in large group situations. Will benefit from amplification, hearing aids, and assistive listening devices.
71–90 dB Vacuum cleaner	Severe "deaf"	Will not hear conversational speech. Speech and language difficulties. Will benefit from a hearing aid(s) and special education placement.	Will not hear conversational speech and requires visual cues. Will benefit from vocational evaluation and personal counseling. Hearing aids, signaling and telecommunication devices, and interpreting services important.
91 dB+ Phone ringing, Lawnmower	Profound "deaf"	May hear loud noises but more aware of vibration. Vision is primary avenue for communication (sign language, captioning, TT use).	May hear loud noises but more aware of vibration. Vision is primary avenue for communication (sign language, captioning, TT use).

Note. From *Keys to Living With Hearing Loss* (p. 10), by M. B. Dugan, 1997, Hauppauge, NY: Barron's Educational Series. Copyright 1997 by Barron's Educational Series. Adapted with permission.

TABLE 2.2

Strategies for Communicating in Different Situations for Those With
Hearing Loss and Those Communicating With People With Hearing Loss

Communication difficulty	Strategies for people with hearing loss	Strategies for communicating with people with hearing loss
Noise	Avoid as much distraction as possible and focus your attention on the speaker. Move to a quieter place, watch people's faces and nonverbals as they communicate.	If possible, remove the background noise (e.g., turn off the radio). Make sure you have the person's attention before speaking and face the person as you speak. Position yourself so the light is on your face and there is no glare in the person's eyes. Speak slowly and clearly but do not exaggerate mouth movements. Raise your voice slightly but do not shout. Rephrase your response (and add facial expression or nonverbal cues) if you are asked to repeat something. Do not chew gum or obscure your lip movements. Try to place yourself with your back to a blank wall or one with an uncomplicated background.
Distance between speaker and listener	Move as close to the speaker as possible. Consider using an assistive listening device. Try to place yourself in an area with as little background noise as possible but where you can have a clear view of the speaker's face and body movements.	Face the audience and speak slowly and clearly. Raise the level of your voice. Try to use gestures and nonverbal cues as much as possible. If an interpreter is accompanying a person with hearing loss, speak directly to the person and not the interpreter.
Multiple speakers	Tell other people you have a hearing problem and tell them they need to speak one at a time, slowly and clearly. Try to position yourself so that you have a view of as many speakers' faces as possible. Let the conversation flow naturally, but ask specific questions about what you missed rather than saying, "What?" Ask people to rephrase, rather than repeat, what they have said.	Make sure each speaker speaks slowly, clearly, and one at a time. Each speaker should face the person with hearing loss when speaking and speak naturally. Make sure the area is well lit and that each speaker will be visible to the person with hearing loss. A person with hearing loss should face away from any windows so as to avoid glare. If an interpreter is present, speak to the group and not to the interpreter.

(continued)

TABLE 2.2 (Continued)

Communication difficulty	Strategies for people with hearing loss	Strategies for communicating with people with hearing loss
Low light levels	Move as close to the speaker as possible. Try to move to a better lit area. Take advantage of all existing light by positioning yourself to have it focus on the speaker's face.	The most important thing is to obtain more light, or move to a better lit area if possible. Raise your voice level, but do not shout. Face the speaker when talking.
Complex information	Ask for written cues if this is feasible (on a blackboard, flip chart, etc.). Ask for a brief verbal outline of key points.	Prepare handouts ahead of time that outline the communication. Define new or unusual words, acronyms, etc. Say what you are going to say, say it, then summarize what you have said. Monitor the listener's facial expressions and check for understanding. If an interpreter is present, speak to your audience and not the interpreter.

Note. From *Keys to Living With Hearing Loss* (p. 10), by M. B. Dugan, 1997, Hauppauge, NY: Barron's Educational Series. Copyright 1997 by Barron's Educational Series. Adapted with permission.

impaired and are being served by some form of special education in the United States:

> These students are an extremely diverse group. Not only do the nature and degree of their visual impairments differ, but so also does the way they adapt to their vision loss. Some students have other disabilities in addition to visual impairment. Their level of academic functioning spans a great range. And in every way they are as disparate as any other group of individuals in terms of ethnic and racial background, religion, geographic location, and income. Given this diversity, it is important to remember that each child needs to be viewed as an individual with unique needs.

Most academic work is structured so that vision is the primary sense through which data are taken in. Limitations on the ability to see and receive information from the relevant environments can affect a child's sense of freedom of movement, perspective of the self within a broader context, and development of a sense of fitting in and belonging.

The education of students who are blind or visually impaired should include all the basic areas of the regular education curriculum but additionally include an "expanded core curriculum" that provides education in areas essential to living and working independently and successfully in today's world (e.g., Ramsey, 1997). The expanded core curriculum might consist of some or all of the following:

- independent living skills, which are methods of carrying out everyday tasks, such as grooming, cooking, telling time, handling money, and so forth;
- social interaction skills;
- compensatory academic skills, including techniques to take in data such as braille reading and writing, the use of optical devices to read standard print, and auditory methods of learning;
- orientation and mobility, which refers to where one is in an environment and methods of safe travel;
- visual efficiency skill, which means finding strategies to make the best use of existing vision;
- assistive technology use and skills in using special software and hardware to take in data, process information, and perform tasks; and
- career education.

Which of the above are most relevant for a given child is determined by an appropriate assessment that considers such individual characteristics as type of vision disorder, age at which vision loss occurred, prior learning experiences, developmental levels, and possible additional disabilities. Probably the most common intervention for taking in printed data is the provision of such materials in the form of enlarged print, audio recording (e.g., books on tape), or braille. Assistive technologies such as adapted input and output for computers and low-vision optical and video aids enable many partially sighted, low vision, and blind children to participate in regular class activities.

TECHNOLOGIES AND ACCOMMODATIONS

Table 2.3 summarizes key strategies for people with vision loss or those wishing to communicate visual information to them in a variety of environmental situations. Note its similarity to Table 2.2 regarding people with hearing loss.

These strategies are very useful for large-area situations (classrooms, meetings, etc.). For most people who are blind or with very low vision, however, independent reading and writing is one of their biggest challenges. Because there are both advantages and disadvantages associated with each strategy, many adults who grew up with vision loss and have experimented with a variety of products have found over the years that a blend of high- and low-tech devices maximizes their options for reading and writing. For

TABLE 2.3
Strategies for Communicating in Different Situations for Those With Vision Loss and Those Working With People With Vision Loss

Communication difficulty	Strategies for people with vision loss	Strategies for working with people with vision loss
Noise	Avoid as much distraction as possible and focus your attention on the speaker. Move to a quieter place so you can hear voices and environmental cues clearly.	If possible, remove the background noise (e.g., turn off the radio). Make sure you have the person's attention before speaking. Even though the person with vision loss may not be able to see you, face the person as you speak to maximize the clarity of your voice.
Distance between speaker and listener	Move as close to the speaker as possible to hear the speaker as clearly as possible. Try to place yourself in an area with as little background noise as possible. If visual information is presented that you cannot see, request descriptive services. If that is not available, request visual material be provided to you in an accessible format.	Face the listener and speak slowly and clearly. Raise the level of your voice. Describe all visual and graphic material as well as particular gestures and nonverbal cues.
Multiple speakers	Tell other people you have a vision problem and ask them to identify themselves when speaking. Try to position yourself so that you are in an area as free of background noise as possible. If you miss key information, ask specific questions about what you missed rather than saying, "What?"	Make sure each speaker speaks one at a time and directly faces the audience. Each speaker should speak naturally. Make sure the area is well lit and free of background and unnecessary noises (e.g., turn off overhead projectors when not using them). Provide verbal descriptions of visual or graphic material.

(continued)

example, many people do not know braille and prefer to have a sighted assistant orally read print material to them. Yet, this results in a loss of privacy when having personal letters, bank statements, and other documents read by another person, who often needs to record the response from the person who is blind. Many people with vision loss use audiotapes of books or prerecorded text and take advantage of radio reading services, but these cannot help with personal correspondence.

TABLE 2.3 *(Continued)*

Communication Difficulty	Strategies for people with vision loss	Strategies for working with people with vision loss
Low light levels	Move as close to the speaker as possible. Try to move to a better lit area. Take advantage of all existing light by positioning yourself to have it focus on the speaker's face.	The most important thing is to obtain more light, or move to a better lit area if possible. Face the audience when talking.
Complex information	Ask for advanced cues if this is feasible and ask for a brief verbal outline of key points.	Prepare handouts ahead of time that outline the communication in large print and on diskette. Define new or unusual words, acronyms, etc. Say what you are going to say, say it, then summarize what you have said. Monitor the listener's facial expressions and check for understanding. Speak to the audience when descriptive services are provided.

What Is Braille?

Braille is named after the person who created it, Louis Braille, which is why the word is frequently written with a capital B. Many good descriptions of braille exist that are accessible on the Web (e.g., American Foundation for the Blind, 2002b; Castellano & Kosman, 1997; National Federation of the Blind, 2002; Wormsley, 2000). Fundamentally, there are three different levels of braille. In Grade 1 braille, one letter is equal to one braille "cell," which comprises six raised dots in a particular pattern or configuration indicating one letter or symbol. Grade 1 braille consists of each letter of the alphabet, numbers, punctuation marks, and specific braille composition signs such as capitalization. Grade 2 braille is a more complex system and, unlike Grade 1 braille, has a system of contractions. *And* and *the* are each just one braille symbol in Grade 2 braille. Also, common word endings like *-ing* and beginnings (such as *dis-*) are represented by one braille symbol. Even whole common words may have a unique symbol or be represented by a single letter (e.g., the letter *d* with a space or punctuation on either side stands for the word *do*). Grade 2 braille is more difficult to learn and is complex because the meaning of a symbol depends on the context in which it occurs. Grade 3 braille is a more highly contracted system of braille.

This is how the basic braille works. It begins with the six dots arranged in a cell three dots high and two dots wide as follows:

1 .. 4
2 .. 5
3 .. 6

The first 10 letters in the alphabet, letters A through J, use the top four dots. For example,

A B C D E F G H I J

When these same 10 characters are preceded by a special sign, they are used for the numbers 1 to 0. To make the next 10 letters in the alphabet (K through T), the lower left-hand dot is added. For the last letters, U through Z, Louis Braille added dots 3 and 6 (the bottom two dots) to A through E to form U through Z. Louis Braille originally did not include W because it was not prevalent in the French language. Twenty years later, however, at the request of people in Britain, he added a W to the braille alphabet by adding dot 6 (the bottom right dot) to a J. There are a total of 63 possible combinations, thus far leaving us with 37 remaining combinations. They are used to create such contractions as *and, for, the, with,* and common letter combinations like *er, sh,* and *th.*

There are a variety of ways to produce braille, one of which is called *slate and stylus.* This is a small device in which paper is placed in a metal template and the stylus (which may look like a small sharp pencil but with a nail on the end of it instead of a pencil point) is pressed down into an array of six-dot cell templates to create each desired dot. According to one user of slate and stylus,

> When you start punching out all those dots, you have a whole new meaning to writer's cramp. Even though you read braille left to right, when using a slate and stylus you have to punch the dots right to left because you're turning the paper over to read it.

The slate and stylus (e.g., American Foundation for the Blind, 2002b) can fit into a shirt pocket very easily, weigh next to nothing, and can accompany the person anywhere. Although this is not a system designed to create pages of text, it is very handy for jotting down notes in classes or meetings. For example, when I traveled to a conference with a colleague who is blind, I noticed him take out his slate and stylus and emboss his name, phone number, and e-mail address on about 20 of his business cards. While I drove us to the conference, another colleague who is blind said to me, "It's the only good way in a meeting to take notes on something I want to comment on later because it provides good random access just like pen and paper do."

Other means of obtaining braille documents include manual braille embossers (much like the old manual typewriters) and braille printers attached to computers.

Blending More High- With Low-Tech

Increasingly, individuals with vision loss are relying on computerized devices to enable them to read and write with privacy. An older, electromechanical device called the Opticon (for "Optical to Tactile Conversion") first became commercially available in 1971 (e.g., Scherer, 1982; University of Illinois at Urbana–Champaign, Graduate School of Library and Information Science, 2002). It transformed a symbol, letter, or number into a vibrating bunch of sandpaper-like pricks that tickled the finger in the exact configuration of the original image. It was slightly larger than a videocassette and had two major components: (a) a camera about $1'' \times 1\frac{1}{2}''$ that was free-moving and would be manually guided over a page of text; a cord attached the camera to the (b) chassis, where users placed their left index finger over a zone of 144 "stimulator rods." The particular arrangement of a combination of the rods originated in the camera's picture, which then was "coded" into the tickling sensations known as, for example, the letter O (which to the user would be a vibrating little crater).

The sandpaper-like pricks were produced when the appropriate rods were raised and then vibrated. It worked well for well-formed and standard letters and symbols, such as those found in textbooks, but not for handwritten text.

A colleague who is blind told me that he had an Opticon back in the very early 1980s. He found it to be very slow and tedious and is grateful for the current optical scanners and screen readers (which are both cheaper and better). He said, "I was reading about 15 words a minute with the Opticon and my finger became numb after 20 to 30 minutes." The Opticon has now been replaced by better technology: optical character recognition (OCR) systems that "scan printed or typed documents automatically and display the text rapidly in either synthetic speech or braille" (Leventhal, 1996, p. 129). It, too, uses a camera to get an image of the printed page. The second component is recognition software to convert the image to text, and the third is a speech synthesizer to convert the text to synthesized voice output. The first two components (the camera and the conversion of image to text) are also found in current machines that scan text into computer files.

Those personal computers that are equipped with synthesized voice output (or "screen readers") use computerized speech to read the text that appears on the screen, and they enable a user to read and write e-mail

Figure 2.1. Example of a refreshable braille keyboard. Courtesy of Deborah Gilden, PhD, The Smith-Kettlewell Eye Research Institute, San Francisco, California.

messages completely independently and privately. If a paper copy of the message is desired, a computer with a braille printer can print it out for the user. As another option, the user can input or type in a message and read it back in braille by using a refreshable braille keyboard, shown in Figure 2.1. This consists of a set of pins, about 1/3 inch long, set in rows with varying numbers of braille six-dot cells. Jay Leventhal, senior resource specialist in the technology center at the American Foundation for the Blind in New York City, describes how it works:

> A refreshable braille display is a separate device that displays 20, 40, or 80 characters of the text. The display attaches to one of the computer's ports. The braille letters are formed by sets of pins being raised and lowered electronically. These displays are refreshable, meaning that they allow the information displayed to change as the user moves the display window around the screen. (Leventhal, 1996, p. 128)

How does a refreshable braille display work from the perspective of the user? The computer translates the message into the appropriate braille symbol, letter, or number and then directs the pins to raise up in the appropriate dot configuration. When the person has run his or her fingers over the pins or dots and receives the message, the pins fall back into place and the next part of the message literally pops up. One user believes it is particularly useful for reading books:

Figure 2.2. The Braille 'n Speak portable notetaker. Courtesy of Deborah Gilden, PhD, The Smith-Kettlewell Eye Research Institute, San Francisco, California.

After a while I get tired of listening to tapes. My mind wanders and it's hard to concentrate. You can't listen forever. The refreshable braille is great for this, but you have to be very careful about running your fingers across the pins because if they bend they'll have to be straightened out or sent back for repair.

The Braille 'n Speak, shown in Figure 2.2, is a popular notetaker for people who are blind (http://www.freedomscientific.com). Invented in 1988 by Dean Blazie, it is a sleek single unit about the size and shape of a videocassette with a Perkins-style keyboard (seven black buttons across the surface to input braille—six dots plus a space key). Three buttons are aligned on the left, three on the right, and the seventh centered below them. In the lower right-hand corner are slots set in a circle about the size of a nickel. This is the speaker. And these are the only visible qualities of this device. Even though it is quite small and lightweight (under 1 pound), it is a computer. It can be small because there is no need for a monitor and circuitry that goes with a monitor. There is no keyboard or mouse, but it can do everything a sighted person would do with a standard keyboard, mouse, and monitor. And it has as much memory—180-page RAM (random access memory) capacity. There are 4,096 bytes in a page, so 1 page in the Braille 'n Speak is equivalent to 3 pages of print or 8 pages of braille. When that is added up to 180, that is how much storage capacity exists. In addition, there is a flash memory that can store as much material as the old and new testaments (over and above the RAM capacity of 180 pages).

The Braille 'n Speak is a very versatile device, as described to me by Charlie, a graduate of the Batavia School for the Blind. He is highly proficient with it and instructs others in its use:

> With a laptop, you would separate your different files into directories and I can do that with this. It also has speech built into it. It has a clock, calendar, timer (real and lapsed, either way), it has a regular calculator and an extensive scientific calculator so that students can take this through their classes, set up different files for each class, and when they get into algebra and statistics, calculus, or whatever, all of the necessary calculator functions are right at their fingertips. It has an amazing personal data assistant.

The Braille 'n Speak is also quite compact and easy to carry in a briefcase, purse, or even a coat pocket. Its accompanying carrying case has a pocket for accessories, where it perhaps offers the greatest versatility. According to Charlie,

> The ports on the side are unique in that one port you can hook up to an accessory disk drive which allows you to download material. Let's say I've written a paper on this and I want to give it to someone. I can download it on a disk and you can take it home and put it in your PC and read it in regular text. Or if you want to give me material that I need to read, I can take your disk, put it into the disk drive, download it into this, and then read through it.
>
> This has a tremendous capacity for back-translating braille. A braille translator takes ASCII text and translates it into Grade II, or shorthand, braille. Now, when I talk about braille. . . . To give you an idea, when we talked about a page, one page of print is probably 2.5 to 3 pages of braille. Now that's shorthand braille. With Grade 1 braille, where you write letter for letter, it would take a tremendous amount of space because braille in itself is big. For example, the Old and New Testaments are 18 volumes in shorthand braille and each volume is 3 inches thick and a foot square. Now you know why blind people don't carry the Bible to church because they would need a wagon. I have a vest pocket edition of a dictionary; it's just a small paperback book, maybe ¾ inches thick, standard paperback size. In Grade II braille, it's 8 volumes for that vest pocket edition.
>
> The other port on this Braille 'n Speak is a printer port. So with this unit I can hook this directly to a regular inkjet printer or laserjet printer. I can write a letter and I can have it in print and send it off. I can do my own work. I don't have to get someone else to write a letter for me. Not that I wouldn't, if I needed to. But this allows me

access to my own personal communications. I can also print this out in braille with a different command. I'd plug this into a braille embosser. Now, if I have material I want to write and send to a braille reader or even if I just have notes I want to keep for myself, or if I want to study a file on a disk you gave me in braille, or if it's something you want me to have in braille, I plug it into this, give it two commands, and in just a couple of seconds I have a braille copy. So this single device allows me to have a disk copy, a hard copy in print or a hard copy in braille. I have three forms of communication I can work with.

This degree of versatility is certainly a giant leap ahead of the slate and stylus approach to braille writing with as much portability. And, as opposed to the slate and stylus approach, braille does not have to be created "backward."

At this point, I observed Charlie enter information into the Braille 'n Speak so that the voice output could be heard. To me, it sounded like a robot was speaking—and very fast. The machine voice had no discernible inflection to me, although it has been designed to provide a little bit of inflection and pauses at punctuation marks (such as with commas and periods). The voice inflection falls with periods and rises with question marks. But, it had been set at a fast speed. I could only pick out about three understandable words and could not detect the inflection. Even Charlie, who is highly proficient in Braille 'n Speak, said:

I don't use the speech synthesizer that much because the speech isn't all that great unless you plug it into a bigger speaker. The speaker on this is about the size of a nickel. So you're not going to get much quality out of that. But I'll turn it on and it'll say, "Braille 'n Speak 2000 . . . ready . . ." and then it'll give the name of the file I was last working on because, when you turn it off, it stays on whatever file you were working on. And it will give me the time. You can slow down the speech or speed it up. So I am now ready to take my notes and when I get home I can print them out in braille and I'll either edit them or file them. It does have the capability to echo back everything I input into it. And if I don't like the way it pronounces a word, I can change it. It has a dictionary in it and I can change the phonics of the way it speaks a word. This is helpful with people's names. It has a 300,000 word spell-checker and it also recognizes apostrophes. So when you write a document, you can go through and spell-check it. It has a "find" mechanism in it so if you download a book into this and you're reading it, and you just want to find some section of the book, you just need to go to the top of the file and hit the search mechanism like on any other computer and you punch in what you're searching for and it will go right to it. It is extremely fast. Faster than some of the PCs I've used.

At present there are three levels to the Braille 'n Speak. The very basic level, which they call the Braille 'n Speak Classic, includes the clock, the calendar, and the regular (not scientific) calculator. The classic has a capacity of 45 pages. The next level, the 640, has a 150-page capability, and the last level, the 2000, is the one described above. The 2000 has many additional programs such as a metronome. According to Charlie,

> I can also plug this from the disk drive port into a modem, into the telephone line, and now I can access the Internet. The other nice technology I have is a scanner. When I first got that, I was able for the first time in 50 years to read my own mail. There is also a checking program I've downloaded to keep track of the balance in my checking account. I can also write checks and print them out. I can do all my checking privately and no one else has to know what I have. I don't need anyone to read my mail, my letters, and bills, so I have privacy. I don't have anything to hide, don't get me wrong, it's just that now I can get the information first.

The above are just some examples of the devices and technological advances that have evolved over a relatively short span of time into products that give many people with vision loss the capability to read and write independently (e.g., American Foundation for the Blind, 2002b; University of Illinois at Urbana-Champaign, Graduate School of Library and Information Science, 2002). And new products are being developed every day. For example, in 2000 a new notetaker, BrailleNote, a competitor to the Braille 'n Speak, came on the market. It features an eight-key Braille keyboard, Braille display (18 or 32 cells), and voice output. Both the BrailleNote and the Braille 'n Speak offer notetaking, word processing as well as some basic organizational functions, speech output, and a calendar, and they can interface to a computer. But they differ in the commands that they use. The BrailleNote has a more intuitive menu system, especially if the person already uses a computer, and gives the option of a Braille or QWERTY keyboard. Both connect to the computer but in different ways. The Braille-Note has a few innovative features (e.g., a global positioning system, or GPS) and is simpler to learn for many. It claims to "produce results that are compatible with those produced by standard Windows applications" (http://www.braillenote.com). However, the Braille 'n Speak has been around for over 15 years and is a pretty stable product (http://www.freedom scientific.com).

Developments in technologies for people with hearing loss have similarly evolved into sophisticated devices that provide the means to take in data, process information, and communicate independently with anyone, anywhere in the world. Technologies have provided important means of rendering many barriers much less significant, barriers that so many people have found frustrating and even overwhelming and oppressive. Yet, technology has not been able to make hearing and vision loss irrelevant. There are many challenges to living with hearing and vision loss, and this is unique to each individual. The meaning hearing or vision loss has for any given person is an individualized construction that has evolved through a complex interplay of one's personality, the attitudes and behaviors of others, and the kinds and quality of assistance and instruction provided. This is the topic to which we turn in chapter 3.

3

THE PERSONAL MEANING OF
HEARING OR VISION LOSS

I always felt I was on the outside looking in. There was a glass window there, and I couldn't get by it.

—An adult woman deaf since birth

Something has to be done about feelings. Because feelings are so elusive and so complex and so painful sometimes.

—A woman with adult onset severe hearing loss

When you use another person to help you, you have no secrets.

—An adult man with complete blindness

People react to changes in their physical and sensory capabilities according to their personality and personal attitudes. These are formed by their history of social relationships and background experiences, lifestyle preferences, established interpersonal networks and communication needs, judgment and outlook regarding their perceived capabilities and functioning in a variety of situations, and the adjustment patterns they have established to deal with loss and change (e.g., Scherer, 1996a, 2000). The characteristics of the environments in which they typically find themselves (including the physical or built environment as well as the attitudes of the people within those environments) also exert a strong influence on how people react to their hearing and vision loss. Of course, one of the biggest factors in determining such reactions is the nature and severity of that loss, at what age it occurred, and whether there is associated pain or additional illnesses or injuries.

Hofstra University professor Frank Bowe has long been an advocate for people with disabilities and was one of the key individuals behind the creation of the 1990 Americans With Disabilities Act. In 1994, he gave a plenary presentation during which he made it clear that the information highway has not always been a smooth road (Bowe, 1994). Told in concert with some rather humorous examples of his early technology use, he underscores the evolution in technologies and the personal reactions of people with sensory loss to them.

> Larry Scadden [Dr. Scadden wrote the Preface to this book] and I both spoke on the phone a few weeks ago. Larry has been blind since he was 4. I have been deaf since I was 3. We were saying how it's kind of amazing that we made it through the public schools despite the fact that there was no technology to accommodate us. Yet, both of us have continued our education. We both have PhDs. We have to in the kind of work we do, collecting information, analyzing it, reporting it. We both use technologies for that today.
>
> Larry and I have made a movement from people to machines. When Larry and I were young, we interacted with information as mediated by other people. Larry had to use braille, and people had to produce that braille for him. People had to read books, translate them to braille, read them into a tape recorder—very people intensive, very labor intensive. That was true for me, too. I was about 20 when I made my first phone call. I was in my 30s before I watched my first TV program and understood what was happening. Virtually every interaction I had needed to be mediated by other people. When watching TV, hearing people had to stop and explain to me what was going on. If someone telephoned me, somebody else took the call. If I was calling my mother, if I was calling for a date, whatever, it was done by somebody else. I can still remember being in my dorm room studying for an exam and somebody comes in and said, "You just got a phone call from Steve. You're going to meet him at the library at 8 o'clock to give him some tutoring." And I said, "Oh, I am?" Other people made decisions for me because it was just too much trouble to involve me in the phone call.

Fitting in and belonging are important goals for all adolescents—actually, for people at any age. According to Erik Erikson (1963), a personality theorist who developed a theory of stages of psychosocial development, adolescence is the crucial time when a person develops a view of the self as an individual and as part of a peer group. The kinds of relationship styles, patterns, and preferences formed here are likely to shape future choices in friendships and potential partners. A primary task of adolescence, thus, is to come to know oneself as an individual and as part of one or more social groups. Dr. Bowe describes his experience of trying to fit in and be like his peers:

> I remember being 14 or 15 trying hard to blend in like all 14- and 15-year-olds. People were watching TV shows and movies in those days, and I was trying to do that, too. I remember standing in front of the TV set for four and a half hours, completely unable to lip-read even one word and getting frustrated (because I'm a good lip-reader), but a half hour went by and I understood nothing. Finally my father came

home from work, stood there for 2 seconds and said, "Here's the problem. They're speaking in French. It's being dubbed into English."

While this was said with humor from the perspective of a well-adjusted and highly successful adult, it is obvious that he had experienced many miscommunications, embarrassing situations, and, as a consequence, frustration when trying to connect with others.

People have a great need to be affiliated or connected with others, and education derives much of its power from connecting teacher with student, and students with each other. Of course, students at different ages have different needs for connection. In this chapter, I discuss Erikson's developmental stages and Abraham Maslow's (1954) hierarchy of needs within the context of educating students with vision or hearing loss. Although I focus primarily on hearing loss in this chapter, many of the experiences discussed will be recognizable to people with vision loss and other disabilities.

REACTIONS TO HEARING AND VISION LOSS DEPEND ON MANY FACTORS

For 7 years I taught "Introduction to Educational Psychology" at the University of Rochester, Eastman School of Music. Broadly, educational psychology is concerned with learner development and diversity, motivation and thinking, and teaching and instructional strategies. Two important aspects of learner characteristics, of prime interest in this chapter, are the ways in which people develop as individuals with unique preferences and characteristics, and the ways in which people are motivated to learn.

Earlier, Erikson's theory of psychosocial development was mentioned in the context of adolescence as a crucial time for coming to know oneself as an individual and as part of one or more social groups. Erikson's theory of the psychosocial development of the normal/healthy personality throughout the life span is very popular in educational psychology (e.g., Eggen & Kauchak, 2001; Ormrod, 2000) because it speaks well to the fundamental personal and educational issues confronting learners from elementary through postsecondary education. It also emphasizes the interaction of personal, social, and educational stresses typically faced during these phases of the life span.

Erikson (1963) believed that people progress through a sequence of stages to a higher or more advanced level of development. Erikson conceived of eight stages or *crises* a person needs to resolve before the healthy adult personality can fully emerge. If a particular crisis is not resolved, it is more difficult to successfully resolve successive crises. Erikson's stages of psycho-social development, with a focus on the positive outcomes of each crisis, are as follows:

1. *Infancy*

   Trust versus Mistrust
   Satisfaction of basic survival needs
   leads to trust in the self and
   others and to hope, optimism

2. *The toddler*

   Autonomy versus Shame and Doubt
   Expression of self-control leads
   to autonomy

3. *Early childhood*

   Initiative versus Guilt
   Positive outcomes of having
   exhibited initiative lead to purpose,
   ambition

4. *School age*

   Industry versus Inferiority
   Success at activities leads to
   a sense of accomplishment and
   adequacy

5. *Adolescence*

   Identity versus Confusion
   An understanding of the self,
   self-confidence, able to make
   choices and to express them

6. *Young adulthood*

   Intimacy versus Isolation
   The capacity to give and receive love

7. *Adulthood*

   Generativity versus Stagnation
   The desire to nurture, produce, create

8. *Old age*

   Integrity versus Despair
   Viewing one's life as complete
   and fulfilled

But what is it like to progress through these stages if one has a hearing loss or cannot see? For some individuals, it may not make any difference. But for others, as Dr. Frank Bowe alluded to above, there are additional challenges and obstacles to the development of self-confidence, making and expressing choices, and feeling that one fits in and belongs. Being accepted by peers, having a source of emotional support from friends, and knowing the rules of acceptable behavior can elude some. An illustration follows.

Like Frank Bowe, Janet was also born with hearing loss. Janet has a PhD in electrical engineering and works for a Fortune 500 company. She never married and lives with her aging mother who, until 3 years ago when her own hearing deteriorated, made all of Janet's phone calls.

Janet is a tall, attractive woman who walks with deliberation, although with a slow pace and stiff posture. She rarely smiles and has a soft-spoken voice with little inflection to it. Her conversational style is as deliberate as her movement, and she uses her analytical mind to carefully select and weigh her words before she speaks them. Thus, our interview started out slowly. I began by drawing a "lifeline" across a sheet of paper and asked Janet to mark off key events in her life. She put her first mark on the lifeline for the day she began school.

> I've worn hearing aids since childhood. It was the aid of the time which made no concessions to my size. It had a battery pack strapped to my leg and I had to wear an aid about the size of three or four packs of cigarettes on my chest. I went to school, and I kept looking around to see if anybody was staring. No one was, and after the first day it was basically all over.
>
> Everything was generally okay until high school. Then I was in an environment that was socially far more difficult, and at that point it did become clear that I was different. And I felt different, socially different. I felt handicapped in not knowing how to play the game. I felt that there were a lot of rules of conduct out there that were not written rules of behavior. I did not know what they were, so I would just violate some code of behavior. There were times when that just ruined my self-confidence. I always felt I was on the outside looking in. There was a glass window there, and I couldn't get by it. This not only made me introverted but unaware of other people's needs. And so I changed from being basically a person who liked other people to a person who was afraid of them.
>
> And a loner. I was developing a self-image of myself as one who was strong and independent. It was a way of living with it. I just incorporated it as part of my persona. That's not to say that I was completely happy with it, but I was beginning the process of developing something that I could live with. And there were some rewards. I get work done. I get a feeling of accomplishment from being able to work by myself. I get some peace. I think other people have to learn some of this and some never do.

I then asked Janet about the lifeline mark for the time she was in college. This should have been a time, according to Erikson's theory, when her focus turned to the formation of intimate, mutually satisfying relationships and the knowledge that such relationships require reciprocity, compromise, and sacrifices. When people cannot learn the relevant "rules of conduct" and form intimate relationships, then a sense of isolation may result. I asked Janet what college was like and whether her friendships were different from those in high school.

In college I read a lot—not studied a lot. I was treating myself with what I chose to read. It was a way of learning, maybe, social mannerisms without having to understand the situation you're in. That's the way I learned the rules. By reading, not by doing. I was not very outgoing, didn't smile that much, wasn't that friendly. The social niceties and rules are things I'm still learning with some regret that I didn't see them earlier.

If I had it to do over again, I'd be much more assertive in forming friendships. I developed a philosophy, probably through a fear of rejection, that I was going to go just halfway and no more. It was like holding your hand out. If they didn't reach right out to take it, I was going to pull it away.

When I asked her what, with this insight, she would try to do differently if she could go back and change things, she replied:

One thing I would try to do is be very much more up front about my hearing loss. And be more assertive. Especially in forming friendships. Also, I think that if I had had the opportunity to go to a school for the deaf instead of a regular school, I often think my personality would have been completely different. Maybe my career would not have been as rewarding, but I might actually have been happier.

As when Janet was growing up, many young people today with hearing loss also feel socially isolated and disconnected from their peers. In any attempt to understand individual differences in adjustment to and views of hearing loss, it is often informative to look to theories such as Erikson's around which such an attempt can be based as they can lead to a deeper perspective of the roots of depression, anxiety, anger, loneliness, and social isolation often encountered when working with people with severe hearing loss.

Within the population of people with disabilities, the disability associated with the most psychological problems is that of hearing loss (e.g., de Graaf & Bijl, 1998; Pollard, 1996). As revealed in the quotes earlier, there is an emotional and psychological adjustment to childhood hearing loss, but people adjusting to hearing loss later in life can find it particularly difficult (e.g., Kristina, 1995). However, adjustment is highly variable and depends on the individual's life experiences, customary ways of managing challenges, and degree of sociability (e.g., Thomas, 1985; Vernon & Andrews, 1995). For example, those individuals who are outgoing, prefer group activities, and have careers that emphasize interpersonal contacts react differently to adult onset hearing loss than those who lead more private lives. And while for some hearing aids are a lifeline, for others they are an inconvenience or embarrassment (e.g., Schirmer, 2001). The personal meaning people attach to technology use is individualized and affects people of all ages with all types of disabilities (e.g., Pape, Kim, & Weiner, 2002;

Scherer, 2000). The bottom line, according to one woman I interviewed, is "You have to make the choice between being connected and not connected. All the devices and modifications are not going to help if there isn't an emotional readiness to use them."

The choice to wear a hearing aid and feel stigmatized or not wear a hearing aid and possibly miscommunicate is a dilemma with strong implications for one's sense of connection and self-esteem. In addition, the personal and social aspects of coming to terms with a hearing loss are often stressful. When under stress, one's ability to hear and participate in interactions becomes compromised. This was articulated well during one of my interviews:

> There are days now when I feel tired and I don't hear as well. When I'm rested I hear better. So, it's very clear to me that my hearing is determined by my well-being. It's important that I reduce the stress and anxiety and exhaustion that comes from having to put forth all these efforts to hear and to comprehend.

A cycle of stress and social isolation can develop for those people who have yet to adjust to their hearing loss and find ways to relax, participate in social relationships (perhaps through the use of hearing aids and assistive listening devices), and make the essential personal, interpersonal, and environmental accommodations needed to be comfortable participating in conversations and social activities (e.g., Thomas, 1985).

NEED SATISFACTION, MOTIVATION, AND SELF-ESTEEM

Maslow developed a hierarchy of five basic levels of needs in the order in which individuals attempt to satisfy them:

1. Physical
   a. survival
   b. security
2. Social/affiliation
   a. belonging
   b. esteem
3. Intellectual/achievement
   a. knowledge
   b. understanding
4. Aesthetic
5. Self-actualization

Maslow maintained that needs must be met at each successive level, beginning with the lowest or physical needs, before one will move on to the next level, and that frustrated needs result in anger or anxiety. A young

TABLE 3.1
Psychosocial Learning and Behavioral Challenges Facing People With Hearing and Vision Loss

Sensory disability	Psychosocial learning challenges	Psychosocial behavioral challenges
Hearing loss	Lack of exposure to verbal dialogue and information presented in auditory media.	Less general information about the world and interpersonal communication styles.
	Lack of exposure to verbal information and cues (e.g., voice inflection, verbal indicators of mood and affect).	Confusion and misunderstandings due to lack of perception of verbal clues to conversational affect and meaning.
Vision loss	Lack of exposure to visual information (e.g., nonverbal cues, body language, films, and other visual media).	Confusion about what is visually happening in group situations or presentations.
	Less opportunity to observe and imitate the behavior of others.	Uncertainty about nonverbal behavior and anxiety when with others.

adult who is suddenly aware of significant hearing loss may have been at the level of achievement only to have to focus once again on self-esteem and social needs. Often such adults will find themselves in the position of having to move through each stage again, meeting the needs for affiliation with new friends and perhaps meeting achievement needs in an entirely new career area than originally planned.

When we consider Maslow's social/affiliation needs for belonging and esteem and overlay this onto Erikson's fifth stage, adolescence, and the development of identity versus confusion, we can see the importance each has placed on self-esteem. Erikson, like Maslow, emphasizes the importance at this stage of developing an understanding of the self, self-confidence, and the ability to make choices and to express them.

Self-esteem involves having a clear notion of self, having a clear identity, and believing that these are valued. The information we receive and give is constantly being fed into our identity. When we cannot receive certain kinds of information, or the information we receive is confused, incomplete, or comes much too fast, it can be overwhelming and lead to identity crises and low self-esteem (e.g., Seppa, 1997; Shirmer, 2001; Tuttle & Tuttle, 1996). Table 3.1 summarizes psychosocial learning and behavioral challenges for people who are deaf or who are blind when they cannot receive some kinds of information.

When going and growing through the developmental process of the adolescent and young adult years, the lack of connections to peers and the formation of firm identity can have a negative effect on self-esteem. One woman, Kate, relates how she did well as a child and teenager, but the transition to college life proved to be very difficult. Once again, I used the lifeline interview technique to get an idea of the key events she recalls most vividly in her life. About her early school years, she said,

> In grade school I was okay. The teachers put me in the front seat of every class and they did all the teaching. They stayed in the front of the class and would make notes on the blackboard. As long as I sat in front of the class, I had a good understanding of what was going on. In high school, it was pretty much the same way except for senior English. The teacher had this method of teaching which was to ask questions and have the class participate. He'd make a statement and get a response and say, "That's great. Now build on that." And I'd be sitting there in the front of the class thinking, "What was that answer? What's happening now?" And I was totally lost. I used to consider that my fault, that I was not paying attention, because that's what used to be written on my report cards so often. It never occurred to me to state that I was not able to hear. I used to consider it my problem and that I was the one who had to adjust to it.
>
> That's why I never finished college. My hearing loss was becoming so devastating to me, I was not hearing, I was doing the wrong homework. I went from being a very, very happy person going into college to a very devastated one. It was the first time in my life I realized I couldn't handle it. I went from being a very outgoing person to the point where I became very withdrawn. I didn't want to see anyone. I wouldn't be with anyone.

She then told me that she had met her husband in college, which was very fortunate as he saved her life.

> If it hadn't been for him, I would have committed suicide due to the depression and social isolation from my hearing loss. Stewart, my husband now, but we were just dating then, said, "We're going to get you a hearing aid." So he and I went and looked at hearing aids and I tried one on. I'll never forget that . . . that was just an incredible experience. I said, "What's that noise, what's that hum I hear?" and it was the air conditioner. I'd never heard an air conditioner before.

With a newfound capability of connecting to her world, one would think that Kate would have begun to experience enhanced self-esteem. But a negative perspective can prove difficult to dislodge. Kate then related how she felt stigmatized by hearing aids even though her real difficulty was the social management of loss of information.

> But after getting my hearing aid, every time I went outside I wore a scarf, so that if the wind blew, people would not see that I wore a

hearing aid. You just didn't see 20-year-olds wearing a hearing aid. It was not an easy thing to get used to.

It's been very hard over the years, because I had gotten into so many situations where I didn't fully understand what is being said. And I'd say maybe the wrong thing or respond to something I heard, but the subject had already changed. And when you feel off-the-track and lost so often, you begin to lose your sense of being okay.

I had people on campus once in a while say, "Oh, I saw you before and you ignored me." Or, "I said hi to you the other day, and you didn't even look up." It was so devastating. I'm a friendly person. I like people and having a social life, and I was slowly becoming a lonely and isolated person.

I then asked Kate, "So, it was you who changed? The people who were out there that you couldn't communicate with may or may not have changed, so was it more of an adjustment in you?"

Probably. The people out there that I couldn't communicate with didn't change, it was me.

Our interactions with similar others can ameliorate or reverse psychological distress when these interactions result in observing and sharing strategies that can be incorporated into a more positive view of the self. From other people we obtain the necessary ingredients for our self-image, self-esteem, and sense of well-being. Communication exchanges help us form a healthy identity or, as in the case of Janet earlier, can lead to confusion and ultimately to isolation when they are not complete or positive. When working with individuals with disabilities, regardless of age or developmental stage, a peer network or support group can be very helpful. These groups are composed of others with similar disabilities and, thus, shared experiences. As Janet said, she might have fared better emotionally if she had attended a school for the deaf. But within the inclusive educational environment of today, such peer support can be obtained within the school and outside of it through activities sponsored by organizations and associations. One such organization is Self Help for Hard of Hearing People with 250 chapters throughout the United States, many of which have children's groups (www.shhh.org). Self Help for Hard of Hearing People has an international membership and a sister organization in Australia.

ADJUSTMENT

For individuals who are born with a hearing or vision loss, adjustment can be a lifelong process. And any given individual can exhibit a combination of adjustment patterns over time and across situations. But for some who acquire a hearing or vision loss in adulthood, adjustment to changed sensory capabilities can be traumatic.

Lee Meyerson, who has a severe hearing loss himself, is Regents Professor of Psychology (retired) at Arizona State University. He is a past president of the American Psychological Association's Division 22 (Rehabilitation Psychology) and the founding editor of the journal *Rehabilitation Psychology*. Meyerson has devoted his career to developing procedures for evaluating and improving the skills of people with disabilities. After World War II, he characterized several adjustment patterns typical of adults with recent onset hearing loss (R. G. Barker, Wright, Meyerson, & Gonick, 1953). Although he addressed hearing loss, many of the same feelings and reactions he characterized then are experienced today and are also shared by those with eyesight loss in adulthood. Meyerson's Adjustment Pattern 1 is adopted by a person like Janet, who prefers to withdraw to the safe and familiar. Janet became an avid reader to attempt to master and control life events without having to actually connect with others. In Adjustment Pattern 2, the person acts "as if" he or she has no hearing loss at all. Great energy may be devoted to reducing, disguising, or compensating for the hearing loss in the face of different communication abilities and the existence of barriers to optimal interaction. Such people may live in limbo between two worlds, feeling ashamed of their hearing loss but sensing that they are not quite up to par with the conversational capabilities of their "normally hearing cohorts." In Adjustment Pattern 3, the person with hearing loss recognizes that fact and accepts it as part of him- or herself without devaluing the self.

A person may be in Adjustment Pattern 1 socially but be in Adjustment Pattern 3 at work, or vice versa. And although some may come to adjust to their hearing loss in several important ways, there may be permanent scars that come to define an individual's preferred lifestyle and even fundamental personality. Janet is an example. While she can articulate the impact it has made on her life, she has incorporated that impact into a permanent part of her identity.

Another person explained to me the sheer fatigue involved in trying to maintain a social life in the context of hearing loss. Even though she has many friends and is socially quite active, there are occasions when she prefers to be alone and enjoy solitary activities. For her, learning to be content while being alone has become a coping strategy.

> I have to feel very energetic to go into situations where there are a lot of people where I'm going to have a difficult time hearing everyone. I avoid parties and prefer lunches with two, three, or four people. I have learned to enjoy my own company. I'm very good at being alone. I wasn't always, but I read a lot. I watch TV and do crossword puzzles.

Many individuals with hearing loss find it helpful to socialize and learn from others with hearing loss. It can be less fatiguing, and there are guaranteed shared experiences. There is a vast literature on the benefits of social support and having available others who understand from firsthand experience one's everyday obstacles and frustrations (e.g., Pillemer & Suitor, 1996; Yalom, 1995). It can be reassuring, and it lets people know that they are not alone in what they are feeling and perceiving. Support groups have also been found to be very helpful in modeling and sharing new strategies for communication. For Kate, the achievement of Adjustment Pattern 3 occurred only after joining just such a support group:

> I finally had enough self-esteem to say, "I didn't hear that, would you mind repeating it?" I can do that now very comfortably. I never would have believed that a support group could be worth anything and I've totally changed my thinking about that. Because they helped me realize that it's not a deficit in me, it's not something I'm doing wrong, just in my hearing. My attitude about myself, my expectations changed. Needed to change. Looking back across this lifeline, I see that it probably took 25 years before I finally felt as though I had really, totally regained my self-esteem.

Dave is an engineer with a major corporation who has a severe hearing loss. According to Dave, too, adjustment to hearing loss requires self-knowledge and self-advocacy.

> As I see it, the issue with people with hearing loss is that if someone has a problem, it's to some extent their own darn fault. There is obviously a loss of hearing, but other people with the same degree of hearing loss are coping really quite well. I think a lot of this is a mental attitude. And I think perhaps the most important thing is being assertive. Until the individual is willing to assert himself or herself, nothing will happen. I know a woman who really has need of a loop system in a meeting situation and yet she will not set up the loop and say, "Folks, I need to have your cooperation in order for me to communicate with you. I need to have you use the microphone." She won't do that because, I think, she's not comfortable asserting her needs.
>
> There is a lot of work I think that could be done on the psychological impact of a hearing loss. I never had an appreciation for what some people have gone through, and what it has done to them, really, as an individual. So much of the effect of hearing loss is dependent on the makeup of the individual. Some, I can perceive, have been significantly changed as far as their personality is concerned. There are a lot of people out there from family situations where the rest of the family will not accommodate the individual or will not make a little extra effort to communicate with them. The biggest need for hard-of-hearing people is to, first, accept their loss and, second, to actively involve themselves

in improving their quality of life by doing something about it and asserting what they need.

According to Dave, he was always Adjustment Pattern 3. He told me that he was more of an introvert and so never particularly felt his life changed as a result of his hearing loss.

> For me, hearing loss didn't represent that big a change in my lifestyle. There are times, when I get in groups at parties, that I feel left out of it, but I accept that and I know there's nothing that I can do about it. So, why worry about it. I try to find one or two people to communicate with, and as long as I can do that, it's fine. I tend to be an introvert anyway, so that I usually spend a moderate amount of time not necessarily by myself, but in solo activities. I like to do a lot of reading.

Unlike Dave, many people who become very hard of hearing or deaf after early childhood and after they have acquired language (termed *adventitiously deafened*) talk about how the world has seemed to have gone "dead," and that they have come to feel isolated and out of contact with the world. For them, hearing aids can be very important and can help them reconnect and develop an adjustment pattern that is close to Adjustment Pattern 3, even though those hearing aids may not restore the person's hearing (e.g., Scheetz, 2001; Tyler & Schum, 1995).

In fact, some interactions can be especially problematic for those with hearing loss, even when they do have hearing aids. As one woman pointed out to me,

> Hearing loss is such a painful disability, psychologically speaking and socially speaking. It impacts every bit of your life. Including your sex life. I had to choose between hearing what my husband said and having a whistle or perhaps breaking my hearing aid. Or not hearing what he said. I'm talking about in bed. So you're losing the endearments and the intimacies. In parent–child relationships, too, you lose intimacy and those little intimate conversations. Who does your child confide in? Because you don't raise your voice to talk about intimate matters. You talk about them softly.

Achieving Adjustment Pattern 3 can be a hard-won battle that requires time, a supportive partner and other family members, and even a social or peer support group. It also depends on the individual's core resources, temperament, and personality. As one person said to me,

> It's been difficult through the years. I was tenacious, and that helped. And resilient. I think I absorbed a lot of hurt and rose above it. When I talked about tenacity . . . the only way you can hang onto your self-esteem is to be tenacious. You can't expect other people to constantly say, "You're okay." And you somehow have to hold onto "I'm okay."

This person went on to say how the psychological effects of hearing loss, the personal meaning of hearing loss to each unique person, has not been given enough emphasis. Today, with time pressures on medical and health care providers, counseling and psychological services have been reduced as a result.

> Something has to be done about feelings. Because feelings are so elusive and so complex and so painful sometimes. It's very hard for people to deal with that, and I understand, and I think that's both the most important and hardest part. And why people have not dealt with it. Feelings are different for everyone and it takes energy and real expertise to try to sort them out. When you have that figured out, only then you can start talking about hearing aids and assistive listening devices.

In summary, as the individuals quoted in this chapter have indicated, both hearing and vision loss occurring at any point in the life span can have a negative impact on mental health, social relationships, and functional status, and these negative effects can be reduced through the use of appropriate technologies (Heine & Browning, 2002; Keller, Morton, Thomas, & Potter, 1999; Wallhagen, Strawbridge, Shema, Kurata, & Kaplan, 2001). The benefit from the use of technologies will be affected by the degree to which the user has realistic expectations of the gains that can occur from their use, and this will be an outgrowth of a person's temperament–personality (Barry & Barry, 2002; Barry & McCarthy, 2001), general outlook, judgment, degree of optimism, and prior experiences and satisfaction with technology use (Scherer, 2000; Scherer & Frisina, 1998).

For people with hearing loss especially, intimate relationships are affected (Hetu, Jones, & Getty, 1993), and a general lack of connection and communication has been chain-linked to constricted social relationships, isolation, and social withdrawal; stress, fatigue, and irritability; depression, loneliness, and low self-esteem; poor subjective quality of life; and a reduced psychological and general health status (Aguayo & Coady, 2001; Knutson & Lansing, 1990; Mulrow et al., 1990). Peer support has been found to be helpful to many. As one deaf person said to me,

> We all have learned from each other. Strategies and skills, and so forth. And feelings. That was very important. It was very supportive to be in a group of people of whom some were having a greater difficulty and some were having the same difficulty. I mean it really gave you a sense of where you fit in and that your observations and assumptions were appropriate . . . because it was confirmed by other people having them. That is a very important thing for self-esteem.

In addition to the difficulties that can occur in trying to find help with these various psychological aspects of coming to terms and living with hearing or vision loss, we all live in a time of flux with all the attendant anxieties associated with change. The technological and information explosions have left many of us feeling overwhelmed; we feel controlled, not in control. There is too much to do with too little time to do it within the workplace, schools are acclimating students to overloaded schedules, and life at home is grabbing fast-food meals between myriad activities. We often have an unclear sense of purpose and our place in the scheme of things. In short, with or without hearing, with or without eyesight, we all feel disconnected at times. But this is compounded when one cannot take in and process information, exchange that information with others, and use information to grow and develop. Fatigue and frustration are frequent outcomes of less-than-successful attempts to understand what one cannot hear, making it all the more difficult to interact and communicate. But today, there are legislative mandates and advances in the development and availability of assistive and educational technologies, and there is a system in place to enable all students to learn equally regardless of their level of hearing or eyesight. Inclusive education exists in which students learn together and interact regardless of their level of hearing, vision, mobility, or speech. The growth in educational technologies and assistive technologies and how they have shaped and are used in educational settings is the topic to which we now turn.

Scherer, 2000). The bottom line, according to one woman I interviewed, is "You have to make the choice between being connected and not connected. All the devices and modifications are not going to help if there isn't an emotional readiness to use them."

The choice to wear a hearing aid and feel stigmatized or not wear a hearing aid and possibly miscommunicate is a dilemma with strong implications for one's sense of connection and self-esteem. In addition, the personal and social aspects of coming to terms with a hearing loss are often stressful. When under stress, one's ability to hear and participate in interactions becomes compromised. This was articulated well during one of my interviews:

> There are days now when I feel tired and I don't hear as well. When I'm rested I hear better. So, it's very clear to me that my hearing is determined by my well-being. It's important that I reduce the stress and anxiety and exhaustion that comes from having to put forth all these efforts to hear and to comprehend.

A cycle of stress and social isolation can develop for those people who have yet to adjust to their hearing loss and find ways to relax, participate in social relationships (perhaps through the use of hearing aids and assistive listening devices), and make the essential personal, interpersonal, and environmental accommodations needed to be comfortable participating in conversations and social activities (e.g., Thomas, 1985).

NEED SATISFACTION, MOTIVATION, AND SELF-ESTEEM

Maslow developed a hierarchy of five basic levels of needs in the order in which individuals attempt to satisfy them:

1. Physical
   a. survival
   b. security
2. Social/affiliation
   a. belonging
   b. esteem
3. Intellectual/achievement
   a. knowledge
   b. understanding
4. Aesthetic
5. Self-actualization

Maslow maintained that needs must be met at each successive level, beginning with the lowest or physical needs, before one will move on to the next level, and that frustrated needs result in anger or anxiety. A young

	...sorted in auditory media.	...about the world and interpersonal communication styles.
	Lack of exposure to verbal information and cues (e.g., voice inflection, verbal indicators of mood and affect).	Confusion and misunderstandings due to lack of perception of verbal clues to conversational affect and meaning.
Vision loss	Lack of exposure to visual information (e.g., nonverbal cues, body language, films, and other visual media).	Confusion about what is visually happening in group situations or presentations.
	Less opportunity to observe and imitate the behavior of others.	Uncertainty about nonverbal behavior and anxiety when with others.

adult who is suddenly aware of significant hearing loss may have been at the level of achievement only to have to focus once again on self-esteem and social needs. Often such adults will find themselves in the position of having to move through each stage again, meeting the needs for affiliation with new friends and perhaps meeting achievement needs in an entirely new career area than originally planned.

When we consider Maslow's social/affiliation needs for belonging and esteem and overlay this onto Erikson's fifth stage, adolescence, and the development of identity versus confusion, we can see the importance each has placed on self-esteem. Erikson, like Maslow, emphasizes the importance at this stage of developing an understanding of the self, self-confidence, and the ability to make choices and to express them.

Self-esteem involves having a clear notion of self, having a clear identity, and believing that these are valued. The information we receive and give is constantly being fed into our identity. When we cannot receive certain kinds of information, or the information we receive is confused, incomplete, or comes much too fast, it can be overwhelming and lead to identity crises and low self-esteem (e.g., Seppa, 1997; Shirmer, 2001; Tuttle & Tuttle, 1996). Table 3.1 summarizes psychosocial learning and behavioral challenges for people who are deaf or who are blind when they cannot receive some kinds of information.

When going and growing through the developmental process of the adolescent and young adult years, the lack of connections to peers and the

III

ENVIRONMENTS
FOR LEARNING

4

THE MOVE FROM SEPARATE TO INCLUSIVE EDUCATION

[M]ainstreaming hasn't been the greatest thing for her. Emotionally I'm
not sure it was worth it.
—Mother of a deaf college student

I don't know who I would be now if I had had that kind of [discussion
group/counseling opportunity], whether I would have managed a better
education, whether I would be a different person, I don't know.
—A deaf adult who was educated in a public school

Most students with disabilities today, regardless of whether their disability involves hearing, eyesight, speech, mobility loss, or learning difficulties, receive their primary and secondary education in schools with nondisabled peers. This was originally termed *mainstreamed education*, but the current term is *inclusive education*. As noted earlier, inclusive education has been made possible in large measure through the existence of educational technologies and assistive technologies (ATs).

With or without a disability, high school students of the 21st century have been living, studying, and playing in a high-tech world of VCRs, computers, CDs, DVDs, the Internet, and the World Wide Web. They share their high-tech world with peers of varying cultural and ethnic backgrounds, and for their entire schooling, they have been more or less integrated with students from diverse backgrounds in their classes.

Just over 25 years ago in 1975, the American vision was not particularly accepting of diversity nor was it particularly global. Then several things happened at once. In 1975 the educational "mainstreaming law" (Pub. L. 94-142) was passed as the Education of All Handicapped Children Act. This law mandated that children and adolescents with disabilities be educated in the "least restrictive setting" and that, as much as possible, students with disabilities should be included in regular classrooms. Over time, students with disabilities were being included in "regular classrooms" all right, but they increasingly began to use ATs and adaptations to educational technologies to compete successfully in those classrooms (e.g., Hasselbring & Glaser, 2000; Parette, 1991). Because of the nature of their unique educational tools, they looked different from other students equipped with little more than the standard textbooks, notebooks, and pens (e.g., Scherer, 1991, 1992b). While classrooms became more physically integrated, they certainly were not integrated socially. And to much the same extent, this is true today.

Microelectronics has enabled machines and computers to become more sophisticated, yet smaller and more portable, and both the capabilities of students with disabilities and the opportunities open to them have expanded significantly. The increased availability of electronic, computerized ATs (such as those used to caption spoken words into real-time text display in large lecture rooms) has meant that students with severe physical disabilities *can* participate in regular classrooms. It has only been since ATs have become more available that significant numbers of students with severe disabilities *have* actually been included in regular educational settings (e.g., McKee & Scherer, 1987). Advances in assistive devices facilitated fuller mainstreaming of students with disabilities, and mainstreaming experiences, in turn, created an increased demand for advances in ATs (e.g., Scherer, 1991). As a result, today many more children with severe limitations in hearing, vision, mobility, and speech are able to attend public schools, function independently, and graduate to attend college and become competitively employed. However, access to computers remains a challenge for many, leading to a digital divide or a grouping of students into the haves and have-nots, and this jeopardizes educational equity (e.g., Scherer, 1992a).

As noted in chapter 1, disability-related statistics have not always been collected systematically or consistently. There is also a considerable delay from the time data are collected to the time they are available in reports and articles. Data in Table 4.1 from The *23rd Annual Report to Congress on the Implementation of the Individuals With Disabilities Education Act* (U.S. Department of Education, 2001) show that during the 1990–1991 school year a total of approximately 4.4 million students in the U.S. and insular areas, ages 6–21, were provided special education services. Nine years later, during the 1999–2000 school year, a total of 5.7 million children and youths with disabilities ages 6–21 were served, an overall increase of 30.3% in nine years. The largest single group served was students with specific learning disabilities, but all categories of disability increased at least 10% in 9 years with the largest percentage of growth occurring among students who have other health impairments. Students with visual impairments increased 12.3% and those with hearing impairments (exclusive of deaf-blindness) increased 21.0%. It is likely that many students with visual and hearing impairments also have learning disabilities.

TABLE 4.1

Changes in Number of Students Ages 6 Through 21 Served Under IDEA by Disability Category, 1990–1991 and 1999–2000

	1990–1991	1999–2000	Difference	Change (%)
Specific learning disabilities	2,144,017	2,871,966	727,949	34.0
Speech or language impairments	987,778	1,089,964	102,186	10.3
Mental retardation	551,457	614,433	62,976	11.4
Emotional disturbance	390,764	470,111	79,347	20.3
Multiple disabilities	97,629	112,993	15,364	15.7
Hearing impairments	59,211	71,671	12,460	21.0
Orthopedic impairments	49,340	71,422	22,082	44.8
Other health impairments	56,349	254,110	197,761	351.0
Visual impairments	23,682	26,590	2,908	12.3
Autism		65,424		
Deaf-blindness	1,524	1,845	321	21.1
Traumatic brain injury		13,874		
Developmental delay		19,304		
All disabilities	4,361,751	5,683,707	1,321,956	30.3

Note. From *Annual Report to Congress on the Implementation of the Individuals With Disabilities Education Act* (p. II-23), by U.S. Department of Education, Office of Special Education Programs, 2001. In the public domain.

In the 1997–1998 academic year, 52.5% of the preschool-age children (ages 3–5) received their services in programs designed primarily for nondisabled children. For students with disabilities ages 6 to 21, the proportion is smaller (see Table 4.2 for other statistics for this time frame). This number will no doubt increase as the preschool-age children advance educationally and move through the system.

When type of education environment is considered for students with vision and hearing loss over a 10-year period, there has been a significant move out of separate facilities, classes, and resource rooms and into regular classes. The breakdown is provided in Table 4.3.

The educational environments described in Table 4.3 are defined by the U.S. Department of Education, Office of Special Education and Rehabilitative Services, as follows:

- *Regular class:* A student with a disability is educated in a regular class if he or she is removed from regular classes to receive special education and related services for less than 21% of the school day.
- *Resource room:* A student with a disability is educated in a resource room if he or she receives special education and related

TABLE 4.2
Percentage Distribution of Students With Disabilities
3 to 21 Years Old Receiving Special Education Services,
by Instructional Environment: 1997–1998

Characteristic	All environments	Regular class	Resource room	Separate class
By age				
All persons, 3–21 years old	100.0	47.0	27.2	21.4
3–5 years old	100.0	52.5	8.5	31.2
6–21 years old	100.0	46.4	29.0	20.4
By type of disability				
Mental retardation	100.0	12.6	29.6	51.7
Visual impairments	100.0	48.1	20.1	17.3
Hearing impairments	100.0	38.8	19.0	25.4
Serious emotional disturbances	100.0	24.9	23.3	33.5
Multiple disabilities	100.0	10.0	17.3	45.1

Note. There are some reporting variations, for example, estimated or incomplete data and nonstandard definitions, from state to state. Data for 3- to 5-year-old children are not collected by disability. Disability data are only reported for 6- to 21-year-old students. Because of rounding, details may not add to totals. From U.S. Department of Education, National Center for Education Statistics, 2000, *Digest of Education Statistics,* Table 54. In the public domain.

TABLE 4.3
Ten-Year Change in Educational Environments in Which Students
With Vision and Hearing Loss Are Educated, Ages 6–21

Environment by disability	% in 1986	% in 1996	% point change
Hearing impairments			
Regular class	20.0	36.2	16.2
Resource room	22.4	18.9	−3.5
Separate class	32.6	26.8	−5.8
Separate facilities	25.0	18.2	−6.8
Visual impairments			
Regular class	32.8	47.7	14.9
Resource room	25.1	20.6	−4.5
Separate class	17.9	17.1	−0.08
Separate facilities	24.2	14.6	−9.6

Note. Based on the number of students served under Part B of the Individuals With Disabilities Education Act, in the United States and outlying areas. From *Annual Report to Congress on the Implementation of the Individuals with Disabilities Education Act* by U.S. Department of Education, Office of Special Education Programs, 2001. In the public domain.

services outside the regular class for 21% to 60% of the school day.

- *Separate class*: A student with a disability is educated in a separate class if he or she receives special education and related services outside the regular class for more than 60% of the school day.

- *Separate facilities*: A student with a disability is educated in a separate facility if he or she does not attend school with his or her nondisabled peers; instead, he or she is educated in a separate day school, a residential facility, or a homebound/hospital setting.

Virtually all students with disabilities (96 percent) are now served in regular school buildings. During the 1998–99 school year, 2.9 percent of students with disabilities were educated in public and private separate day schools; 0.7 percent were educated in public and private residential facilities; and 0.5 percent were educated in home/hospital environments. Specific data for students with hearing and visual impairments is in Table 4.4.

According to the statistics from the U.S. Department of Education, as the students continue to move through all levels of educational programs in the 21st century, from preschool through postsecondary education, there will be a tremendous need for technologies to accommodate their learning needs as well as personnel trained in the use of those technologies. This will become all the more important as the population of students with hearing and vision loss in our public schools increasingly bring with them challenges such as additional disabilities (e.g., learning disabilities) or lack of proficiency in English (e.g., Easterbrooks, 1999).

SEPARATE FACILITIES VERSUS INCLUSIVE EDUCATION

Rochester, New York, is home to the Rochester School for the Deaf (RSD), which is primarily a residential school serving deaf students from preschool through high school. Rochester is also home to the National Technical Institute for the Deaf (NTID), one of eight colleges of the Rochester Institute of Technology (RIT). The National Technical Institute for the Deaf is the world's largest technological college for deaf students and the first effort to educate large numbers of deaf students within a college campus planned principally for hearing students. Students come to NTID from all over the United States, as well as several other countries to prepare for a variety of technical careers and to enter bachelor degree programs at RIT. Students in RSD and NTID have the benefit of social and learning environments and instruction adapted to their needs as students who cannot hear. One deaf educator, who is very familiar with both schools' programs and mission, commented to me:

> While the education of deaf students since the mid-'70s has seen a shift away from residential schools towards inclusive education, even today several deaf students at the National Technical Institute for the Deaf who attended inclusive schools believe that socially they would have

TABLE 4.4
Number of Children With Hearing or Visual Impairments Ages 6–21 Served in Different Educational Environments Under IDEA, Part B During School Years 1989–1990 Through 1998–1999

Hearing Impairments

	<21%	21-60%	>60%	Public separate facility	Private separate facility	Public resid facility	Private resid facility	Home hosp envir	Total
1989–1990	15,146	10,170	17,782	3,908	2,028	6,423	479	117	56,053
1990–1991	16,157	11,844	19,693	3,504	1,988	6,261	383	315	60,145
1991–1992	16,469	12,477	19,017	3,512	2,327	6,548	474	80	60,904
1992–1993	18,276	12,227	17,435	3,448	1,674	8,146	542	234	61,982
1993–1994	20,266	13,230	20,295	2,701	1,963	7,030	531	147	66,163
1994–1995	22,539	12,443	18,381	2,447	1,850	5,894	652	133	64,339
1995–1996	24,034	12,532	17,778	2,818	1,791	6,648	663	175	66,439
1996–1997	25,607	12,523	18,142	3,372	1,883	6,046	586	124	68,283
1997–1998	26,697	13,102	17,445	3,168	1,888	5,746	585	161	68,792
1998–1999	27,893	13,177	17,835	3,192	1,820	5,737	592	145	70,391

Visual Impairments

	<21%	21-60%	>60%	Public separate facility	Private separate facility	Public resid facility	Private resid facility	Home hosp envir	Total
1989–1990	9,250	5,561	4,960	778	274	2,181	375	129	23,508
1990–1991	11,177	6,159	5,295	925	410	2,125	219	260	26,570
1991–1992	9,937	5,325	4,923	767	1,370	2,379	286	106	25,093
1992–1993	10,769	4,987	4,266	930	399	2,029	191	120	23,691
1993–1994	11,252	5,299	4,567	630	404	2,366	173	135	24,826
1994–1995	11,534	5,295	4,322	729	474	2,384	234	132	25,104
1995–1996	12,021	5,186	4,299	869	488	1,978	201	145	25,187
1996–1997	12,526	4,972	4,561	990	597	1,897	268	159	25,970
1997–1998	12,535	5,233	4,505	1,263	493	1,522	337	172	26,060
1998–1999	13,042	5,093	4,340	1,226	554	1,589	277	147	26,268

Note. Excludes those with deaf-blindness. Beginning in 1989–1990, states were instructed to report students in regular class, resource room, and separate class placements based on the percent of time they received services outside the regular class (<21, 21-60, and >60, respectively) instead of the percent of time they received special education. resid=residential; hosp=hospital; envir=environment. Data based on the December 1, 1998 count, updated as of September 25, 2000. From *Annual Report to Congress on the Implementation of the Individuals With Disabilities Education Act* (pp. A-193–A-193), by U.S. Department of Education, Office of Special Education Programs, 2001. In the public domain.

been better off being in a residential school—in spite of their belief that inclusion prepared them very well for the academics of college.

A student expressed this sentiment as well as anyone when he said, "I was mainstreamed in high school. When I came to NTID, it was wonderful to meet a lot of other hearing-impaired students and not to feel so weird anymore."

Many deaf students at NTID have told me that students in inclusive educational settings frequently form particularly strong ties—even dependencies—on their parents. They often need parental help and support academically as well as emotionally (e.g., Bondi-Wolcott & Scherer, 1988). For this reason, NTID sponsors special sessions for parents during orientation week to help parents and students "let go" of one another. I had been asked one summer to interview parents and students about their relationships and their experiences with mainstreaming. The mother of one student recalled that, for her daughter,

> high school was difficult—more so socially than academically. Her social experiences were very negative being in a regular classroom. There were no other deaf students in her class. . . . In the end I think she was academically better prepared than she would have been had we left her in with the other deaf students. But mainstreaming hasn't been the greatest thing for her. Emotionally I'm not sure it was worth it.

Another mother felt mainstreaming had limited her own sources of support. "Because she was mainstreamed, I lost contact with some resource people and others to lean on, to have people I could bend their ears when I was having problems."

Solutions to the challenges faced by people with hearing loss often become apparent only when they are far removed from the situation. For example, one adult woman shared her educational and personal experiences with hearing loss from the time she first noticed it at age 12. While her education and social life are no doubt different in many ways from that of today's teenager with a hearing loss, her observations and feelings are just as true now for a lot of people as what she experienced many years ago, despite advances in assistive and educational technologies. "When I was in school, if you had a disability you were on your own. There was no such thing as a support system." This echoed what I was being told by many mainstreamed or included NTID students and their parents. I asked this woman to share her "life story" with me. She began in her adolescent years when she first had appreciable hearing loss.

> I had a drop in hearing the summer before I was 14. I went camping and the other girls I was with were talking about hearing the chipmunks and the rain on the roof of the tent, and I wasn't hearing those sounds. So when I got back home, I went upstairs and I was testing sounds and

I couldn't hear them. I couldn't hear my fingernails tapping on the banister. I had heard a roaring in my ears and I thought it was the wind and the trees and the waves, but when I got home, I still had that noise in my ears. So something happened, and I was so frightened. I prayed that when I woke up in the morning it would be all right, but it wasn't.

I somehow sensed this was going to hurt my parents a lot, and I began to cry to my older sister. I said, "Margie, I can't hear. And I can't go back to school." Well, my sister began to cry. She put her arms around me and she said, "Oh, honey, you have to go back to school." And my parents said that, too. I did go back to school, but I couldn't hear. And I was miserable. My teachers didn't believe me when I said I couldn't hear. They thought that I wasn't paying attention. Even though I couldn't hear the teacher, I did my homework so I got along okay.

I was curious to find out what she would think about being in a different kind of educational setting, one in which students with hearing loss received assistance to participate in school both academically and socially. She had received no help. With the kinds of support available now, what does she think might have happened differently?

The culture from when I was in high school has changed so much. Certain things would not have been possible then that are possible now. What I wish would have happened in high school was the formation of a discussion group. A group led by a trained leader, say a counselor, who understands teenagers and understands hearing loss who would have hearing and hard-of-hearing teenagers who are in the same class together—and the teachers, too—so they could draw them out about their personal experiences and let them share their frustration. Not only the frustration of the hard-of-hearing person in not hearing what the other one says, but the frustration of the hearing teenager in communicating with the hard-of-hearing teenager. Teenagers are self-conscious and they don't want to be different from other teenagers, and they're suspicious of others who are different. I didn't want to be different from them, but they didn't accept me when I was different either. But once you start sharing, then you're getting rid of some of the inhibitions on both sides. A hard-of-hearing teenager doesn't understand his or her own hearing loss that well and the hearing person doesn't know anything about it. So they need to foster that kind of sharing and understanding. And then discuss communication strategies. Here's the situation and here's what you can do about it. For the teachers, how can they use visual aids and assistive devices.

It's important to share feelings and share experiences and understand that you're not alone. It's stressful not knowing what people are saying, so stress management should be a part of it. Another big part that's needed is assertiveness training. Being able to raise your hand in class and asking the teacher to slow down. Otherwise, the hard-of-hearing students miss out on so much of the instruction. I don't know who I would be now if I had had that kind of help, whether I would have managed a better education, whether I would be a different person, I don't know.

Many people who are now adults with significant hearing loss have wished that they had attended a school for the deaf—or wondered how different their lives would be now if they had. They also, like the woman quoted above, offer ideas for how inclusive educational settings can better help deaf and hard-of-hearing students integrate with their peers. Despite advances in technologies for people with hearing loss, many of the fundamental issues around being connected, forming a positive identity and sense of self, and attaining a sense of true belonging have remained the same. Many students today still experience the loneliness and frustration that have been described in the preceding paragraphs and chapters.

INCLUSION HAS CLOSED THE DOORS TO MANY SCHOOLS FOR THE DEAF

Receiving an education in a residential school for the deaf is an option fewer and fewer students are likely to have in the future. Because of the 1975 educational mainstreaming law, subsequently reauthorized as the Individuals With Disabilities Educational Act or IDEA, residential schools for the deaf have experienced a significant reduction in student enrollment, and, as a result, many have closed.

A number of schools for the deaf in the United States have been in continuous operation from as early as 1817, when the first school was opened in Hartford, Connecticut. This was followed by schools in New York in 1818 and Philadelphia in 1820. These schools were the primary foundation for and means of transmitting deaf culture and American Sign Language as the language of deaf culture. *Culture* has been defined in Lang (1994) as "a consistent pattern of thought and action," a phrase he took from Ruth Benedict (1887–1948), whom he profiled in his book, *Silence of the Spheres*. Benedict became deaf as a child from measles and went on to become an eminent anthropologist. Lang (1994) wrote, "The 'consistent pattern of thought and action' is seen in the contributions of deaf people, their languages of signs, their art and poetry, and other aspects of their heritage" (p. xxix).

It was in the schools for the deaf that students with hearing loss learned not only sign language but also ways to learn, live, and work in a silent world existing within the broader hearing culture. With a built-in peer support system, schools for the deaf provided a regular school curriculum, including all-deaf sports teams that played against individuals from hearing schools. For example, the hand signals used today in football originated with a deaf student football team.

About the same time as schools for the deaf were being established for students who could not hear, schools were being built for students who could not see. They, too, were residential schools, and many students going to a school for the deaf or a school for the blind had to travel hundreds of miles from their families to receive an education. One example of what a school for the blind was like is described next.

MANY SCHOOLS FOR THE BLIND
HAVE BEEN CLOSED OR TRANSFORMED

The New York State School for the Blind in Batavia, New York, is a beautiful place. Located on professionally tended grounds, it sits on a small hill across the street from a park. It looks just like a private college campus with its red brick buildings, white pillars and rotundas, well-tended lawn, and lush shrubbery.

The school was founded in 1868 as the "Asylum for the Blind" and was intended for Civil War veterans who "were blinded in the war." At the time of its founding, it was in a rural area, but as with many 19th-century institutions, the city has grown around it. Through the years, it developed into a school.

In the 1950s there was a worldwide rubella epidemic that resulted in babies of infected mothers being born with disabilities such as deafness or blindness. Throughout the late 1950s and the 1960s, the numbers of students attending residential schools that specialized in their education exploded. According to one staff member at the Batavia School:

> At one point, the school was very exclusive. When I came here in 1975, one of the old timers was here and she had an English class where the average IQ was 135. In the 1970s when PL 94-142 was passed, the mainstreaming law, we lost all of the kids considered to be "normal blind" [those without additional learning, sensory, or physical disabilities]. That's when we made our transition, not overnight, but over 7 years to a school of a little under 70 multiple handicapped students ages 5–21 who are legally blind (because that's our charter—to serve those who have 20/200 vision or less with the best correction), but who also have additional disabilities such as mental retardation, hearing impairment, autism, who are medically fragile, the full range—but all at the lower levels of functioning. Given the needs of the children, 70 is quite a large number to educate now.

But the campus has not physically changed very much since the school educated many more students. There are two brick buildings on campus that are mirror images of one another on either side of the main high school building. They used to be the boys' and girls' dorms. There was a separate junior–senior high and elementary school as well as a separate health center and gym.

Because the Batavia School is still the designated school for the blind in New York, the campus also houses the book depository for braille and large-print books. This depository serves people who have vision loss regardless of age or where they live in the state. Through interlibrary loan, people in other states can also use the materials here.

The depository has books in large print as well as books in braille. They also make instructional materials. The biggest benefit of the textbook depository is conservation and sharing of resources. For example, a high school biology text could be several volumes in braille and cost several hundred dollars to produce. Because braille books are so expensive and there is such a limited market for them (many small districts may have just one student with vision loss), it makes sense that when one student is done with the book, it can go to the depository and be available to another one perhaps in a different state.

A federal quota system has been set up by the federal government to compensate for the fact that blind students require more expensive instructional materials. Nationally, the American Printing House for the Blind (APH; http://www.aph.org) was originally mandated by Congress in 1879, under the federal Act to Promote the Education of the Blind, to supply educational materials for visually impaired students below the college level in the United States and its territories. The American Printing House for the Blind manufactures braille, large type, recorded, computer disk, and tactile graphic publications as well as supplies a wide assortment of educational and daily living products (e.g., braille slates, tactile rulers, special reading lamps, paper designed for embossing braille, bold line paper for handwriting) for students and individuals of all ages. In addition, the APH offers a variety of services to assist consumers and professionals in the field of vision, such as a database listing materials available in accessible media from organizations across North America.

The funds appropriated under the Act are used by each state to purchase educational materials from APH for their blind students of less than college level. Each U.S. school district is given a dollar allotment that is determined by the number of children they serve. From this pool of funds, they determine how best to meet the needs of their students and distribute technologies and adapted instructional materials among them. Thus, in New York, resources are provided statewide through the Batavia School for the Blind. This is how the process works according to the director of the Resource Center:

Students are registered with their state education departments (in this case New York) as "legally blind." They have to be legally blind. The application form for federal registration explains what legally blind is and defines eligibility as a student. The student must have an educational plan before college level for at least 20 hours per week. So that includes preschoolers as well as those over 21 but who are in an educational program less than college level (for example, people in developmental centers). I go all over New York to deliver materials—except New York City and Long Island. Textbooks go through the American Printing House for the Blind and they have a computerized system to locate the books across the country and it's done through IDEA funds. We're allotted a certain amount each year and when those monies run out then we have to wait until the next year. It usually works out that the students get what they need because of this Resource Center because we know where the materials are and can recirculate them.

Charlie was first discussed in chapter 2 when he described his Braille 'n Speak device. I asked Charlie about his experiences there when the school educated only the "normal blind." He mentioned many of the same issues that I have heard from deaf students—that the ones who were together at the schools for the deaf, or blind, developed better social skills and (in the words of Erikson, Maslow, and Hansell) a sense of belonging and identity. Yet Charlie, like many deaf students, believes the best academic preparation is obtained in inclusive educational settings. Charlie is well educated and a successful professional, but he went through the educational system many years ago. How would he fare now going through the system? Who teaches braille in the schools? What is the current educational experience like for students with vision loss? This is explored in the next chapter.

5

CONTRASTING INCLUSIVE WITH EXCLUSIVE EDUCATION

A lot of what I do is around systems and structure as opposed to adapted equipment or specialized equipment.... I believe motor patterns or doing things in a certain pattern is very important in order for blind students to feel like they have control of the space they live in and have to function in. And so I use everything. But you've still got to have that system to go back to check, "Did I get all the holes, did I fill all the spaces?"

—Teacher, New York State School for the Blind

In this chapter I contrast two very different learning experiences, each involving different educational goals and technologies. The first is an inclusive program for kindergartners and fifth graders; the second is an exclusive program for students with vision loss. I also introduce additional technology, such as service animals, for students with vision loss.

WHAT IT TAKES TO BE INCLUDED

This is what it is like early in the 21st century when you are in a fifth-grade class in a public school district rated as one of the best in the United States, and you cannot see. As I enter the inclusive classroom, I see students sitting at tables of two or three, and the tables are arranged to encircle the front of the room. The student I am here to observe, Stephen, is sitting at a table with another boy, and the vision teacher is immediately behind him. The classroom teacher is working at the blackboard on adding positive and negative numbers. The vision teacher leans in toward Stephen and I see she is talking with him. Stephen's eyes are on the teacher in the front of the room.

The classroom teacher asks the students to stand. He divides them into two halves, with one half on the right side of the room and the other

73

half on the left. He takes one of two piles of papers and distributes the sheets to the students in one half. Then he takes the other pile and distributes that to the remaining students. The students in one half have the math questions; the students in the other half have the answers. Their task is to find the student on the other side of the room and match Question with Answer.

As Stephen got up and moved to join the other students in his half, the vision teacher got up and moved in synchrony with him. As the students slowly mingled and tried to find their match, the vision teacher was right there checking answers for Stephen's question. Some of the boys started throwing their sheets at one another in the form of paper wads or airplanes. But not Stephen. He stood very quietly with his Question and the vision teacher. After about 5 minutes, the Question and Answer pairs stood together and waited for the teacher's instructions on what to do next.

The teacher took each matched Question–Answer pair in turn and asked the Question student to repeat what was on his or her paper. Then he asked anyone in the class for the correct answer. Stephen remained standing with his Question and the vision teacher. When all Questions and Answers had been checked for their match, the exercise was done and everyone sat back down, including Stephen with his vision teacher right behind him.

Two things struck me. The first is how smothering special education support must seem to some students as they mingle with their classmates and try to have peer interactions. The other is the way the teacher never gave commands to the students. Rather than saying, "Do this," he would ask the students, "Can you do this, please?" The tossing of the paper wads and airplanes drew, "I would appreciate it if you stopped doing that. Will you do that for me?" This classroom of upper-middle-class fifth graders complied, but I had the distinct sense that while their bodies stopped tossing and became quiet, their minds were saying, "Well, okay. This time."

Stephen was the only student with significant vision loss in his classroom. This is not unusual. Issues of social isolation, lack of peer relationships, and dependence on others continue to challenge educators and parents. A research study by Sacks, Wolfe, and Tierney (1998) revealed that many students with vision loss, like those with hearing loss, have not always had a range of social experiences or positive social encounters from which to develop interpersonal skills. Sacks et al. (1998) stated the following: "Opportunities for social integration and acceptance by sighted age-mates appeared limited at best. . . . Many of these students spent their time alone involved in primarily passive activities: watching television, listening to the radio or CDs and sleeping" (p. 477).

This is what it is like early in the 21st century when you are in a kindergarten class in the same school district, and you cannot see. The following information is taken from the observation notes I took while in that classroom.

The classroom is loosely partitioned into one large classroom area with two smaller working areas around one corner. Colorful student artwork has been hung all around the room. Small storage bins are in the back of the room. On the opposite side of the classroom from the small work areas is a row of windows running the full width of the room and under these are bookshelves filled with books and educational materials.

In this inclusive class of about twenty 5-year-olds, there are two parent volunteers, the vision teacher, a personal aide, and the kindergarten teacher. Most of the students are sitting in small groups of three to four children at round tables, and they are reading and coloring. At the back of the room, Ellen is working on something else entirely with her vision teacher. She sits very quietly. Demurely, actually. She is slight for her age, and she looks like she had rolled out of bed and into school. Her hair needs to be brushed and her clothes don't quite match one another and appear to be hand-me-downs. She is very soft-spoken and quiet, but friendly. She yawns frequently.

Ellen is blind and also has cerebral palsy (she can walk independently but is slow and walks with a high-stepping gait and often appears as if she is about to stumble or fall). As an integrated student in her kindergarten class, she is expected to do what her class does and keep up with them academically. She has been given a seat closest to the door because of her mobility. Like the other students, she has her own drawer for crayons, and so on, but hers is labeled in braille.

Ellen works with her vision teacher 5 hours per week (an hour per day) on braille, technologies, and some academics. She has a full-time personal aide, an integrative–inclusive education teacher 5 hours each week (for standards, classroom academics), lessons on how to use a long cane, occupational therapy, physical therapy, and instruction in orientation and mobility.

Orientation and mobility, or what is informally called O&M, trains individuals without eyesight (a) to develop an awareness of their position and relationship to significant objects in the environment and locate themselves in space ("orientation") through the use of fixed landmarks (doors, fences, etc.), surface changes in the pavement or floor, echos ("echolocation"), and environmental sounds and smells and (b) to walk safely and confidently in and around their environments (mobility; e.g., Blasch, Wiener, & Welsh, 1997). An information sheet on "Orientation and Mobility for Teachers" produced at the New York State (NYS) School for the Blind is worth quoting here, as it well describes a process that can sometimes be difficult to understand:

You may recall the story of the three blind men who, after examining different isolated parts of an elephant each developed a totally different image of the elephant, by extrapolating the whole from only one of its parts. When a normally sighted child visually locates an object, he or she can comprehend it as a whole at a glance, whereas the totally blind child must explore it with his or her remaining senses, putting together a sequential series of parts observed tactually, supplemented with other sensory observations (auditory, olfactory and gustatory) to form a whole which may or may not be accurate.

Orientation training involves concentrated assistance in concept development and body imagery. Key spatial–environmental concepts such as *above, below,* and *near* need to be taught in order for children who are blind to develop an awareness of the structure of their environment.

Mobility can be aided by the use of a long white cane, electronic devices, a sighted guide, or a service animal (or guide dog; Blasch et al., 1997). Many individuals use a combination of these mobility assistance devices.

SERVICE ANIMALS ARE KEY RESOURCES FOR PEOPLE WHO ARE BLIND

The Americans With Disabilities Act of 1990 recognized the value of service animals for people with disabilities and set forth a definition:

> Service animal means any guide dog, signal dog or other animal individually trained to do work or perform tasks for the benefit of an individual with a disability, including but not limited to guiding individuals with impaired vision, alerting individuals with impaired hearing to intruders or sounds, providing minimal protection or rescue work, pulling a wheelchair or fetching dropped items. (CFR 36.104)

Service animals assist individuals in many ways. They are trained to fetch and return dropped or needed items and to pull wheelchairs up ramps or across distances that individuals with disabilities are incapable of attaining independently (e.g., Arkow, 1989; Sachs-Ericsson, Hansen, & Fitzgerald, 2002). Service dogs are also trained to do other tasks, such as turning switches on and off, opening doors, carrying materials, handing in paperwork, and mailing letters. In addition to providing instrumental services, the presence of an animal appears to aid in the removal of social barriers by enhancing the social perception of people with disabilities (Lockwood, 1983) and by facilitating conversations (Messent, 1984).

Today there are over 35 service and hearing dog organizations training animals to assist individuals. Many of these organizations are funded by donations and benefactors and provide trained service animals at virtually no cost to the recipient. However, candidates are on waiting lists for as long as 3 to 5 years because of limited funding. This can be frustrating for individuals wanting to regain independence in their lives.

According to Zapf and Rough (2002), most of these service dog agencies use service dog trainers to train the animal to learn a variety of commands that will assist the client (person with a disability). The service dog trainer will work with the client and service animal to develop a good working team. Although most service dog trainers have a background in animal obedience and training, they do not have the background knowledge and expertise in assessing people with disabilities. Currently, many service animal programs do not use properly trained individuals as evaluators in assessing the needs of their clients to appropriately match clients with service dogs. To remedy this situation, Zapf has developed an assessment process and series of assessments, called the Service Animal Adaptive Intervention Assessment (Zapf & Rough, 2002), which is divided into a series of steps. The first step is deciding whether a service animal is an appropriate form of assistance for a particular individual and involves assessing the person in three clinical domains: physical, cognitive, and psychosocial. Subsequent steps assess the person's predisposition to the use of a service animal and involve evaluating the person's background knowledge and experience with animals, level of skill activity, personal characteristics, and the requirements of the animal compared with the resources or abilities of the person.

DAYS FILLED WITH PULL-OUT AND PUSH-IN ACTIVITIES

There is a lot for Ellen to learn. And this learning is a considerable responsibility for her school district. While Ellen had attended a preschool for students who are visually impaired, and could have stayed there for kindergarten and elementary school, her parents wanted her to have an inclusive education but with support in the form of services like braille, O&M, and so on. Consequently, Ellen's day is filled with *pull-out* and *push-in* activities. She is *pulled out* of her classroom for O&M, occupational and physical therapy, and learning to use a long cane. The last involves training the person who is blind to use a white cane (which may or may not fold) individualized in length for that user as well as the use of a method such as the *touch cane technique* (or Hoover technique), which involves moving the cane in an arc in front while walking and having it touch on the side opposite the forward foot (e.g., Blasch et al., 1997).

Ellen's vision teacher comes into her classroom (*push in*) to work with her. The vision teacher had just come from another school, and in preparation for her arrival the aide had rolled the cart of supplies into the classroom so that it would be ready and waiting for her. My observation notes continue with the following.

> The aide hands a notebook to the vision teacher, who goes to the cart and pulls out a Perkins Brailler (for manual brailling). Then she brailles

entries for Ellen's journal (each student in the class is to maintain one). After this, she pulls a set of index cards from the cart. On each she had earlier brailled one letter of the alphabet. The letter was also written in pen. She now sits at a child-size table with Ellen and, one at a time, hands the index cards to Ellen. For every two Ellen gets correct, she receives a penny to put in a small paper cup sticky-taped to the table in front of her. If Ellen plays with the cup, she has to give a penny back. When she accrues 15 pennies, she will get a reward. In this case, it is listening to an audiotaped version of the Helen Keller story. Throughout this exercise, Ellen tries hard to concentrate. Everything seems to be hard work for her—even cracking a smile. She keeps yawning. She also keeps losing her concentration. Her vision teacher frequently requests that she pay attention and keep her hands still.

Eventually, Ellen accrues her 15 pennies and we move to a section of the room where there is an electrical outlet for the tape recorder. The location of the outlet requires each of us to sit on the floor in front of the bookshelves under the windows. As Ellen sits down, the vision teacher immediately begins to focus on Ellen's poise and posturing while getting into a comfortable seated position on the floor. As we sit there listening to the Helen Keller tape, other students come over to deposit their schoolwork in one of three boxes on the bookshelves behind us. But they cannot get access to the boxes because we are in their way.

At the end of the hour, the vision teacher puts everything back into the cart and leaves for another school. Ellen is left to rejoin her class for lunch.

DAYS FILLED WITH BASICS AND ADAPTATIONS

While Stephen and Ellen were being educated in a highly respected public school, 30 miles away about 70 students were also being educated at the NYS School for the Blind. As mentioned in chapter 4, the students there are all legally blind, but they may also have additional disabilities such as mental retardation, hearing impairment, or autism and may be medically fragile (e.g., respiratory arrest, hour-long seizures).

Table 4.3 (see chap. 4, this volume) shows that between 1986 and 1996, the percentage of children ages 6 to 21 with hearing or visual disabilities who were educated in regular classrooms increased substantially, whereas the percentage served in resource rooms, separate classes, and separate residential facilities decreased. According to the U.S. Department of Education, Office of Special Education and Rehabilitative Services (1998b):

The types of environments in which children with disabilities are educated and the extent to which their educational environments have changed over time vary greatly by disability type. For example, in the 1995–96 academic year, about 89 percent of children with speech or language impairments were educated in regular classrooms, compared with about 10 percent of those with mental retardation. There has been a general downward trend in the percentage of children with disabilities who were educated in resource rooms and separate classes, but this pattern does not hold true for children with all disability types. Among children in 8 of the 12 disability categories, where disabilities tend to be more severe, placements in either resource rooms, separate classes, or both increased between 1985–86 and 1995–96 (between 1991–92 and 1995–96 for autism and traumatic brain injury). Even so, children in many of these 8 disability categories show relatively high decreases in placement in separate facilities.

The 13 disability types referred to above and listed in chapter 1 of this volume (including hearing and visual impairments) are those classified according to federal law under the Individuals With Disabilities Education Act. They are defined in Exhibit 5.1.

The current students at the NYS School for the Blind represent the 13 categories listed in Exhibit 5.1 in a variety of combinations, depending on the student. Because of the severity of the students' disabilities and health conditions, the school has its own health center that is staffed around the clock with nurses. Doctors representing a variety of specialties come in 4 days a week.

The vision loss and health conditions of most of these students are a result of prematurity and birth accidents, including oxygen deprivation (genetic disorders and trauma are minor causes). The majority of the students' disabilities come from dysfunctional areas of the brain. Many are cortically visually impaired, which means that nothing is physically wrong with their eyes. They can see, but not perceive, so they cannot use their vision functionally. There are some students who function intellectually at the infant level and a lot of students with very difficult behaviors. I was told by the school, "A big part of our program is helping students relate to others in a positive way; just to engage some of the students is very challenging."

This is what a typical day is like for these students.

At 7:00 a.m. the instructor assistants all arrive. They go directly to the cottages and get the students up. There is one assistant for every two students. This is an opportunity to work on dressing and bathing skills, such as selecting clothes, doing buttons, whatever level the child can handle. Then the teachers come in at 7:30 a.m. and assist. Two cottages are intermediate-care facilities, or ICF units. They are for those 15 to 16 kids who, for whatever reason, have families who are not able to provide them with the kind and level of care they need. Basically, these students are wards of the state, and this is where they live 7 days a week, 12 months a year. They get their education here and they live here. My impression is that it resembles more of a hospital than a residential unit. The students

EXHIBIT 5.1
Individuals With Disabilities Education Act's
Thirteen Disability Types in Alphabetical Order

1. *Autism*: a developmental disability significantly affecting verbal and nonverbal communication and social interaction, generally evident before age 3, that adversely affects a child's educational performance. Other characteristics often associated with autism are engagement in repetitive activities and stereotyped movements, resistance to environmental change or change in daily routines, and unusual responses to sensory experiences.
2. *Deaf-blindness*: concomitant hearing and visual impairments, the combination of which causes such severe communication and other developmental and educational problems that they cannot be accommodated in special education programs solely for children with deafness or children with blindness.
3. *Deafness.* And . . .
4. *Hearing impairments*: an impairment in hearing, whether permanent or fluctuating, that adversely affects a child's educational performance, in the most severe case because the child is impaired in processing linguistic information through hearing.
5. *Mental retardation*: significantly subaverage general intellectual functioning existing concurrently with deficits in adaptive behavior and manifested during the developmental period that adversely affects a child's educational performance.
6. *Multiple disabilities*: concomitant impairments (such as mental retardation-blindness, mental retardation-orthopedic impairment, etc.), the combination of which causes such severe educational problems that they cannot be accommodated in special education programs solely for one of the impairments. The term does not include deaf-blindness.
7. *Orthopedic impairments*: a severe orthopedic impairment that adversely affects a child's educational performance. The term includes impairments caused by congenital anomaly (e.g., clubfoot, absence of some member, etc.), impairments caused by disease (e.g., poliomyelitis, bone tuberculosis, etc.), and impairments from other causes (e.g., cerebral palsy, amputations, and fractures or burns that cause contractures).
8. *Other health impairments*: having limited strength, vitality, or alertness, due to chronic or acute health problems such as a heart condition, tuberculosis, rheumatic fever, nephritis, asthma, sickle cell anemia, hemophilia, epilepsy, lead poisoning, leukemia, or diabetes that adversely affects a child's educational performance.
9. *Serious emotional disturbance*: a condition exhibiting one or more of the following characteristics over a long period of time and to a marked degree that adversely affects a child's educational performance:
   a) an inability to learn that cannot be explained by intellectual, sensory, or health factors;
   b) an inability to build or maintain satisfactory interpersonal relationships with peers and teachers;
   c) inappropriate types of behavior or feelings under normal circumstances;
   d) a general pervasive mood of unhappiness or depression; or
   e) a tendency to develop physical symptoms or fears associated with personal or school problems.
   The term includes schizophrenia. The term does not apply to children who are socially maladjusted, unless it is determined that they have a serious emotional disturbance.

(continued)

EXHIBIT 5.1   *(Continued)*

10. *Specific learning disabilities*: a disorder in one or more of the basic psychological processes involved in understanding or in using language, spoken or written, that may manifest itself in an imperfect ability to listen, think, speak, read, write, spell, or to do mathematical calculations. The term includes such conditions as perceptual disabilities, brain injury, minimal brain dysfunction, dyslexia, and developmental aphasia. The term does not apply to children who have learning problems that are primarily the result of visual, hearing, or motor disabilities, of mental retardation, of emotional disturbance, or of environmental, cultural, or economic disadvantage.
11. *Speech or language impairments*: a communication disorder such as stuttering, impaired articulation, a language impairment, or a voice impairment that adversely affects a child's educational performance.
12. *Traumatic brain injury*: an acquired injury to the brain caused by an external physical force, resulting in total or partial functional disability or psychosocial impairment, or both, that adversely affects a child's educational performance. The term applies to open or closed head injuries resulting in impairments in one or more areas, such as cognition; language; memory; attention; reasoning; abstract thinking; judgment; problem-solving; sensory, perceptual, and motor abilities; psychosocial behavior; physical functions; information processing; and speech. The term does not apply to brain injuries that are congenital, degenerative, or induced by birth trauma.
13. *Visual impairments*: an impairment in vision that, even with correction, adversely affects a child's educational performance. The term includes both partial sight and blindness.

Note. From *Twentieth Annual Report to Congress on the Implementation of the Individuals With Disabilities Education Act,* by U.S. Department of Education, Office of Special Education and Rehabilitative Services, 1998 (Code of Federal Regulations, Title 34, Section 300.7, 1995). In the public domain.

have their own bedrooms but share a common living area. Through the window I can see outside to the Sensory Park. This is an area where kids can climb around a wooden castle with steps, play with adapted swings and slides, participate in water play and sound activities, and play miniature golf. There is also a section with a lot of scented herbs.

The classrooms are well equipped. In one room, for example, I saw a lot of tumble forms and mats. The school tries to concentrate equipment in as few rooms as possible so that they do not need to purchase as many items and scatter them around the facility.

Compared with the public schools, this school also offers all the related services—physical therapy, occupational therapy, speech, and audiology—and they follow the same school calendar with all the typical breaks and vacations, but that is where the similarities end. Many of the students are content just to sit and do nothing. Some fear if they get up and try to move around they will get hurt. Others do not have the mobility or the desire to move.

The school offers adapted physical education 5 days a week. There are three teachers who are dually certified in adapted physical education and in teaching the visually impaired. All classes are structured to have six students, two instructor assistants, and one teacher; there is a lot of one-to-one attention given to each child.

Physical education includes the use of a unique pool. The floor can be raised so the entire pool can have between 2 to 4 feet of water, and it is heated to 92° F. This is a therapy pool and, for some students, it is the only time they have freedom of movement because they can only move their limbs under water.

The teachers have all become adept at using and modifying whatever is available to them. In one class I observed, they were focusing on helping students develop a "mental map" of one or more objects within entire environments. According to one teacher,

> Our understanding of a meaningful picture does not always translate into anything tactilely meaningful for the blind person. So our job is difficult. You can't just take a tactile picture and put it in front of the child and think they will understand it. There are skills involved in teaching them how to read and interpret these diagrams. And then to generalize it well. You have to get them to see the big picture, too.
>
> We use a lot of thermoform and tactile paper where the heat recognizes the ink drawing and makes a design raise up. For botany class, I took the leaves and made them raise up. We also use super glue and glue string to create a raised surface.
>
> Over here on this computer is a game we adapted. We put felt on the switch mechanism so they can tactilely feel it. We also have braille on the keys. There is music with it and they can recognize the songs and anticipate what will happen. I just printed out an Intellikeys keyboard and traced everything with super string.

When a new student transfers to this school from somewhere else, a teacher will go to the current program and observe the student. I was told,

> I've never seen a child go backwards. I've never seen a child worse off here. And almost always the changes are remarkable. But center-based programs are very "out" right now. They're the opposite of inclusion. But when children's needs are as intensive as these kids, there's just no comparison. Many of our students are inclusion dropouts. Many of our parents say, "My child was the class gerbil. The other kids just loved her, but she wasn't learning or doing anything."

For the highest functioning students, there is "total community-based functional programming." The students stay in the cottages in the morning and work on simple meal preparation, cleanup, laundry, and so on. They plan entire meals and go into the city to shop for groceries. They will also eat in restaurants, go to baseball games, and participate in community activities. The school has vans to transport them and the students are, as one teacher said, "hard to catch because they're so often off-campus doing all sorts of things." Some students attend a program to prepare them for employment. Students with less vocational potential may use a simulated apartment where they prepare to live as independently as possible and practice such activities as meal planning and cooking prepared meals.

At the end of the school day, the students return to their residences. The ratio is still one assistant for every two students. There is also a recreational therapist at night who designs various evening programs and activities and who tries to get the students into the city as much as possible for concerts, baseball games, and so on. According to one of the staff, "We try to integrate as much as possible, but we have many kids for whom that is not appropriate and it is overstimulating for them."

When they reach the age of 21, the students will go to whatever adult programs exist in their home county, with assistance in the transition provided by staff at the school. According to one staff member,

> Day treatment is where the bulk of our students go. We have some who are sheltered workshop candidates and in the past, maybe one or two who could handle supported employment. But the blindness is such a big factor. In supported employment with the other disabilities, it is just very difficult. Sheltered workshops are not popular now, either. But for us, a placement in a sheltered workshop is like a public school getting a student into a top university.

The characteristics of students with vision loss (as well as those with hearing loss) have changed over the past few decades, and there has been a movement to include these students as much as possible in regular classes in public schools. This evolution—some would say, revolution—in education has been made possible in large part by the increased availability of services and technologies for educating students with vision or hearing loss. Trained specialists can select from a wide array of products, devices, and techniques. The students themselves have opportunities to learn in a variety of educational environments. But what is striking about the examples of Stephen, Ellen, and the students at the NYS School for the Blind is that the emphasis is primarily on a personalized, hands-on approach to instruction, on *teaching and learning strategies*, and much less on the use of technology per se. Although such hands-on attention can appear to be socially stifling for the students, it does offer each student the opportunity to maximize his or her learning according to what has been found to work best. What follows is a further discussion of an individualized approach to instruction from the perspective of one teacher at the NYS School for the Blind.

TEACHING AT THE NEW YORK STATE SCHOOL
FOR THE BLIND FOR OVER 35 YEARS

I was talking with Betty in her classroom. It is obviously an old room in an old building and has high ceilings and drab paint on the bare walls. No student artwork is posted on the walls to ring the room with color and student creativity. There was not even much furniture in the room, which caused Betty's large desk and the few available chairs to appear imposing.

Betty has more energy and a younger countenance than someone usually does at her age. As we talked, she would suddenly pause every now and then and listen or glance over at one of the three students. She would never miss, and usually anticipated, everything the students did while we were talking. She described how she works with her students:

> You can, if you think hard enough, adapt for almost anything. But if that adaptation creates an awkwardness for other people, you're not enabling them, I think, and you have become part of their disability.
>
> I am strict and demand a great deal. I'll pull out of you everything I can get because I don't have much time to get at all that's in there.

In chapter 4, I pointed out that the population of the school has changed over the years from serving "normal blind" students to those with multiple disabilities in addition to vision loss. Betty mentioned, too, how they used to teach carpentry skills and chemistry and all the typical subjects of the earlier era. Then she said:

> Now, in the public schools, they're afraid to let them. They work in teams and the blind student may just put one substance in a test tube. So they don't develop an understanding of the whole process. And they only know it on an auditory level.
>
> One of things we know very definitely about normal blind is that their verbal skills are very advanced over their actual functional skills because they can learn anything they hear. They can give it back to you and sound like geniuses and not have a clue about what they're talking about or what it means. But in public school, the usual mode of imparting information is auditory and verbal. So they can give it back but there's no concreteness to it.
>
> Here's another example of what I mean. In the public schools, when they talk about animals, they will have plastic models. We had a library of animals prepared by a taxidermist so students could understand the size, smells, texture, and everything about an animal. As an example of the perceptions of a blind person who has never seen and, therefore, why would they know, we had this animal library, but we could not have a full-grown elephant. But we did have the foot of an elephant. "See how big this foot is? You can imagine the size of the animal." And we'd go on explaining about the size of this elephant and how tall and

long and so on. They'd always nod and say, yup, okay. And we thought we were doing one terrific job. We went on one of our senior trips to Washington, DC, to the Smithsonian and there was an elephant there. So I had arranged that we could climb over the ropes because there was no way they could know anything if they couldn't touch it. Well, we climbed over the ropes. And this one girl . . . I can see her face today and it was like, Oh, my God! She said, "You know, I did not have an idea of how large this was from that foot you used to show us. I didn't have a clue." So you can describe until the cows come home, you can even take one part of the whole. But they can't imagine it. So when I teach about trucks, I don't give them little toy trucks. We go to a real one.

But how do you teach a child who is completely blind who has never experienced light, let alone color, what color is? How do you teach *concept development* such as body image and spatial concepts such as directionality (above, below), sequence, quantity? Listening skills and auditory comprehension? Appropriate behaviors? Betty shared her approach.

We would sit down on the grass and we would have our lesson and we would talk about the sun feeling like yellow, and "put your face down and smell the grass. That's green. You've been told the color of grass is green, but I'm telling you that it looks to me like it smells to you."

Betty, ever vigilant toward the students in her room, looked over at a student when he sat back in his chair and stretched. Once he had settled back to focus on his work again, she turned back to me and said:

That's Jamie. He is deaf, blind, and autistic. But Jamie does have vision. We don't know a lot about his vision, but we know he sees. And there isn't a child in here who does not have attention deficit. It just comes with the package. Jamie has a lot of problems with impulse control, even with medication. It has taken the edge off, but it has not been sufficient for me to be able to get him focused long enough to learn communication. I'm a firm believer that if we don't have communication, we're not going to go anywhere no matter what we do. We've just got to have a way to communicate. So with him I use manual signs as well as pictorial ones because we don't know a lot about his vision. But we're learning.

Jamie has been passed from person to person, program to program, and no one has been able to address his needs. And I'm just stubborn. I'm somebody that says, it may take me a while, but there's just got to be a way. We work with him in that small room over there (which appeared to be a large closet off the main classroom), which I created just for him. When we started with him, he would trash a room. So I put everything on a board and screwed the board to the wall so that he couldn't throw it. There was nothing in there on the table, on shelves, nothing. I had to get the stimuli out of here. There were just too many things and he couldn't handle all that stimuli. I took all the lightbulbs out except that one. And I worked with him with the light directly over his work area. For Jamie, and kids who are cortically visually impaired, it's great because they can just focus on the one thing. So his focus was only right here (Betty points to a small area on the table). And now he has come to prefer this. I thought, this boy is now 15 years old and he's never going to have this kind of opportunity again. Now he'll go through an average of 20 tasks in a couple of hours. We intermix and alternate fine motor, gross motor, fine motor. We have rewards that are gross motor based, because that is very rewarding for him, and it is now predictable. He knows that this is coming.

He can't hear anything, so I can't use a buzzer. Lights have a different significance for him. So I had to use something that was still sensory that he could interpret as either there or not there. I chose the fan because I thought he'll know when it goes on and when it goes off that something starts and it ends, starts and ends. So we use the fan as a signal. That goes on, when that goes off, this is finished. And he's just getting that, he's figuring out that he can control when he doesn't have to work and he can take a time-out. This will probably be the thing, once we get him cued to it, that will help him control his environment.

This seems to be a form of basic operant conditioning, which involves the shaping of desired behaviors by reinforcing and rewarding each successive step toward the desired behavioral goal. I was curious to know more about what Betty does to try and reach and teach Jamie and her other students. So I asked Betty for more details.

They know they have to do what I ask and we can do it the hard way or the easy way, but we're going to do it. You have to establish the relationship. It doesn't happen overnight, but in 6 weeks there's not a kid in my room that doesn't know.

Like Jamie. He was a hitter. He'd just come up and whack everyone, whack, whack, whack. So I kept repeating, no, you don't do this. And whenever I touched him, like patting his hand, I would be gentle. So when he'd do it incorrectly we'd go back. Yesterday, he was glad to see me, and he isn't always, but he was glad yesterday morning and he smiled from ear to ear and he reached over and patted my hand. So in a year he's beginning to try and make those connections and what is appropriate touch. And, of course, we have to translate that to his peers.

After a while I began to introduce things back on the shelves. We used to work out of trays that we would carry in here. Now I can leave them in here.

At this point, I wanted to know what happens when Betty is out ill for a day or for some reason needs to have another teacher work with her students. Once again, her response indicated that her approach tended to be a behavioral approach.

When I set up my activity books for staff, I give them all of the step-by-step task-analyzed directions for everything. It may be 12 steps long for the simplest thing, but that will make sure it's always the same. A sub can walk in, pick that activity up, and do it exactly the same way I do it. I finally put them on cards so that now I don't have to rewrite every time, I just photocopy the methodologies in the order I want for a student.

Betty paused and suddenly seemed to grow pensive and introspective. I sat there and let her think in the silence. After a few minutes she looked at me and said:

There's so much I want to learn, need to learn. I want to know how does Jamie know it's me. Is it because of the perfume I wear? What is it that he uses? If it's not my face, what is it? Because we need to know that. If I can get clarity on some of these issues I want to then "event" his day. He is so compulsive, that if we can figure out how to give him the information he needs, he could go through his day without a lot of assistance. You could just put it up on a board on little hooks or whatever and he just does this, then this. Eventually, we're going to give him pictures of different people around here and he will match the person with the picture. He will take the photograph around and put it to the person.

Because Betty had focused so much on behavioral approaches to learning, I wanted to know what she thought about assistive and educational technologies, and whether she used them. When I asked her, she replied with an example:

I might get a student who has a great deal of difficulty scooping, for example. Whenever I decide to use an adaptation in that student's training, I never do it thinking this is a lifetime commitment. It's like what I said earlier about overadapting and that it may create an awkwardness. The adaptation is a temporary thing that will enable me to be able to do skill building one part at a time. So I might start with an inner-lip plate, but in my mind I'm going to move from that inner-lip as quickly as I can to a regular plate with a plate guard on it. Now, once I get there, and we don't have this little actual bump that you come into when you bring your spoon up, and it kind of pushes the food over the lip of the plate and pushes it onto the spoon, now with this new plate guard it bumps, but it doesn't necessarily fall into the spoon. Also, I'm very careful to be sure eating will always be a two-handed task. With many of the students with multiple disabilities, I make sure that the left hand (if they are right-hand dominant) is always near the plate. The next step is to take the plate guard away and put a knife there. So you do things in graduated steps. But I don't want to leave them with all these adaptations. How many grandmothers have a lipped plate? How many restaurants have an inner-lip plate? Many who are seeing the child as an inconvenience in the first place say, "Now I have to have all this besides? This is even more inconvenient."

So a lot of what I do is around systems and structure as opposed to adapted equipment or specialized equipment. I have communication boards which are electronic and I use those along with nonelectronic ones. I believe motor patterns or doing things in a certain pattern is very important in order for blind students to feel like they have control of the space they live in and have to function in. And so I use everything. But you've still got to have that system to go back to check, "Did I get all the holes, did I fill all the spaces?" If I am consistent, and I do it the same way and I do it in multiple experiences or exposures, that base pattern is there, it becomes part of them. And it affects them being able to visually map the environment that they're in.

I asked Betty whether there was a specific instance in which she had used a communication device and how well it worked with a student with multiple disabilities. She related the following example.

I have a student right now that when I first started working with him almost 3 years ago he just wandered and hummed. That was his life. He now can travel all over the school. He anticipates what's coming up and that visual mapping is happening. He's one of the highest functioning now with the communication board. We're just buying his own after moving him from a training board down to a very small square . . . [at this point, Betty gets up, moves away, and retrieves a board off the shelf in the classroom] . . . I designed this training board so that I can teach tracking. It has a jelly bean switch . . . I always start with yes and no. If the child is left-handed, yes is on the left. If the child is right-handed, we put yes on the right so that the first reach will be a success and you get something positive. And once they get the idea of it, then I begin to build the skill. I use the standard technique of, OK, let's track and find "drink" so [she operates the switch and the machine responds with "drink" "drink"]. They're taught to hit it twice. When that's what you want, then you hit it again and then I'll know that's the one you want. Once they get the idea that this empowers them, then they use it consistently. My next challenge is to get them from this size, which is way too big, down to a smaller size which can be personalized and they can carry around.

Betty uses primarily behavioral approaches, which can be effective with the current student population at the NYS School for the Blind. These approaches have made a lot of difference in her being able to manage them and achieve gains in their independent functioning. Yet, when one considers Maslow's hierarchy of needs, Erikson's theory of psychosocial development, and Hansell's vital connections, it is clear that much of what occurs today at the NYS School for the Blind is at the basic, most fundamental levels.

Most public schools have only a small enrollment of students with vision loss, but even this small number would not be able to take part in inclusive education without the aid of assistive technology. Inclusive schooling would not have happened and would not continue were it not for legislation passed in recent years to strengthen education for those with disabilities. In the next chapter I discuss the technology and legislation that have made inclusion possible.

6

TECHNOLOGY MADE INCLUSIVE
EDUCATION POSSIBLE

I gave myself a week to calm down and then I went to the principal
and said I'm going to look for an alternate placement for my son, and
I did. I knew from then on it was going to be a struggle, and it was.
— Betty, a teacher and also mother of a student with a disability

As described in chapter 5, it is not unusual for a student with vision
loss to be the only student in his or her school with such an impairment,
which can lead to feelings of isolation and dependence for this student.
Severe vision loss, as well as severe hearing loss, in students age 18 and
under is considered to be a "low-incidence disability." The opportunities of
these students in the typical public school to interact with peers who have
the same disability and who are at the same age are minimal. Students with
vision loss in public schools are often left feeling isolated and separate from
their classmates. Although legislation can mandate inclusion, it cannot
legislate the formation of relationships and connections to friends.

THE INCLUSIVE EDUCATIONAL ENVIRONMENT
NOW IS LARGELY DETERMINED BY LEGISLATION

Many laws have been passed that ensure students with sensory impairments have the best possible education at the elementary, secondary, and
postsecondary levels (e.g., the Individuals With Disabilities Education Act,
due to be reauthorized in 2003, and the Higher Education Act [Pub. L.
102-325]). This section discusses key legislation related to secondary public
school education.

IDEA Amendments of 1997

In June 1997, the Individuals With Disabilities Education Act (IDEA) was amended by Public Law 105-17 as the "IDEA Amendments of 1997." This is the fifth set of amendments to the Act since its initial passage in 1975; each set was designed to strengthen the original law and to help ensure better results for students with disabilities and their families. In 2003, it will be authorized again. Over the years, IDEA has fostered significant changes in the lives of children with disabilities and their families as well as in the roles of schools and teachers in the education of children with disabilities.

The basic tenets of IDEA have remained intact since the original passage of the law in 1975 as Pub. L. 94-142, popularly known as the "mainstreaming law." The IDEA Amendments of 1997 retain much of the previous version of the law but with some important revisions in each of its six core principles:

1. Free Appropriate Public Education
2. Least Restrictive Environment
3. Appropriate Evaluation
4. Individualized Education Program
5. Parent and Student Participation in Decision Making
6. Procedural Safeguards

The complete text of the 1997 revised law can be obtained online at the U.S. Department of Education (http://www.ed.gov/offices/OSERS/IDEA; case sensitive).

Children with disabilities ages 3 through 21 receive services through Part B of IDEA; Part C relates to services for infants and toddlers ages 0 to 2. Under this legislation, eligibility for services is determined by whether a student has a disability in one of the following 13 categories: (a) specific learning disabilities, (b) speech or language impairments, (c) mental retardation, (d) emotional disturbance, (e) multiple disabilities, (f) hearing impairments, (g) orthopedic impairments, (h) other health impairments, (i) visual impairments, (j) autism, (k) deafness, (l) deaf-blindness, and (m) traumatic brain injury.

For students in each of these 13 categories, the importance of assistive technology (AT) has been recognized. Within the IDEA Amendments of 1997, emphasis is placed on identifying the supplementary supports and services needed to enable a child to be educated in the general education classroom and with the general curriculum. As of July 1, 1998, all Individualized Education Program (IEP) teams had to "consider whether the child requires assistive technology devices and services" to receive a free and appropriate public education. Schools must provide AT for students at no cost to their parents if the student's IEP team determines a need for the technology.

The federal definition of *assistive technology device* used in IDEA is the same as that first set forth in the Technology-Related Assistance of Individuals With Disabilities Act of 1988 (see chap. 1, this volume). *Assistive technology service* is defined as:

> any service that directly assists a child with a disability in the selection, acquisition, or use of an assistive technology device. The term includes:
>
> (a) The evaluation of the needs of a child with a disability, including a functional evaluation of the child in the child's customary environment;
>
> (b) Purchasing, leasing, or otherwise providing for the acquisition of assistive technology devices by children with disabilities;
>
> (c) Selecting, designing, fitting, customizing, adapting, applying, retaining, repairing, or replacing of assistive technology devices;
>
> (d) Coordinating and using other therapies, interventions, or services with assistive technology devices, such as those associated with existing education and rehabilitation plans and programs;
>
> (e) Training or technical assistance for a child with a disability, or if appropriate, that child's family; and
>
> (f) Training or technical assistance for professionals (including individuals providing education or rehabilitation service), employers, or other individuals who provide services to employ, or are otherwise substantially involved in the major life functions of children with disabilities. (Golden, 1998, p. 3)

Within the mandates of the IDEA Amendments of 1997, service providers must be prepared to fully incorporate caregivers/parents as primary in the assessment and intervention process and the development of the IEP, and to provide services within the child's natural environment.

IEP Teams

Each student's IEP spells out the special education and related services that he or she will receive. Individualized programs that address the specific needs of children with disabilities and their families are developed, described, implemented, and evaluated by a multidisciplinary IEP team. An IEP is developed for and in collaboration with families with school-age children. Teams are comprised of individuals who are knowledgeable about child development and particular types of impairments that a child might have. They may include an educational administrator, occupational therapist, special educator, physical therapist, speech/language therapist, audiologist, nurse, and psychologist. Members of the IEP team recommend strategies, devices, accommodations, support services, and so on that will enable the child to participate to the fullest extent possible in all developmentally appropriate activities in an inclusive school setting.

When AT is being considered for a child, a member of the IEP team might be able to assess the child if the IEP member has had training or experience with the selection and use of AT. Frequently, however, a specialist from the community is called in to evaluate the child's AT needs (e.g., Golden, 1998; Judge & Parette, 1998). School districts often identify individuals/agencies with expertise in AT who are able to assist the district and IEP teams with the evaluation of AT needs of a student, as well as in the selection, design, fit, and customization of devices as appropriate. In each case, the AT evaluator works with the child's IEP team to identify AT solutions that meet desired student outcomes.

Because the AT evaluators do not know the child on a day-to-day basis, they must gather information provided by the members of the child's IEP team. When working with the student's IEP teams, each AT evaluator incorporates his or her own evaluation process, including the type and amount of information to be collected from family and other team members. Often the focus of information sharing dwells on the disability of the child, what he or she is unable to do, and what technologies are available that may address these deficits. What too often results is a recommendation of a device that does not take into consideration the learning preferences of the child, his or her personality and temperament, or the physical and attitudinal characteristics of the environments in which the technology is used (e.g., Judge & Parette, 1998).

While the IDEA Amendments of 1997 (Pub. L. 105-117) mandate incorporating parents and caregivers in the assessment and intervention process, this does not always occur to everyone's satisfaction. Parents need to be prepared to present and discuss the child's abilities, preferences, and strengths as well as limitations; the child's frequent environments, the activities within those environments, and the types of adaptations that help the child participate; the physical and attitudinal aspects of the environments and how they impact participation; and their expectations and desired outcomes for the child (Flippo, Inge, & Barcus, 1997; Jary & Jary, 1995; Judge & Parette, 1998).

The IEP Is the Basic Blueprint for Building an Education

Individualized Education Programs are a helpful means of organizing goals for a student and incremental means for achieving those goals. The concept of the IEP as a "personalized service plan" as a concept is one that has existed for years. In vocational rehabilitation it is called the Individual Plan of Employment (formerly it was the Individual Written Rehabilitation

Plan), and it was originally made a requirement by the Rehabilitation Act of 1973 (Pub. L. 93-112). The purpose of these plans is to ensure joint goal setting and decision making on the part of the service provider and recipient and the right blend of technologies and accommodations in light of the person's needs and strengths (e.g., D. R. Maki & Riggar, 1997). Key aspects to these individualized plans are annual (or more frequent) reviews and an openness to amendment. They are also meant to pull together in a unified way all the information about an individual that has a bearing on that person's success in school or in a rehabilitation program.

Section 504 of the Rehabilitation Act of 1973, Amended in 1998

This legislation prohibits discrimination against people with disabilities in all programs and activities conducted by recipients of federal financial assistance. It applies to students in elementary, middle, and high school as well as students with disabilities in postsecondary education.

Section 504 requires that all children with disabilities be provided a free, appropriate public education in the least restrictive environment. A person with a disability under Section 504 is any person who

   i. has a physical or mental impairment which substantially limits one or more major life activities,
  ii. has a record of such an impairment, or
 iii. is regarded as having such an impairment.

This definition differs from that found in the IDEA, which defines specific disabling conditions.

Section 504 states that educational programs for students with disabilities must be equal to those provided to students without disabilities:

> No otherwise qualified handicapped individual . . . shall, solely by reason of his/her handicap, be excluded from the participation in, be denied the benefits of, or be subject to discrimination under any program or activity receiving federal financial assistance. (29 U.S.C. 794)

Thus, individuals who are not qualified for special education under IDEA may be qualified for special services and accommodations under Section 504. For example, let us consider a student who just received a cochlear implant, which is an electronic assistive listening device surgically implanted within the inner ear to stimulate hearing.

Candidates for cochlear implants have a severe to profound sensorineural hearing loss (cannot discriminate sound in words and language) and do not benefit from high-powered hearing aids (which primarily just amplify sound). Cochlear implants are systems that transmit sound information through multiple electrodes (or channels) and are designed to provide useful sound information by directly stimulating the surviving auditory nerve fibers in the inner ear (cochlea).

Research at Johns Hopkins University indicates that profoundly deaf children (80-dB loss or greater) receiving a cochlear implant are more apt to be fully included in school and use fewer school support services than similarly deaf children without an implant (Francis, Koch, Wyatt, & Niparko, 1999). But cochlear implants require intense auditory and language development training. Thus, students with hearing loss who have cochlear implants may not require special education, but they may require special accommodations under Section 504.

Like IDEA, Section 504 requires identification, evaluation, provision of appropriate services, notification of parents, an individualized accommodation plan, and procedural safeguards. These activities must be performed in accordance with Section 504 regulations, which have some requirements that differ from those of IDEA (Katsiyannis & Conderman, 1994; Pardeck, 1996).

Services and facilities for students with disabilities must be comparable with those provided to nondisabled students. For example, transportation schedules must not cause students with disabilities to spend appreciably more time on buses than students without disabilities; arrival and departure times must not reduce the length of the school day. The length of time spent in a school bus for students with disabilities should not be much longer than those of nondisabled students.

Classes for students with disabilities should not be held in inappropriate locations such as storage rooms or partitioned offices. Room sizes must be adequate to accommodate the educational, physical, and medical needs of the students. Teachers of students with disabilities must be provided adequate support and supplies to give their students an education equal to that of students who do not have disabilities. If teachers of students without disabilities receive clerical support, teachers of students with disabilities must also receive clerical support.

Educational agencies that receive U.S. Department of Education funds, either directly or indirectly, must comply with Section 504. The Office for Civil Rights, U.S. Department of Education, is the enforcing agency for Section 504 and it conducts compliance reviews and investigates complaints. Federal funds for a school that is not in compliance with Section 504 may be terminated.

Recent Initiatives

The No Child Left Behind Act of 2001 (Pub. L. 107-110) is the Reauthorization of the Elementary and Secondary Education Act and was signed on January 8, 2002 to help close the achievement gap between disadvantaged and minority students and their peers in K–12 education (President's Commission on Excellence in Special Education, 2002). It is based on four basic principles: stronger accountability for results, increased flexibility and local control, expanded options for parents, and an emphasis on teaching methods that have been proven to work.

The President's Commission on Excellence in Special Education was created in October 2001 to study "issues related to federal, state, and local special education programs in order to improve the educational performance of students with disabilities." The Commission's report, "A New Era: Revitalizing Special Education for Children and Their Families" (President's Commission on Excellence in Special Education, 2002), highlights key findings and recommendations for change. One key finding is that too much emphasis is put on the bureaucratic aspects of special education provision and not enough on academic achievement and social outcomes of learners from K–12 through postsecondary education. The Commission points to the low rate of transition to full employment and postsecondary opportunities and calls for a new commitment to individual needs. Other findings focused on the current system waiting for a child to fail and placing too little emphasis on prevention of failure, early and accurate identification of learning and behavior problems, and aggressive intervention using research-based approaches. The Commission calls for general and special education to work better together, and it cites current funding arrangements as creating an incentive for special education identification and separation. Additionally, there is a need to better prepare, recruit, and support teachers working with students with disabilities. As of this writing, it is likely that many of the Commission's recommendations will be included in the 2003 reauthorization of IDEA.

In the near future we can expect to have an increased emphasis on evidence-based practice. This entails the achievement of outcomes and results based on research and proven strategies of *what works*. As you will see in subsequent chapters, this will emerge largely from the proven benefits of a comprehensive, upfront assessment of student strengths and needs that involves both the students and the parents regarding required services. Such parental involvement will likely help curb the dissatisfaction so many parents have voiced that has often led to litigation. An early and comprehensive assessment will also identify additional obstacles to learning and participation that may have otherwise gone unrecognized. When left unaddressed these can result in student frustration and behavior problems. Academic success is the ultimate goal, but it is paramount that students feel that they belong to the educational environment and fit in with their peers. Such a dual emphasis is in line with other efforts worldwide (such as those by the World Health Organization) to achieve a society inclusive of all.

Other legislation that remains pending includes the following:

- The Instructional Materials Accessibility Act of 2003, which would improve access to printed instructional materials used by blind people or other persons with print disabilities in elementary and secondary schools, as well as for other purposes.
- The Educational Excellence for All Learners Act of 2003 is designed to encourage lifelong learning by investing in public schools and improving access to and affordability of higher education and job training.
- The Higher Education Act (HEA) was last amended in 1998 (Pub. L. 105-244), was first passed in 1965, and it dictates federal postsecondary education policy. Pell grants, student loans, and work-study options all come under this legislation as does the TRIO program, which provides support services to postsecondary students with a documented disability who have an academic need for support services and one or more of the following:
  - Low income status
  - First generation or minority status
  - Demonstrated motivation to excel
  - Evidence of steady progress in educational goals

  Although program authorizations in the HEA do not expire until 2004, there is growing interest in the U.S. Congress in the issues that might be considered during the reauthorization process. One of many of these is distance education.
- The Assistive Technology Act (ATA) is due to sunset in 2004. A new Act will need to be created by Congress if this effort is to continue.

In summary, students with disabilities in all levels of education are entitled to accommodations in instruction and assessment, the provision of instructional materials in alternate formats, and educational services matched to their learning needs and preferences. Recent legislation and advances in assistive and educational technologies have made all this possible, available, and affordable. Although there are many problems with the current special education system, many of the essential foundation blocks are in place. How they can best be organized to enhance a particular student's learning, quality of life, role performance, and participation in desired activities is the substance of the remainder of this book.

THE EDUCATIONAL ENVIRONMENT TODAY IS TECHNOLOGY RICH BUT CONNECTION DEPRIVED

While the intent of legislation such as IDEA and Section 504 is to help students with disabilities succeed in obtaining an education, the results for too many students have fallen short of this intent. Also, despite the legal mandate to consider AT devices and the services to support their use, and given that approximately 20,000 AT devices are currently available (as listed by a federally funded project called ABLEDATA; http://www.abledata .com), professionals and parents often feel overwhelmed by technology and the choices available and do not believe they have the essential knowledge to sift through these choices and identify those products that best meet the needs of the individual learner (e.g., Flippo et al., 1997; Judge & Parette, 1998; Kelker, Holt, & Sullivan, 2000; Overbrook School for the Blind, 2001). Being aware of ATs is only the first step. To select the most appropriate AT for a child, professionals must obtain information that will match the planned educational outcomes of a child, his or her abilities and preferences, the context of the environment(s) in which the AT is used, and expectations of professionals and parents regarding the selection of AT devices as solutions to existing difficulties (Judge & Parette, 1998). This can seem very overwhelming, indeed.

Researchers examining AT use by children (e.g., Judge & Parette, 1998) make the following key points. First, a significant number of professionals are ill-prepared to make informed decisions about what constitutes appropriate AT and also lack family-centered practices. Second, more family involvement in AT assessment and decision making is needed as well as training on ways to integrate the use of AT in naturally occurring activities. When family members are involved in the selection and use of AT, there is a greater likelihood that the device will both promote the child's overall development in the natural environments and have a positive impact on the whole family (Judge & Parette, 1998; Kelker et al., 2000).

Of all the members of the IEP team, family members know their child the most intimately and in the most varied environments. Often, families have to incorporate the child's technology use into their accustomed routines and lifestyles. They are the ones who will take the blind child who has yet to master mobility to a shopping mall or family vacation. Without the family's or parents' involvement, the child's AT may go unused, be used inappropriately, or be used in limited situations (Kelker et al., 2000).

Too often, however, parents feel outnumbered and intimidated by the IEP team, and IEP team members may view parents' hopes and aspirations for a child as unrealistic or their request for a specific AT as costing the school district too much money (Judge & Parette, 1998). There are times when parents' wishes and the IEP team's responses do not match. Even those parents who are educators themselves can feel the IEP team is missing the mark with their child.

Betty, the teacher at the New York State School for the Blind discussed previously, has a son with a learning disability, which in her words is "no big deal, really no big deal, compared to what I work with here." She was also on a school board for 7 years and served a term as president. Her experiences illustrate the kind of adversarial relationships that can develop between parents and teachers.

> I remember when he was in second grade, he was having a particularly difficult time. So I went to school and visited for a day. Oh my! They just saw me as the ignorant, overreactive, emotional mother. I watched him struggle all day long.
>
> I gave myself a week to calm down and then I went to the principal and said I'm going to look for an alternate placement for my son, and I did. I knew from then on it was going to be a struggle, and it was. But there were good teachers in those years as well. But as a whole, the system is not prepared. And if they had to work with the students I have now, they wouldn't even know where to begin. They're not even equipped to work with my son.
>
> When I was on the school board, I would have to be political to get what was best for the kids. The teachers were not happy when I didn't see things their way, as they expected I would as a teacher myself. I tried to see things the students' way and what was best for them educationally. That's the difference between the person who is a teacher and the person who teaches as a job.
>
> There's something missing in the way we are preparing and screening teachers. If I were going to teach just one course at the college-level, it would be observational skills. What are you looking at and what does it mean? Don't be curriculum dependent. You're not teaching a curriculum. You're teaching human beings who have a potential to learn—every one of them. The rate of learning may be different, the methodology may be different, and the technique may be different, some adaptation may be needed, but they all can learn. And I don't think we're getting that across to the teachers today.

When discussing AT, the students' limitations too often become the focus, not their capabilities. Parents may or may not have an understanding of what their child is capable of learning, thus they look to the IEP team to provide clarity as well as hope for their child's future success in school. But too many times parents leave IEP meetings feeling anxious and depressed about their child's progress, or the lack of it (Judge & Parette, 1998). Or parents may see strengths that are not acknowledged during the meeting. Should parents and professionals feel each is misunderstanding the other, that they have different and unshared goals for the child, then there is potential for conflict, which in turn may lead to an adversarial relationship (Judge & Parette, 1998). Then, as was the case with Betty, parents may decide to change the child's placement or school (see Table 6.1).

Parents want to see their child's strengths and abilities and know the school is focusing on those with their child. Technology in this way is presented as a means of helping the student achieve success in school both

TABLE 6.1
When the Decision Has Been Made to Take a Child Out of One School
and Put Him or Her in Another: Some Strategies for Parents

Exiting a school	Entering a school[a]
1. If an adversarial relationship with one or more school professionals has developed, try now to minimize this as much as possible.	1. Have key school professionals meet your child. Apprise them of your perspective of the student's needs, why you have changed schools, and so on. It is important to be very candid and honest; remember, you are counting on them to help your child succeed.
2. Acknowledge helpful and supportive professionals by writing them letters of appreciation and apprising them of your decision.	2. Learn everything you can about the many activities, services, and programs offered in the new school.
3. Read through the student's records and flag anything that you disagree with or that you believe has the potential to be damaging to your child in the future. Meet with school officials to get such information removed.	3. Consider the potentially beneficial effects of counseling for your child or a discussion group or a peer support group.
4. Discuss with your child his or her feelings about changing schools. What friends does your child most want to continue to see? Can continued time together with those friends be arranged?	4. Discuss with your child his or her feelings about the new school, what a typical day is like, and so on.
5. Do not promise your child that things will suddenly become better. Do say that an opportunity exists for things to improve.	5. Monitor your child's emotional and social growth as well as academic growth. Continue to consider options in No. 2 above.

[a]Many of these apply to home schooling as well.

academically and socially (Kelker et al., 2000). But when the emphasis is put on the student's limitations and strategies to address them, such as technology use, then using that technology can take on a negative sheen or have a negative stigma. This attitude on the part of IEP teams permeates the school culture and becomes pervasive (known as the "hidden curriculum") and affects how teachers and peers view students with disabilities (Jary & Jary, 1995).

Edyburn (2002) did a systematic review and content analysis of the scholarly literature in special education technology for 2001. He included (a) 5 special education technology journals, (b) 17 special education journals, and (c) 9 educational technology journals. The dominant themes identified were accessibility, AT, implementation issues, Internet use and Web resources, technology integration, and universal design. He also found articles featuring new developments in assessment accommodations, ethics and measurement, and instrument development and validation. While he found literature demonstrating a commitment to capturing and communicating the voices of students with disabilities, their parents, and teachers, the overwhelming emphasis was on the means of implementing legislation, equipping students with products and accommodations to enable them to participate in learning, and adapting educational environments to students of diverse capabilities. There was no theme identified having to do with special education technology as fostering the formation of relationships, connecting the student to teachers and peers in quality and meaningful ways, or helping students deal with a sense of isolation and disconnectedness.

On their own, students do not develop either positive or negative views of themselves. It is only in interacting with teachers, students, parents, and others that they come to form a perspective of who they are as individuals, what activities they want to pursue, what goals they have, and with whom they feel most comfortable. When students participate equally, they are more apt to perceive themselves as capable and as fitting in and belonging in that classroom. Where are the hotlinks to sensitivity, the emotional and social curb cuts?

LEARNING OCCURS BOTH INSIDE AND OUTSIDE OF SCHOOL BUILDINGS

Although classrooms are now only one of several learning environments in formal education, they continue to be key learning environments for most students. The classroom is the center for didactic presentation, dynamic demonstrations, and interpersonal inquiry and discussion.

Legislative support for widening the quality and amount of educational opportunities available to people with sensory disabilities has focused most attention on the classroom environment. Lifelong learning requires equal attention to laboratory settings, libraries and other repositories of information, community-based centers for learning, the home, sports, and other arenas for social activity, and these should be considered priority areas as well.

Laboratories

Full participation of students who are deaf or hard-of-hearing does not often require adaptations in scientific laboratories as long as good communication is established between lab partners. Students who have limited vision usually can operate effectively and safely in scientific laboratories with appropriate optical or electronic magnification devices. Full participation of blind students, however, has long been a concern of schools and faculty despite the fact that there are many successful scientists with disabilities (including blindness). The National Science Foundation (www.nsf.gov) has made it a priority to support research into making science, engineering, and math careers more attractive and accessible to students with disabilities, and this has meant the support of projects to develop new technologies for access to laboratories. According to Larry Scadden (1994), former senior program director at the National Science Foundation Program for Persons With Disabilities:

> Today we are on the threshold of exciting technology that should make science labs far more accessible to all students including those with sensory impairments, namely: digital measurement instruments, computer generated graphics, virtual reality and sonifications. An interesting byproduct of visualization research is the translation of dynamic, digital displays into audio transformations. The resulting dynamic auditory displays are now called "sonifications," to parallel the term "visualizations."
>
> Regarding computer generated graphics, it is the case that many people cannot produce good graphics or drawings in science laboratories. Computer-aided drawing, and design software packages are used today by many scientists and science students to produce precise graphical presentations of data gathered in laboratory investigations. Raw data are arranged in tables, and appropriate graphical formats are selected. The computer then generates and prints the graphic for use in papers or manuscripts. With such software, individuals without help of vision or coordinated movements can produce precise graphical displays for their experimental findings.

New visualization tools are appearing seemingly daily. There is a program that allows people who are blind to know where they are at all times when working with charts and graphs (Internet TV for Assistive Technology, 2003), and this program can be useful in every field that produces these visual tools. Tactile innovations include haptic devices that

> apply differential units of force into gloved fingers, thimbled fingers, or a finger-held stylus in order to create a touch-based two- and three-dimensional computer experience as an alternative to the standard, visually-based one-dimensional graphical user interface. . . . Haptic devices enable users to "feel" and manipulate the features/shape of two- and three-dimensional objects (i.e., shape, weight surface textures, temperature) through the use of tactile and force feedback mechanisms, which are actively or passively sensed by the fingertips. (Marullo, 2002, pp. 3, 6)

Haptic devices combined with nonspeech sound have also been found to help students access graphic information (Brewster, 2002).

Most students in labs work together in pairs because there is seldom sufficient equipment and supplies for everyone. A student who is blind can participate without any specialized technology or accommodations through the selection of a good lab partner and appropriate division of labor. For example, the lab partner can give verbal descriptions of microscope images and identify color changes obtained in chemical reactions and the partner who is blind can record the information.

Libraries and Community-Based Learning Environments

Most libraries and community-based learning environments (e.g., museums, exhibits, zoos, historical sites) today have alternative forms of printed materials (braille, audio recordings, large print, and even computer diskettes). Multimedia presentations contain both captioning and video descriptions. Tactile diagrams and three-dimensional replicas should be available for hands-on exploration. Above all, these facilities should have staff knowledgeable about the needs of deaf and blind patrons and who can communicate adequately with them and answer questions appropriately. Technologies for people who are deaf include TT/TDDs and captioned video. These facilities should have an adequate number of text-phones that will provide for telephone inquiries.

Today, most community-based facilities have Web sites, and libraries have converted to computerized searching and reference lists. For individuals who are blind, this information can be obtained through voice output as long as the information is in a nongraphical user interface format. Many individuals with low vision accessing such information require adaptations to computers (e.g., Scherer & Craddock, 2001). The background colors of monitors may be adjusted so that people with low vision can better see the text appearing on the screen. For example, some people may be able to see best when the background screen color is yellow and the text is in bold black print. Another simple adaptation easily achievable includes enlarging the screen text by increasing the font size and using the "zoom" option.

A trend that is increasing is remote access to library and museum materials over computer networks and the use of alternative means of both computer input and output (Scherer & Craddock, 2001). With the appropriate software, information can be input into computers through voice commands rather than by keystroke. Synthesized voice output, which reads the text on the screen, is beneficial not just for people with low vision or blindness but also for students with learning disabilities as they can have the dual output of print and audio information.

It is critical that users have a choice of options and that libraries and community-based facilities make them available because each individual will find that some of the available options are more productive and work better than others. The concept of universal design (or "design for all" or "everyone fits") will increasingly predominate, which means that redundancy in ways multimedia information is presented will become standard (Scherer & Craddock, 2001).

Universal design ideally results in environments and products that are usable by everyone, and thus their relevance to and usability by people with disabilities are assumed and are as invisible as possible. As the outcomes of human factors research advances, we will continue to see more ergonomic keyboards, voice input and output, better arrangements of icons, and improved methods of information display so that individuals with varying learning needs and preferences (such as aging people, people with learning disabilities, and young children) can all benefit from the same technologies through easily achieved adaptations that take into account unique user characteristics.

Personal Residences

Personal residences are likely to become key learning environments in the future, especially with an emphasis on lifelong learning. Today electronic reading machines and access to remote resources via the Internet and the Web make accessing professional and educational materials quite easy and straightforward. A growing area is taking academic courses over the Web via distance learning. This has become an important option for students who are either deaf or blind because they can benefit equally with those without disabilities from this educational medium. Yet, the inaccessibility of course materials, and even entire courses, remains problematic. Still, distance learning is increasing at such a rapid rate that more attention will be given to it in subsequent chapters.

Together with legislation mandating the inclusion of students with disabilities in regular classrooms, assistive and educational technologies have already done much to eliminate the challenges and barriers posed by hearing or vision loss. As our current high school students mature from the classroom to the boardroom, they will be even more crucial to the educational and vocational success of this population. Yet, many barriers remain to the use of technologies by learners with or without disabilities, regardless of age, due in part to their lack of knowledge of available technologies and training in their use. For people with vision loss, graphic–pictorial information still presents a tremendous challenge; for people with hearing loss, the challenge is sound and auditory information in all forms of media and in most environments. In the next section, we review technology options now available for access to information and instruction with an additional emphasis on ways to ensure that future advances adequately meet the needs of learners with hearing or vision loss.

IV

TECHNOLOGIES FOR ACCESS TO INFORMATION AND FOR INSTRUCTIONAL DELIVERY

7

COMPUTERS: MIXING ASSISTIVE, INFORMATION, AND ACCESS TECHNOLOGIES

Access to information by people with sensory impairments must be put on an equal plane with physical access to public premises for people with mobility impairments.

—Dr. Larry Scadden (who is blind)

Now, instead of 3–4 hours, it takes me 45 minutes to an hour. . . . For the first time in my life I am interested and excited about reading and I am realizing how restricted I was.

—A high school student

Education has traditionally been devised in a very generic fashion. Educational materials are not designed so much to meet the particular needs of individual learners but rather those of the most common learner. Thus, learners with vision loss or hearing loss, regardless of age, who share the goal of having complete access to information often feel left out. As discussed in chapter 6, the greatest challenge for people with vision loss is print and graphic/pictorial information; for people with hearing loss, it is sound and auditory information. These challenges can work in opposition. How can the needs of people in one group be met without compromising access to information for the people in the other group?

Ideally, teacher-delivered instruction (a lecture or demonstration) would be delivered to a class so that it would be equally accessible to those with hearing or vision loss. Techniques for accomplishing this were touched on briefly in chapter 1 and are discussed in more detail subsequently. When it comes to a program of study or a conference or symposium, accommodations ideally would be kept in mind so that learning would be equally accessible to those with hearing or vision loss. For example:

- A computer and technology lab would be available to all learners, and some computers would have refreshable braille displays, voice output, and a variety of input devices. Staff would be available to increase the size of the text on the screen and convert relevant documents to braille or large print.

- For each major presentation, sign language interpreting would be available as would real-time captioning (the presenter's words are displayed as text on a screen in real time). Infrared listening systems would be available, and participants would only need to pick up a receiver on arrival at the door to each session.
- Participants with vision loss would have the option of having a sighted guide available to them as well as information printed in braille and large print, audio recordings, descriptive video services, and the text of relevant materials available on disk.

These accommodations depend on the successful mix of assistive, information, and access technologies. While there is considerable overlap among these categories, these terms refer to different products. Assistive technology (AT) in general refers to devices to enhance the personal and independent functioning of individuals with disabilities and has been discussed quite thoroughly in earlier chapters. Therefore, the focus of this chapter is on information and access technologies.

INFORMATION TECHNOLOGIES

Information technology, also referred to as electronic and information technology or information and communication technology, refers to computer and network resources (including both hardware and software), the World Wide Web and Internet, as well as such telecommunications products as televisions, telephones, fax machines, and pagers. It also includes documentation, help (software), and customer support services per Section 508 and Section 255 of the Telecommunications Act of 1996 (http://www .access-board.gov/about/Telecomm520Act.htm).

The Telecommunications Act of 1996 requires manufacturers and service providers of telecommunication equipment to address the access needs of people with disabilities when they design and fabricate equipment. In 1997, the Federal Communications Commission (FCC) approved adding to the Telecommunications Act of 1996 a mandate to close caption virtually all U.S. television programming by 2006. Then in 1999, the FCC ruled that telecommunications equipment manufacturers and service providers must design equipment and services with the needs of people with disabilities in mind so that they are accessible to and usable by people with all types of disabilities. Manufacturers and service providers must also evaluate the accessibility, usability, and compatibility of relevant equipment and services and give people with disabilities access to telephones, cell phones, pagers, and operator services. This is inclusive of providers of voicemail or an interactive menu service.

CAPTIONING

As noted above, there is now a federal mandate to close caption virtually all U.S. television programming by 2006. Captions are translations of the spoken word into text that looks like subtitles on the screen, thus allowing deaf and hard-of-hearing people to read what they cannot hear. There are two kinds of captioning. *Open captions* are permanently part of the picture and always visible on the screen, whereas *closed captions* have to be "opened" to be visible. Decoders may be attached to televisions built prior to 1993; televisions with 13 inch or larger screens manufactured after July 1993 for sale in the United States must have a built-in decoder chip. According to the National Captioning Institute (www.ncicap.org), closed captions are converted to electronic codes placed on videotapes or inserted into the regular television signal (specifically on Line 21, a portion of the picture not typically visible). There are 525 horizontal lines in a television picture; line 21 is at the top just before the start of the picture-information-carrying lines. Thus, captions do not obstruct key parts of the picture. They typically are white letters against a black background, and their size is proportional to the television screen. On a 19-inch screen, for instance, captions are 0.5 inches high.

To "open" the captions requires a decoder or a television with the built-in caption decoder chip. This service is free to anyone, and there is no special service to subscribe to in order to receive the captions. A program or video that has been captioned will have a (CC) symbol or registered service mark of the National Captioning Institute.

There are many forms of captions. *Real-time captioning* is the simultaneous appearance of captions while the speaker is talking. This is most frequently seen with live speeches, news, and lectures, as shown in Figure 7.1. The image of the speaker appears on a screen and the captions appear along the bottom. Real-time captioning uses trained stenotype operators or individuals otherwise specially trained. Researchers at the National Technical Institute for the Deaf have developed a training system that uses a laptop computer and requires only specialized training in learning and using an abbreviation system (e.g., Stinson & McKee, 2000).

Live-display captioning is used when a copy of a script or videotape is available in advance. The text of the program is transcribed and stored on a computer disk. The prepared captions are then displayed as line-by-line rolling text synchronized with the accompanying speech or recorded audio.

Figure 7.1. This photo shows simultaneous live captioning and sign language interpreting. Courtesy of the National Technical Institute for the Deaf/Rochester Institute of Technology, Rochester, New York.

The FCC Caption Decoder Standard of 1991 (as revised in 1992; EIA-608, 1992) included specifications that caption decoders be capable of displaying seven colors, which can be used for either foreground or background (although a standard black background must always be a user-selectable option). One of the more popular choices for this option has been color-coding of speaker identification, as mentioned by Phil Bravin, former president and chief executive officer of the National Captioning Institute, Inc. and a 15-year veteran employee of IBM Corporation, during his plenary address for the 1994 National Symposium on Educational Applications of Technology for Persons With Sensory Disabilities:

> Ultimately we would like to allow users to select from different options those that will best suit their needs and their desires in terms of the form and the shape. You might be able to select color captioning. You might want red captioning for the woman character or orange for a male character. . . . You have that flexibility as the user.
>
> Our goal is not to provide rules but resources so the user can design their own use of the technology. We can also look at captioning as multilevel—captioning in university-level English, first-grade-level English, fourth-grade-level English. The user can decide which level is appropriate and then, if they so choose, develop through increasing

levels of difficulty. Still using the same video source, but modifying the level of the English language as it's presented in the text; again, allowing the user the power to make the choice. We can also look at captioning as multilingual captioning. Maybe you want to watch the evening news in French. Or Spanish. It's possible to give that option to users, to make those tools available. Another wonderful tool that's available through captioning is selecting what font you want. Maybe you like Helvetica, Times Roman, or script, maybe you want to change the type size, larger or smaller. Giving these options to the user should be our goal. . . . These are all adaptive forms of captioning. Other adaptive forms of captioning are decoding into braille . . . increase the point size for people with vision impairments. We could also make the captioning speed up or go slower. It could be geared to the speed of the video image, going slow when the video is slow and fast when the video is fast. (Bravin, 1994)

Today, however, users do not control the style and look of captions and really cannot; captioning agencies and TV receiver manufacturers do. Varying the size or speed of captions would be appealing to anyone who cannot process visual information quickly, or who prefers not to. Such flexibility has many merits. A Gallaudet University project developed a multimedia environment for computer users where they can watch a captioned video and then click on words or phrases in the captions, which then stops the video and takes them to a glossary in which they can obtain additional information. A glossary entry might include text, graphics, animations, sound, and video. Sign language explanations, as well as audio pronunciations, are available for those deaf and hard-of-hearing people who want such features.

Larry Goldberg, director of the National Center for Accessible Media sponsored by Public Broadcasting Service station WGBH in Boston, Massachusetts (WGBH was the first site for open captioning on television), has designed computer video disks that offer such choices as multilevel captions, enhanced glossaries, and the use of a sign-interpreted window on the computer screen (Goldberg, 2000).

Captions for deaf television viewers can provide more than just a transcription of speech and can indicate information that can be heard but is not spoken—like laughter and music and a person's manner of speaking. These features can greatly enhance learning. Toward the end of his presentation, Phil Bravin provided the following results from research done at the National Captioning Institute:

We found out at that captioning did assist learning for the general and special education populations as well. Secondly, comprehension was reduced when the captioning was withdrawn, and when it was restored, comprehension improved again. The majority of the students surveyed responded very positively to the presence of the captioning. The most surprising thing, though, is that this was a survey of hearing students, not deaf students. (Bravin, 1994)

Other research studies have shown that not only does captioned television provide a successful learning environment for deaf and hard-of-hearing students, but it has also been found to be beneficial for students with learning disabilities, those learning English as a Second Language (ESL), and young children learning to read. Individuals in these groups have significantly improved their listening comprehension, vocabulary, word recognition, overall motivation to read, and self-confidence (e.g., Jensema & Rovins, 1997; Koskinen, Gambrell, & Neuman, 1993). Prior preparation, class discussion, and related handout materials coupled with captions that highlighted important key words, resulted in the overall highest performance.

Parents of young students, however, may not appreciate the value inherent in captioning. For example, some parents will not buy a decoder until their child can read well, but that is akin to saying they will not buy their child a book until he or she reads well enough. Many such parents rely on the schools to structure their child's learning and are reluctant to introduce anything in the home that they view as potentially interfering with the child's educational plan. There is also a digital divide, between the haves and have nots, when it comes to technologies and software. Not only is their expense an issue, but parents who have not themselves been exposed to these products likely do not place as high a value on them as those who have experienced them.

As with the universal availability of captioning, we are increasingly moving toward products and systems designed with *universal design* features built in from the beginning. Universal design (or "everyone fits" or "design for all") refers to features in a product or system that enable it to be used by individuals regardless of ability or capability. There is also a movement in education now termed *universal design in learning*, which refers to the general accessibility of instructional content and its goals, methods, materials, and manner of assessment (e.g., ERIC Clearinghouse on Disabilities and Gifted Education, 2002). A printed textbook, for example, is not accessible to a student who is blind and, thus, a barrier exists to learning for that student. A textbook with universal design would have additional representations of the printed information (perhaps by having an accompanying CD with audio content, an audiotape, or text in braille). And a CD or DVD would have accompanying video description. For a person who is deaf, the CD or DVD would be captioned.

There are many advantages to universal design (such as keeping costs down and not having to make separate accommodations for each student), but a big disadvantage is that individualized/personal services and options become deemphasized. As is discussed in subsequent chapters, more than access is required to engage and motivate students to learn and to ensure their academic success.

ACCESS TECHNOLOGIES

Interfacing assistive and information technologies for people with hearing or vision loss often requires specialized access technologies, which make it possible for almost anyone, regardless of disability, to access and use most functions of a computer. Alternative computer access might involve adapting the means of input, navigation, and output. Determining the best access methods and making appropriate recommendations can be challenging and require that a good assessment be conducted to find out which methods will work best for any given individual.

People who are deaf or hard-of-hearing do not usually have problems using the computer, although there are accessibility features in Microsoft Windows that display visual signals for some of the sounds on the computer (e.g., a chime or ring can be replaced with screen blinks). People with hearing loss (as discussed by Dr. Frank Bowe in chap. 3) often use electronic mail or online chat systems as an alternative means of communicating with friends, instructors, or coworkers. Because computers pose many challenges to those with vision loss, the remaining discussion relates primarily to people with low vision or who are blind as well as those who have difficulty with dexterity and hand control.

Ramon Castillo, occupational therapist, and Kevin Daugherty, rehabilitation engineer, employed at the Assistive Technology Exchange Center (ATEC), a division of Goodwill Industries of Orange County in Santa Ana, California, led online discussions on access technologies for the course Applications of Rehabilitation Technology sponsored by San Diego State University's Interwork Institute (personal communication, August 12–18, 2002). This section has been taken in part from the information they provided during their online discussion.

Computer Display and Output

As pointed out by Ramon and Kevin, many students with vision loss benefit from the use of large monitors and screen-enlarging software (e.g., software that enlarges a computer's visual display output) which is built-in or added as a software program. Microsoft Windows has many built-in features (e.g., Gilden, 2002), such as ones that allow users to change the display settings to make text larger (as few as two or three sentences may be displayed) and easier to see (e.g., white text on a black background or vice versa). Windows 98 and later versions also include a magnifier. Examples of software products are ZoomTextXtra, MAGic 8.02, Magnum, or Lunar (http://www.dolphinuk.co.uk/products/lunar.htm). For people who are blind who want voice output, Job Access With Speech (JAWS) for Windows allows the user to navigate Windows folders, browse the Web, and engage in other common computer tasks. WindowEyes (GWMicro.com) and HAL (http://www.dolphinuk.co.uk/products/hal.htm) are popular programs, as are the Kurzweil products (which scan a document, convert it to text using optical character recognition [OCR], and read it back). The functions are fully accessible by keyboard (key labels in large print can be adhered to keys) or a refreshable braille display.

Computer Control, Input, and Navigation

When we typically think of inputting information into or controlling a computer, we think of a computer mouse and keyboard. But people who cannot maneuver a mouse or reliably touch the keys on a keyboard require adaptations to these methods or alternative means entirely. One such option is *voice input* using speech recognition software.

Speech recognition is commonly considered a tool for people with motor problems. But anyone who has difficulty writing can find it helpful to be able to forgo a keyboard and just "speak" to a computer. Speech recognition programs (e.g., NaturallySpeaking Professional or IBM ViaVoice) must be trained to understand the speaker's voice and pronunciation and may not recognize what a person says when he or she has a cold or is fatigued. For example, if the person says "up high," the computer may type "a pie." If the user has difficulty with reading or spelling, the error may go undetected because a spell and grammar checker will see the words as correctly spelled and even used appropriately in context. Such errors can best be identified with the additional use of a text-to-speech program (such as TextHELP!) that will read back the displayed text.

Some people may not be good candidates for speech recognition. This includes individuals with inconsistent or unclear speech and those who are able to use a keyboard, albeit slowly, and who do not need to generate much text.

Keyboards

Most people can find a means to access a keyboard, either with their fingers or with some sort of pointer or "stick." There are many different types of keyboards that lend themselves to the needs of various individuals.

The alternative keyboard most commonly recommended by ATEC is the Datalux SpaceSaver keyboard. This is a small keyboard that has a standard QWERTY layout and includes all the function, numeric, and arrow keys in a very accessible layout. It is helpful for some one-handed users, as well as mouth-stick and typing-stick users. There are smaller keyboards, such as the TASH Mini keyboard and the MagicWand keyboard. Each has positive features that must be compared with the needs of the individual users. There are also large or "expanded" keyboards such as the IntelliKeys Keyboard, BigKeys, and DiscoverBoard. If the user does not know how to touch type and has the use of only one hand, the BAT Personal Keyboard is a possible solution. It works by using "chords." It has one key for each of the four fingers and three keys for the thumb. Different combinations correspond to different characters and functions. At first, it appears difficult to learn, but with practice a person can become a skilled user fairly quickly.

The shape of a keyboard is not as important as the position, placement, and typing habits of the user. However, if an individual has limited range of motion because of stiffness (arthritis) or pain (carpal tunnel syndrome), the shape of the keyboard does become more important. As with any product, the best strategy is to contact a center that has several different ones available and try each for about 10–20 minutes.

There are also features within Microsoft Windows that enable people with disabilities to more effectively access computers with their keyboards. StickyKeys allows people who use typing sticks or who type with one hand to control combinations of various keys (Ctrl, Alt, delete). FilterKeys enables people with tremors or poor motor control to access a keyboard by "filtering out" accidental depression of keys.

Navigation: Pointers and Mice

As with the keyboards, there are many different types of pointers or mice. Examples are the trackball, roller ball, or joystick as well as a remote-controlled mouse. If the user has controllable but weak or difficult movement, he or she may be able to benefit from a touch pad (common on most notebook computers). There is also the NoHands Mouse that is operated by the user's feet. Head pointers are options for people who have their best motor control in their head and neck. Eye-gaze systems are used by people to control navigation with their eye movements.

Pointing devices can be used in conjunction with an on-screen keyboard to allow text input and the control of applications. Microsoft also includes MouseKeys as part of the accessibility options of Windows. This utility allows users to control the mouse pointer by using the numeric keypad of a keyboard.

Switch Access

For some users, even moving their head is not possible. If they are able to activate a switch by any means in a controlled manner, they can operate a computer. Switches can be accessed by eye-blinks (e.g., Infrared/Sound/Touch [IST], Self-Calibrating Auditory Tone Infrared [SCATIR]), muscle twitches (e.g., the P-Switch from Prentke Romich), or even brain waves (e.g., Mind/Eye/Muscle Controlled Switch [MCTOS]). Switches can be used to access either an on-screen keyboard with scanning or to control navigation by Morse Code. For example, a sip-and-puff switch registers a dot with a sip and a dash with a puff. Special hardware and software then translate the Morse Code into a form that computers understand so that standard software can be used.

COMPUTER ACCESS ASSESSMENT

New products are being developed continuously, and some of the products listed in the preceding pages may be obsolete in the near future. Therefore, the products named here should be considered examples of what is currently available.

More important than a particular product is how well any given individual can use it and benefit from its use. It is crucial that the consumer's needs and preferences be the driving force behind any product selection. As noted by Kevin and Ramon,

> If a person's goal is to be an artist, computer scientist, mathematician, occupational therapist, or rehab engineer, it may not be necessary to type 50 WPM [words per minute]. On the other hand, if one wants to be a writer and can only type 2 WPM and have clear and consistent speech, speech recognition may be the best tool. Some people are content using a transcriptionist and aren't interested in speech recognition. We always have to ask the client what is important.

Any good, comprehensive assessment is conducted in partnership with the consumer and establishes the person's goals, needs, current and near-term physical and sensory functioning, history of support and technology use, available support, and so on. The Initial Worksheet for Matching Person and Technology (Scherer, 1998; see a portion of this form in Appendix A) inquires into general goals, strengths, and limitations across many areas of functioning (vision, hearing, speech communication, reading/writing, etc.). But additional questions need to be asked when someone is being matched with a computer or computer-based device or system. This would include having the consumer:

1. Demonstrate basic computer skills (turning on the computer, typing, correcting mistakes, using the mouse)
2. Demonstrate, if appropriate, intermediate and advanced computer skills
3. Describe what he or she will be using the computer to accomplish
4. Show that he or she can type and at what rate:
   a. with fingers/hands
   b. with typing sticks or a mouth stick
5. Show that he or she can use a mouse or other pointer
   a. Alternately, assess head control
   b. Assess switch control (What is a good site? Single or dual switch?)
6. Describe the support available to set the system up and provide help if things "don't work"

It is important to not neglect this last area—the amount of support needed and available. Some individuals are unable to turn on their computer or don a headset microphone independently. Knowing as much as possible prior to recommending or providing AT will save frustration for that user and result in a much better match of person and device.

The environments of use, available support in those environments, and the user's needs and preferences must all be considered. Ideally, a trial period of use is provided before a commitment to any given product is made. In order for a user to be successful with a technology, he or she should receive proper training in using it; the need for and preferred mode of training will become apparent in a good assessment. Once specific kinds of products have been identified for trial use, the checklist in Exhibit 7.1 can be used to record the consumer's success and satisfaction with it.

RESOURCES EVERY SCHOOL SHOULD HAVE AVAILABLE TO ITS STUDENTS

If we were to consider combining the devices discussed in the past several pages into a computer lab or work area in a school or university for students with all types of disabilities, what additional products or systems would be desirable? As noted earlier, many individuals, not just those with vision loss, benefit from the use of text-to-speech software. Hearing a word while looking at it combines auditory and visual stimuli, which additively aids comprehension and memory. In this way, students who have difficulty reading benefit from audiotapes of books or computer programs that convert text to speech. Thus, a scanner, OCR software, and a text-to-speech program

EXHIBIT 7.1.
Checklist for Rating Products Tried

Rate each product you tried according to the following scale, and put that number in the box beside that product. When there is a match with some situations, but not others, make a note in the comments section at the end of the checklist:

5 = An excellent match with my needs/preferences
4 = A good match with my needs/preferences
3 = A neutral or average match with my needs/preferences
2 = A poor match with my needs/preferences
1 = An unacceptable match with my needs/preferences

❑ Textbooks/publications on audiotape
❑ Portable cassette recorder
❑ Large-print materials
❑ Hand-held magnifier
❑ Camera-based, visual enhancement system
❑ Desktop computer with visual enlargement (21″ monitor, zoomed text)
❑ Desktop computer with scanning and synthesized speech output
❑ Desktop computer with touch screen access
❑ Desktop computer with speech recognition capabilities
❑ Portable or laptop computer with speech synthesis and printed output
❑ Braille notetaker
❑ Braille typewriter
❑ Refreshable braille display
❑ Modified computer keyboard: _____
❑ Voice input software: _____
❑ Voice output software: _____
❑ Word processing software: _____
❑ Adapted keyboard: _____
❑ Switch: _____
❑ Alternate mouse/pointer: _____

Comments: _____
_____
_____

that vocalizes the text would be excellent choices to add to the lab. For students who use a wheelchair, one or more computers in the lab should sit on an adjustable table. Flexibility in the positioning of monitors, keyboards, and tabletops is important for those with mobility disabilities.

To further ensure that the lab meets the needs of as many students as possible, there should be at least one computer with a large-screen monitor (21-inch) and text enlargement software, another with a refreshable braille display keyboard and braille printer. Options for input (regular mouse, trackball, etc. as well as voice input software, and a keyboard overlay) should be available. Software mentioned earlier, such as Kurzweil 3000 and JAWS, should also be loaded into one or more of the lab's computers. Outside of the lab, key support services would include sign language interpreting, video description, and a note-taking service.

At the postsecondary level, much of the same technology should be available. Cunningham and Coombs (1997) emphasized academic computing centers, discipline-specific computing areas, print and online information services, hardware and software tools, and general technology support and training. In the future, especially as universal design for learning becomes more widespread, support services for students may be more technological and less individualized and personal. But it is not enough just to make technologies available; it is imperative that all students (with or without a disability) have equal access to and know how to use the technologies designed to help them succeed academically and socially and develop self-confidence, autonomy, and a subjective sense of well-being.

Research conducted in the Republic of Ireland (Central Remedial Clinic, Client Technical Services [CTS]) on ways to help students benefit from technology and become personally empowered as well as academically successful has resulted in the development of a model called Statement of Assistive Technology Need (Craddock, 2002; Craddock & Scherer, 2002). The "STATEMENT" project (Systematic Template for Assessing Technology Enabling Mainstream Education—National Trial) was funded as a 1-year pilot program by a European Horizon Programme grant. The aim of the project was to develop a model of good practice in identifying the AT and training needs of students through the provision of a formal Statement of Assistive Technology Need prior to students moving from second-level education (high school) to third-level education (college), employment, or vocational training.

A comprehensive initial AT evaluation/assessment was part of the process that CTS has studied in-depth. This process consists of determining people's various needs and requirements in relation to AT. It has been shown that an assessment of people's multiple needs cannot be done in isolation because their needs are complex and involve all aspects of their lives, that is, environmental, psychosocial, educational, and so on. The Matching Person and Technology (MPT) model, along with accompanying assessment instruments (Scherer, 1998), was chosen and modified for the Irish context because it is a consumer-driven process following the social model of disability as adopted by CTS. This enabled a uniform approach to the preevaluation, evaluation, and postevaluation phases in the overall service delivery process and allowed for the assessment of outcomes resulting from AT.

From this assessment, each student received a written statement of need, which was then used to negotiate his or her AT requirements with the prospective college, training center, or place of employment (see sample in Appendix B). When necessary, the student then received training in whatever AT was recommended.

The overwhelming positive reaction from participating students is illustrative of the effectiveness of the approach used in Ireland. Many have publicly described their experiences, and this has proved to be particularly effective in demonstrating the impact of the process and the value of the technology recommended on students' experiences in education. Additionally, their testimony points to the fact that the development of effective assessment/evaluation systems is central to ensuring the optimal use of technology. The following is a quote from one of the students showing the dramatic impact the technology had on both her education and her well-being.

> Since I received the technology, my life has become unbelievably easier. Now instead of 3–4 hours it takes me 45 minutes to an hour. The pressure that I was under is practically gone. For the first time in my life I am interested and excited about reading and I am realizing how restricted I was—I could never have believed that reading and studying could be this enjoyable. (STATEMENT Pilot Programme, 2000, pp. iii–iv)

In the future, more consumers like this student will receive college degrees and enter the workforce as professionals and managers. These consumers will demand access to a variety of global information and will be lifelong users of libraries. As important as being able to access information in the most individually appropriate means, consumers will seek out experts who are person- and user-centered and not technology-centered. Increasingly, consumers will "partner" with those experts and service providers, as happened in Ireland, in product evaluation and selection. For these partnerships to be effective, however, perspectives, preferences, and needs should be openly explored and acknowledged. The Matching Person and Technology assessment process was found to be useful in the STATEMENT project as a means of making such a discussion possible, and its use in primary, secondary, and university institutions in the United States and other countries is proving to be equally fruitful.

Together, advances in technology options and legislation/policy combine to assure that students with hearing and vision loss can receive the highest quality education and have access to the information and resources available to the larger society. As technology becomes an even more significant part of education, recreation, and contemporary life in general, students with disabilities will more than ever require the technical skills, information, and technology resources to help them achieve a quality, equitable education. One means gaining in popularity for educating students with a variety of disabilities is the use of online courses or distance learning opportunities. Because a majority of these courses are Internet- or Web-based, they tend to follow many of the principles of universal design for learning. The use, effectiveness, and perspectives of Internet- or Web-based courses is a topic we turn to in the next chapter.

8

DESIRABLE AND LESS DESIRABLE EFFECTS OF EDUCATIONAL TECHNOLOGIES

I did not like the e-mail discussions. The feedback was different. I did not know who was saying what. In a classroom I can see the students' faces, their opinions, etc. You can have a hot discussion in class but [with e-mail] you just sit and face a computer.
  —A student commenting on a course via distance learning

I prefer discussions through the computer because I do not have to worry about people looking at me. I feel more comfortable.
  —Another student in the course via distance learning

The purpose of educational technologies is to make learning accessible to as many people as possible through the most appropriate blend of instructional media, information/access technologies, software programs, and access to the Internet and World Wide Web. The remarkable increase in the availability of these products provides educators with many options for addressing an individual student's particular learning style and preferences and for enhancing that student's learning. There are educational technologies that enable students to interact with other classrooms via telecommunications, to concentrate on a particular area through a computer tutor, and to access information from a wide variety of sources via the Internet and World Wide Web.

Guidelines for the accessibility of Web sites have been established by the World Wide Web Consortium's Web Access Initiative as well as Section 508 guidelines from the Architectural and Transportation Barriers Compliance Board (Access Board) of the U.S. federal government. One tool that uses these guidelines to check a Web site's accessibility is the "Bobby guidelines" (http://www.bobby.watchfire.com). In September 2002, the U.S. Department of Education's Learning Anywhere Anytime Partnerships program supported a collaboration among international players in the online learning field, resulting in a set of guidelines for Web site accessibility, particularly in the area of distance education. The "IMS Guidelines for Creating Accessible Learning Technologies" are available on the Web in a screen-reader friendly format as well as in PDF (http://ncam.wgbh.org/salt). The IMS Guidelines, jointly published by the IMS Global Learning Consortium and the CPB/ WGBH National Center for Accessible Media (NCAM), are expected to be a comprehensive source on accessibility.

In this chapter I discuss selecting software on the basis of individual user strengths, provide ways to help make successful use of educational software with children, and discuss the pros and cons of distance learning, an educational option made possible with computers and the world wide web. Throughout the chapter I quote students' and teachers' experiences with and opinions on the technology discussed.

SELECTING AND CUSTOMIZING EDUCATIONAL SOFTWARE

Personal computers have been called "freedom-givers" because well-designed software programs are truly interactive and can provide students with individual attention and continuous feedback; this allows the student to be in complete control of the learning process. Personal computers can be freedom-givers to teachers as well, by simplifying decision-making processes through the use of computerized instructional planning and computerized student data management. Yet, special education or regular classroom teachers not fully attuned to individual student abilities and interests or adept at selecting good educational software and customizing it for an individual student discover that the classroom learning situation can quickly develop into one of confusion and disappointment when they try to fit one software package to all students. Software programs that are helpful to some students may give other students too little reinforcement, too much, or the wrong kind. Some students may want to linger with particular problems, but the computer program continues to present new problems. Some students are distracted and overstimulated by the computer's "bells and whistles," and some have even had epileptic seizures induced by them. Other students deliberately input wrong answers just to get the bells and whistles; still others are disappointed when 15 minutes of steady work is rewarded with nothing more than the display and calculation of a total score.

The bottom line for many teachers who have effectively used computers to enhance student learning is that the value of computer-based learning varies according to the characteristics of a particular student. There are physically abused children who feel more comfortable with an inhuman, impersonal computer, but there are as many other children who may act out more because they crave interaction, personal contact, and human response.

To many users, computers can seem to possess superhuman virtues. Robert Kanigel, who wrote the highly regarded 1997 book on how American factories were made efficient by technical changes in the late 1800s, offered the following observations almost 20 years ago that remain current to this day (Kanigel, 1986):

> A computer does not mind repeating itself. It does not grow bored. It is not distracted by other students. It waits patiently for the slow learner to finish. It lifts no disapproving eye to the student unsure of himself as a result of past school or social failure. It can be programmed to furnish reinforcement and praise. . . . If the computer lacks human qualities like love and caring . . . it displays an abundance of "superhuman" qualities— patience, and energy, and an availability limited only by access to electricity. . . . [Yet] the exceptional person may discover, cruelly, that the same system of computers and advanced tech that offers him new opportunities, contains barriers which impede the growth of his independence. . . . Increased dependence on computers brings with it a vulnerability to machine and computer failure and those individuals without the training, intellect or skills to manipulate information may become "the peasants of the Knowledge Society." (p. 44)

Even the most skilled computer users experience frustration at times. One university faculty member expressed this well when he said:

> Computers are stupid! They require the user to jump through some very strange and very particular gyrations. They can waste a huge amount of time, and generate corresponding frustrations. There are days when I feel this so strongly I think I'm ready to chop my machine into little bits! Still they're useful, and with work, can be made to do things at a prodigiously fast pace. Also, I couldn't write a word any more without my word processor or text editor!

When computers and software programs are helpful, they are used. But when they place more demands on the user than he or she wants, they can, indeed, be a source of anxiety and frustration. Rather than anxiety around a computer being attributable to a state or trait of the individual user, it is more often a statement about the poor quality design of the program or system.

THE KEYS TO CHILDREN'S ENTHUSIASTIC USE OF COMPUTERS: FUN, FREEDOM, AND SUCCESS

Make It Fun

Children will benefit the most from programs that offer meaningful activities. Offering different ways to practice a concept and using sound and graphics will entertain students and hold their attention. This can be especially valuable for drill-and-practice programs. Math programs should randomly order problems, and reading programs should provide a wide range of pictures, words, and phrases. Interactive adventures should have a number of different branches to keep it interesting and unpredictable to the child. Graphics, sounds, animation, and other features should be inherently interesting to the child. For example, watching a treasure chest open to reveal overflowing brightly colored and interesting objects is a lot more interesting than seeing a yellow happy face appear.

Give the Child Freedom

Children like to experiment. Good software programs foster experimenting with new concepts as well as familiar ones in a variety of ways. Children also like the freedom to choose. Good programs incorporate open-ended features to allow them to create (stories, artwork, etc.) according to their individual preferences. It is important that programs provide an easy means of reversing or undoing an action (e.g., through a back arrow) so that the child does not experience negative effects of experimentation.

Build in Success

If children feel competent and experience success with computer activities, they will be motivated to return to them. Good programs allow children to easily navigate around them independently and are picture-based as well as text-based. Good programs also allow children to figure out how to get in and out of them, choose among alternatives, and save and print their work.

- *Select the right level of difficulty*. If a program is too easy, it will bore the child and will not be used. If it is too difficult, even for as short a time as a minute, it may frustrate the child and dampen enthusiasm to try another program. Good software programs offer a range of levels of difficulty and will automatically adjust to what the child can do. Good programs do not "talk down" to a child, nor do they talk over their heads. See Exhibit 8.1 for example levels of computer use children of different ages can handle.
- *Don't make them wait*. Children like immediate gratification, and good programs load quickly, snap to life when an option is selected, and avoid long descriptions or directions. Reinforcing sounds, pictures, points, and other feedback should be given instantly.
- *Sharing success*. Software that tracks the child's progress or prints out an award or certificate of recognition that can be shown

EXHIBIT 8.1
What Children at Various Ages Can Do With Computers

Age group	Ability
0–18 months	Will pay attention to screen colors and movement as well as sounds. Enjoys the tactile sense of moving the mouse and touching the keyboard (even though they probably will not make the connection between mouse movements and events on the screen).
18–30 months	Will begin to notice their actions result in effects on the screen. Touch-screen computers further enhance this, as can software programs that allow them to press any key on the keyboard to hear a favorite song or display pictures or animation.
30–36 months	Tolerance for sitting at a computer increases. Fine motor control exists to use a mouse independently. They can negotiate activities in programs and will enjoy singing along with music while watching events on the screen. They will also enjoy working with parents, teachers, or older siblings on computer activities.
3–5 years	Independent computer use is possible. Can use a variety of programs and manipulate the mouse expertly. Will enjoy working at the computer with a friend. Electronic storybooks and creativity programs that let them print their work are good for this age range.
5–7 years	Can identify keys on the keyboard. Can make choices from pull-down menus to independently launch programs. Can use the computer for simulations, creativity, and reference. With assistance, can access the Web and research a topic.

Note. From *Young Kids and Computers: A Parent's Survival Guide*, by W. W. Buckleitner, A. C. Orr, and E. L. Wolock, 1998, Flemington, NJ: Children's Software Revue. Copyright 1998 by Children's Software Revue. Adapted with permission.

to parents, teachers, and friends is desirable for helping the child derive a sense of accomplishment.

HIT WITH TECHNOLOGY EVERYWHERE, FOR JUST ABOUT EVERYTHING

As noted earlier, technologies have made it possible for students with hearing and vision loss to better access and participate in regular educational classrooms, yet these same technologies are often markers of disability and difference. So, too, are accommodations and support services in general. This begins in the early grades and carries through to postsecondary education. For example, deaf students at the Rochester Institute of Technology (RIT) who are in classes primarily with hearing students are usually found sitting together in the front of their classes so that they can best see the interpreter (who stands in the front with the teacher or professor). This grouping serves to set them apart from their hearing peers, the latter perceiving the deaf students as being separate and "different," so that, indeed, it is uncommon to see deaf and hearing students engaged in the more informal communications that occur among students and between student and teacher.

Even with interpreters, however, deaf students may not pick up on or process all the information they need. A lack of self-esteem may prevent some of them from asserting their needs for additional accommodations. Because they do not let the teacher know they are missing out on key information, the teacher may assume all is fine. Then, when the student tries to obtain additional assistance or information later, a circle of misunderstanding can develop. The following excerpt from an interview with a deaf engineering major at the RIT illustrates this point.

> I feel that I miss out on a lot compared to the hearing students. So many times, even though I attend the lectures, I come out afterwards saying to myself, "What are they talking about?" I find myself lost 90% of the time. Even though I understand what the interpreter says, it doesn't compute because I have to hear it. To be honest, I feel stupid a lot of times because I feel that I miss out in the classroom. I can't make myself appear to be bright to the faculty because they ask me questions in class I can't even answer because it hasn't processed. I go to the teacher afterwards to ask a question and they say, "But we've already gone over it and it's in the notes."

This student believed a particular technology held promise for enhancing her in-class participation and learning—and ultimately her self-esteem. This technology was first referred to in chapter 7, and it is really a system that has been evolving at the National Technical Institute for the Deaf over the past several years. Called "C-Print," this technology has several components (e.g., Stinson & McKee, 2000). First, it requires a person trained to use a dictionary of abbreviations to sit at a laptop computer and type in what the teacher says as close to verbatim as possible. Then, special software converts the abbreviations into complete words and sentences that are displayed on students' desktop or laptop computers or a screen in front of the classroom. While we have all seen captioned films and television, the availability of this technology for instant display and for everyday classroom use is a recent technological advance. But as with most technologies, some students benefit from its use more than others. As wonderful as it seems to be able to read what the teacher says almost immediately, students with poor English skills and lower reading abilities tend to prefer interpreters to this new text-based system. One student articulated this preference as follows:

I know having a teacher stand and lecture and having the lecture go on and on . . . with line after line of captioning, that gets a little tedious. Some or most of us are a little behind. I like using the interpreter because a lot of the vocabulary that I might not understand in print, the interpreter has an understanding of the concept and can sign something related to that to give me a little better understanding of the word.

While educators who advocate the use of educational technologies, and the engineers who design them, are often excited about the possibilities they have for enhancing the capabilities and education of students with disabilities, there are also many teachers, and parents, who see them as not yet fulfilling their promises. Many assistive and educational technologies do not help a student to overcome barriers—architectural or attitudinal—and may even heighten the user's sense of being different and socially isolated. The usefulness and value of other technologies, such as C-Print, are perceived differently by individuals because they vary in their capabilities to take advantage of them. In fact, most technologies used in education today balance advantages with shortcomings.

DISTANCE LEARNING AND TELECOMMUNICATIONS TECHNOLOGIES: BALANCING THE PLUSES AND MINUSES

For more than 10 years it has been recognized that the benefits of distance-learning instruction are many, as are its shortcomings (e.g., Cravener, 1999; Morris, Buck-Rolland, & Gagne, 2002; Ohler, 1991; VandeVusse & Hanson, 2000), and several successful models exist (e.g., Palloff & Pratt, 2001; Simonson, Sweeney, & Kemis, 1993; Withrow, 1991). Yet, course expenses are often high (e.g., B. O. Barker & Burnett, 1991; Palloff & Pratt, 2001), and there is evidence that students do not benefit equally from computer-based instruction (e.g., Abouserie, Moss, & Barasi, 1992; Cravener, 1999; Kay, 1992; Morris et al., 2002; Palloff & Pratt, 2001) and there is often over time a decline in students' preferences for computer-based instruction (Krendl & Broihier, 1992). In addition, little is known about the success of distance-learning instruction with people who have special learning needs (e.g., Johnstone, 1991; Sax, 2002a, 2002b), and there is evidence that Internet use for some has reduced social involvement and increased loneliness and depression (e.g., Kraut et al., 1998).

Thus, as was discussed earlier, distance learning brings challenges as well as opportunities. It offers much promise in enabling institutions to reach geographically dispersed learners in a manner that saves travel time and costs. It enables an instructor in one location and students in other locations to interact. This interactivity may be accomplished through a variety of technologies. Yet, these same technologies often make course expenses very high, present challenges to students who have hearing or eyesight loss, and can result in frustration for both students and faculty.

An Example of a Successful Distance
Learning Course in Secondary Education

A project I had the good fortune to be a part of was a distance-learning project funded by a grant from the U.S. Department of Education to deliver instruction in American Sign Language (ASL) to schools throughout the state of Maine (Keefe, Scherer, & McKee, 1996). MainePOINT (Providing Opportunities for Integrating New Technologies) has been described in an earlier article (Keefe, 1994). The target audience was Maine high school students in four groups: (a) deaf, (b) hard-of-hearing, (c) with learning disabilities, or (d) hearing. In Maine, ASL fulfills foreign language requirements.

In brief, the University of Maine collaborated with the Maine Department of Education and Governor Baxter School for the Deaf to implement an ASL telecourse. A deaf instructor taught the telecourse from the University of Maine, Augusta. Certified teachers monitored the ASL classes at all schools 5 days a week. Not all of the on-site teachers were trained ASL instructors, although three of the first eight were teachers of the deaf.

Because sign language is a visual language, one of the eight schools used a fiber-optic (two-way video) channel that allowed students to see the teacher and to be seen by the teacher. The other seven schools used a microwave channel that allowed students to see the instructor but did not allow the teacher to see the students (one-way video). The fiber-optic (two-way) link was not used at all the high schools because the school buildings had not been equipped with the links.

The ASL course was designed for broadcast 4 days a week, Monday through Thursday, to all eight high schools. Fridays were reserved as lab days and devoted to videotaping student assignments, to reviewing videotaped signing classes that week, and for "conferencing" around various assigned topics posted on a computer bulletin board. Each of the eight high school sites had at least one room with a television monitor, VCR, and a cordless phone. MainePOINT students communicated via e-mail and chat rooms rather than telephones during class broadcasts and outside class for completing homework assignments.

Each day of ASL instruction, the students convened in their classrooms with their "on-site" teacher who monitored the ASL instruction delivered from a distance over the statewide education television network. During the instruction, students could communicate with the instructor via a software package that enabled quick computer interaction throughout the state.

Students worked on assignments using the communication program after class to chat with the teacher and with classmates at other sites. The weekly lab day required students to use camcorders to videotape signing assignments, which were mailed back to the broadcast site for evaluation by the ASL instructor.

The challenge of the program was to deliver visual content (ASL) effectively over the network that existed in Maine at that time. The solution lay in the design of the course and the mix of technologies. The technology base is divided into three areas: technology used to deliver the course (at the University of Maine, Augusta), technology used by teachers to communicate with students statewide, and students' classroom technology used to communicate with the instructor and classmates.

Traditionally, all classes on the University of Maine Network used the phone system. But such a method of communication did not seem appropriate for content such as ASL. Therefore, an alternative approach using multimedia was selected. A software program called TEAMate was selected to help support the multimedia instructional delivery. The program included an "alert" feature to allow students to "talk" with their teacher during broadcast time and "conference" and "mail" features for student-to-student communication. The communication features plus a compact-disk photo file system enabled student pictures (and names) to be broadcast whenever the student addressed the teacher during the class period or when the teacher read an e-mail message from that student. During class time, the university-based technician "split" the screen whenever a student asked a question or made a comment, so the remainder of the class could see both the student and the instructor.

The instructor of the course needed to become familiar with some different teaching technologies. For example, instead of a blackboard, the instructor presented materials on the television screen in computer-generated text (Chromakey). When the teacher wanted to focus on key points, those points emerged in Chromakey text as she signed. The instructor manipulated the Chromakey text with a mouse when emphasizing a specific point.

Overhead cameras were used to display information that would be displayed on a blackboard or overhead projector in a traditional classroom. Print materials needed to be prepared in a large font with few words per line.

Video "roll-ins" are a media tool used to make classes more interesting. Roll-ins are segments of videotapes produced prior to broadcast and introduced into the lesson to illustrate certain examples. The roll-ins can be commercially developed segments or segments produced in-house.

Finally, students were also faced with becoming comfortable with new technologies to fully participate in the course. Each school was given a camcorder, videotapes, TV monitor, fax, VCR, computer, telephone, modem, and communication software. (The equipment did not have to be devoted exclusively to the ASL course.) The students received training on using the communications hardware and software and other equipment. They were asked to use camcorders to videotape their ASL signing, VCRs to review their tapes, and the TEAMate software to communicate with the teacher and with one another.

Students attended a Summer Institute for 2 days just before school started in the fall to foster student integration and introduce the project to them. At the Summer Institute, students met their teachers, interacted with members of the deaf community, worked cooperatively with one another, and received instruction in operating the course technologies. They completed survey forms to assess their existing knowledge of Deaf Culture and proficiency in ASL, their learning preferences, and their predispositions to using the course technologies.

One hundred and eighteen students completed all course requirements, and their grades reflected the distribution found in any foreign language course. The following were some of the key general results from the experimental course (Keefe et al., 1996):

1. There was enhanced social interaction among deaf students who often were one of few, if not the only, deaf students in a class. Deaf students throughout the state of Maine became connected.

2. Throughout the year, student self-confidence in general improved, as did their confidence and comfort with the course technologies. One deaf student in particular, who had been in a mainstream situation for several years, used ASL as his primary language and was followed around by an interpreter. As a result of the ASL course, he had available to him a group of students who could communicate with him, and he blossomed socially. This student had been invited to participate in the class because his teachers wanted him to become more comfortable around technologies. He helped the hearing students with ASL, and they helped him feel more comfortable with the technologies. At the end of the year, he used each technology proficiently.

3. After initial skepticism, the ASL instructor felt that the instructional delivery system was an acceptable way to teach a three-dimensional, visual language over the "flat" computer and television media. She said of her experience:

   > When I was first asked to teach ASL through the television system, my gut reaction was HOW? How could I teach ASL through one-way TV? ASL is based on visual

interaction. It's got to be person to person, face to face in order to communicate. But nonetheless, I accepted the challenge, and we have found that it really is a beneficial way to teach sign language. It has been a true learning experience and there's been a lot of exchanges going on that have made this possible. I believe it's important to have ASL offered by this means, especially to those schools in the rural communities. It would be impossible for them to have their own ASL classes. For me, it's been a way of reaching out and making connections throughout the state to students who otherwise would not have been able to take an ASL class. (personal communication, June 15, 1995).

4. It was very difficult and time consuming for the instructor to evaluate the student-produced tapes of their signing on a weekly basis. Help in this area needs to be provided.

All in all, the educational technologies used by these ASL students had some clear advantages, such as enhanced access to information and instruction and increased self-confidence through the mastery of another language. Although some of these technologies have been replaced with new or competing products, it is still the case that in technology-rich classes, every opportunity can also bring obstacles and barriers to academic success and the sense of being connected to school or a group of peers.

An Example of Distance Learning in Postsecondary Education

Distance learning and telecommunications technologies offer much promise in enabling colleges and universities to reach geographically dispersed learners by allowing an instructor in one location and students in other locations to interact (Sax & Duke, 2002). This interactivity may be accomplished through a common telephone linkup, through a network of computer networks (e.g., Internet), satellite, and broadcast technologies. The growing availability of fiber optic cables means there will be more cost-effective two-way communication in the very near future.

Dr. Norman Coombs has been a pioneer in distance learning and is chief executive officer of Equal Access to Software and Information (EASI). EASI's mission statement is as follows:

[T]o serve as a resource to the education community by providing information and guidance in the area of access-to-information technologies by individuals with disabilities. We stay informed about developments and advancements within the adaptive computer technology field and spread that information to colleges, universities, K–12 schools, libraries and into the workplace. (Equal Access to Software and Information, 2002)

As a professor of history at the RIT, which houses the National Technical Institute for the Deaf, Dr. Coombs often had deaf students in his classes. Deaf students depend so much on their sight, and Dr. Coombs depends largely on his hearing since losing his eyesight at the age of 7. Needless to say, this presented some challenges for student–teacher interactions. Out of this challenge grew Dr. Coombs' use of the computer to interact with his deaf students.

Being a pioneer in distance learning, the idea occurred to him and a colleague at the deaf liberal arts college, Gallaudet University in Washington, DC, to pilot two distance learning courses with students and faculty at both institutions. The course, "Black Civil Rights in the Twentieth Century," was taught by Dr. Coombs with a Gallaudet co-teacher and a "resource teacher." A professor at Gallaudet University taught "Mass Media and Deaf History" with an RIT faculty member and with a "resource teacher." The resource teachers were to facilitate student access to and usability of the delivery system; they were not to provide instruction per se. Both courses were open to students at Gallaudet University and RIT. The maximum student enrollment for each course was set at 26, with the goal of having equal numbers of Gallaudet and RIT students enrolled in each course.

The instructional delivery involved (a) captioned videotapes and movies, (b) assigned readings using a variety of print materials, and (c) class discussions via electronic mail over the Internet. Students had computer access days, evenings, and weekends. Students were given an orientation prior to the beginning of the course on how to use the Internet. All assignments were read and graded through the use of electronic mail. At the end of the course, students from each institution were asked to participate in an evaluation of the courses by completing survey forms and participating in an interview about their experiences. While the results of this evaluation have been reported elsewhere (McKee & Scherer, 1994), the general findings bear repeating here, as many of the students' reactions to those courses mirror those of today's distance learning students.

At that time, only about half of the students said that they felt comfortable communicating through the computer. Students expressed some frustration with the technical difficulties of interacting via the Internet, and both faculty and students agreed that at times, using e-mail was frustrating when there were long wait times for responses to their questions and continued dialogue about an issue. Most students (87%) said they missed seeing other students in face-to-face situations, and half agreed with the statement that they sometimes felt isolated talking only through their computer. Particular student comments were as follows:

I find it hard for me to express myself on the Internet instead of using ASL. Deaf people need to depend on eyes and hands. Therefore I suggest we have more discussion.

It was difficult for me. I would have to force myself to do my work in the morning when it [computer response time] is a little better than in the evenings.

One instructor felt that the discussion was qualitatively better than in a traditional classroom and attributed this in part to the fact that the delivery system encourages reflection before responding. The delivery system also is text-dependent, thus enhancing deaf students' English skills.

There was a great deal of variation in students' perceived interactions with their instructor. Responses ranged form "I had a lot of interaction with him" to "I did not have a lot of interactions with him . . . he would respond to me but that is it." One deaf student found that

It is difficult sometimes to have to watch the interpreter and sometimes I miss things. I wish the teacher would sign for himself or have it on the computer. I prefer between the teacher and me or me and the computer. I do not like the middle person.

Other students clearly did not perceive communication via computer as *interaction*: "I never saw the teacher . . . there was not any interaction, too impersonal." And one student believed the course was taught via distance learning because of the lack of campus space or teacher availability:

I was puzzled at first with the style of the course. I wondered if the teacher did not have any time to teach or if he cannot find a classroom and that is why the course was on the computer.

Other comments by students were the following:

I did not receive as much feedback as I would have liked. For example, I feel I would have received more feedback from a traditional class compared to this course.

I talked to the professor through e-mail. It was very superficial. If it was a regular style classroom, I could have face-to-face meetings with him, conversations would be more serious. It limits your creativity when you cannot express feelings in person.

Students generally felt more positive about interactions with their peers than with their instructor. Almost all of the students said they enjoyed reading the different opinions from the other students. One student found it interesting reading the comments from students from the other college. When comparing traditional instruction to distance learning, students were divided as to whether or not they had more interaction with other students in a distance course: 37% felt they did have more interaction, but 50% did not. One advantage of a distance learning course over a traditional one for deaf students is being able to enter a discussion without worrying about interrupting someone or entering the discussion at an inopportune time. Particular student comments include:

> I feel shy in the traditional classroom because others look at me when I am talking. It makes me feel self-conscious. I prefer discussions through the computer because I do not have to worry about people looking at me. I feel more comfortable.

> No, I did not like the e-mail discussions. The feedback was different. I did not know who was saying what. In a classroom I can see the students' faces, their opinions, etc. You can have a hot discussion in class but [with e-mail] you just sit and face a computer.

> You can have a good discussion in the regular classroom. But it loses something on the computer because there are not facial expressions. Also the discussions lose something because you have to wait too long for a response. The heat goes out of the "heated discussion."

The course's major strength was in the flexibility it allowed students. It was perceived most favorably by those students who were off-campus, needed a flexible schedule, would not otherwise have access to content specialists in certain subject areas, and are motivated and have a self-disciplined learning style. Students who were on-campus and accustomed to the structure found in a traditional classroom were less satisfied and less successful. They tended to miss the structure of regular classes and the support of peers.

Students did recognize that it was up to them to manage their time better in these types of courses, and 50% of the students agreed it was *more* difficult for them to keep up assignments in the distance learning course. One student captured this best when saying,

> I can do the work when it is convenient for me. If something comes up, I don't have to worry about skipping class. I can just go. But, I can get lazy. I can put it off too easily. I have to have good disciplinary skills.

Less than half of the students agreed that they would like to take another course in the same way. Twenty-five percent of the students felt they would not like to take another such course, and 25% of them were not sure. Most students felt social science or discussion classes would best fit this type of format:

> History classes would be good because they are easy. All you have to do is read the book, watch the videotapes. You don't need the teacher's help that much. English would be good too because we could all help each other with our grammar. We can correct each others' grammar and mistakes and help edit. Psychology of Deafness would be a good course, it forces you to analyze on your own and read more.

Technology does not eliminate the need for good teachers. Its strength is that it can get good teaching out to more people. It can also bring in guest Web lecturers and expose students to leaders in the field. Our recommendations for future courses using this means of instructional delivery focused on the need for instructional faculty and students to have initial or periodic face-to-face contacts (such as was done in Maine) to achieve the desired level of human interaction. Then e-mail discussions can be used to supplement discussion-based courses by providing the means for freer and less inhibited discussions.

We also noted the importance of informing students before they register for a course that it will be offered via computer and that face-to-face contact with faculty and other students will be minimal. When students are surprised and their expectations are not met, there is interference with their learning. The method of so informing students may vary from course to course or campus to campus, but it is important that the information be available to potential students to allow them to decide if such an instructional delivery system matches their learning styles and preferences. Once a student enrolls, both faculty and students agree that there is a need to ensure the availability of materials and to provide training in the use of the Internet and course technologies.

That the above findings and recommendations remain current was borne out through my experience in the past five years as one of four facilitators for a distance-learning course for professional rehabilitation counselors pursuing their master's degrees (e.g., Sax, 2002a, 2002b; Scherer & Sax, in press) as well as comments made during a symposium held at the RIT in winter 1998. During the latter, faculty members representing a variety of disciplines discussed their experiences and recommendations for new distance-learning faculty. Although some of the technologies have changed and become more sophisticated (e.g., larger numbers of students are now seen carrying portable laptop computers and personal digital assistant (PDA) devices with them between classes), a number of issues remain the same. According to one presenter:

> At first, in teaching telecourses 8 years ago, I thought I needed to replicate the classroom and get as much interaction going as possible. I started with picture telephones and each student had a remote classroom on their desktop and could see students from all over the country. It was not the way to go. There was a slow transmission time for the images and the lack of clarity on the monitors got in the way. An image would stay on the screen until someone sent another image. You couldn't match the speaker's voice with the face sometimes because the new image would come in so slowly. Then, this technology would only be used to show images of mathematical equations, which worked perfectly for the math professor when face-to-face interaction wasn't important.

From an interactive communication perspective, it failed. So, the moral is pick the right technology for what you want to accomplish. I've come to realize that trying to simulate live interaction is not necessary. With this whole asynchronic mode I guess all of us teach in with distance learning, it's really impossible.

A philosophy professor was the next speaker. For many years he used "at most, chalk on a blackboard," but now he regularly teaches his courses via distance learning. His courses are discussion-based and so he relies on e-mail quite heavily. He shared his experiences as follows:

> Now the only things my students know about one another are their ideas and thoughts and how those are expressed. Nothing about gender, disabilities, or the things that make people shy, aggressive, or whatever. The conversations they can have electronically, especially since it's asynchronous, the conversations go on with more thought, it blows away shyness and also the factor that the loudest student can no longer take control and distract thoughts that otherwise might lead to some coherence in the presentation of the material. In electronic conversations, everyone gets to participate who wants to. They have to go and look things up to make sure of what they want to say and I, too, get to look things up if they ask a question and I don't have the answer. All of this has shown me how much traditional classroom teaching is lacking.

The symposium participants continued to share their perspectives of distance learning from their own standpoint—that is, what it means for the teacher, not the students. Additional responses included the following:

> I find I'm sometimes overwhelmed by the number of e-mail messages waiting for me, all needing immediate attention. And I can really resent having to spend hours sitting and reading and responding to them all.
>
> The more sophisticated the technology, the more dependent you are on it. The more sophisticated the technology, the more support it needs. For me, I need to feel on top of and in control of the class. As I've become more and more dependent upon these technologies, it's more and more a committee enterprise with photographers, computer technicians, and so on. And that's expensive, too. That's why we need to be cautious about applying technologies. I've made the commitment to use these technologies, but I can't do it all by myself anymore, and that makes me feel a little helpless.
>
> It will be obvious how much care and attention you put into the class. You will get the full range of students with technology, too. Those who need a lot of help in using it, those who will be independent and already know it, and those in the middle.

Technology will not make a good teacher out of a poor one, nor will it ensure that all students in the class will master the course content. Today's distance-learning course instructor must be adept at multitasking. The content has to be defined, the presentation style selected to match course objectives, online discussion managed, and so on. The faculty representatives in this symposium as well as the course instructors for the graduate rehabilitation counselors are in a continuous cycle of course presentation, evaluation, and refinement. Accordingly, when the student counselors who participated in the distance-learning course were asked about their experiences, most reported that it had enhanced their learning and performance. Many said they would not have been able to take the course otherwise and continue their education. They liked being able to work at their own pace and time. But, according to one student, this is both an advantage and a disadvantage:

> The brain is not always ready to receive information at 8 a.m. on Tuesday and Thursday. This is also a drawback. If you don't have to do it at 8 on Tuesday then you can push if off to 8 on Sunday. Then it's three weeks down the line and there's this bottleneck.

As we found out in evaluating Dr. Coombs' courses, distance-learning courses are most successful for those students who are motivated enough to keep themselves on track. For those who are not, assignments can slip to the point at which the student cannot catch up.

The asynchronic nature of distance learning and e-mail interactions is beneficial to those students who find it difficult to think on their feet, formulate their ideas, and articulate them in front of a number of people. For these students, e-mail allows them to formulate what they want to say and express it clearly. However, students who are deaf with poor writing abilities and who prefer oral communication find e-mail a hindrance to their participation. "It all depends on the type of student" is an often-heard comment from faculty.

Technology has made it possible to make presentations much more interesting and more visual. It can enliven a dull topic through the use of graphics and better focus students' attention. Yet, other students can become overwhelmed by a rapid succession of graphic material. According to one faculty member:

> There is also a risk that with on-line presentations, we can present too much information too fast simply because it can be presented fast. And too many graphics, etc. can lead to overload. I actually had a student come up to me and say that there were just too many words and images to have to absorb in a short amount of time. We have to remember that students need soak time.

The Council for Higher Education Accreditation (2002) collected data in December 2001 to January 2002 to learn about distance learning in 17 accrediting regional and national organizations. They found that "of the 5655 accredited institutions, 1979 of them offered a form of distance-delivered programs and courses, some of which lead to degree acquisition" (p. 4). The focus on assuring quality from the accreditors' perspective requires that programs demonstrate competence in offering alternative instructional designs as related to curriculum, faculty support, and student learning outcomes. As colleges and universities increase their offerings in online courses and degrees, research has focused on the credibility of this type of instruction. According to a literature review undertaken by the 28th Institute on Rehabilitation Issues (Dew & Alan, 2002), "supporters of distance learning cite an abundance of research that shows no significant difference in the effectiveness of distance education compared with the traditional classroom experience" (p. 26). The study group found evidence from critics stating the opposite opinion as well as other information from those who claim to need more information to judge the effectiveness of the medium. Clearly, there is no definitive answer as yet. This is all the more the case when we consider that online education requires a computer and access to the Internet, which is associated with higher income, education, and employment—areas in which people with disability still lag.

Online access for people with vision or hearing loss (as well as those with other disabilities) is law. Section 504 of the Rehabilitation Act of 1973 (amended in 1998) requires that they cannot be "excluded from the participation in, denied the benefits of, or subjected to discrimination under any program or activity receiving Federal financial assistance." That includes higher education. The 1998 Amendments to the Rehabilitation Act include Section 508, which requires that electronic and information technology developed, procured, maintained, or used by the federal government be accessible to people with disabilities. This applies to all universities with federal government contracts. While Section 508 does not cover access to technology for private use away from federal facilities, when an employee's home becomes his or her place of work, necessary accommodations must be provided. Other initiatives include the following (National Council on Disability, 2002):

- A report from the National Web-based Education Commission, who conducted an investigation of the key issues around the use of the Internet for learning, highlights the necessity for ensuring that all learners have equal access to the capabilities of the Web.
- The "e-rate" program is designed to make Internet access and telecommunications services more affordable for schools and libraries by subsidizing the rate they pay for such services. Although it has been concluded that the e-rate program is covered by Section 508, no steps have been taken to ensure that this program is accessible.

- Section 255 of the Federal Communications Act requires that providers of telecommunications services (such as local and long distance phone companies) and manufacturers of telecommunications equipment and customer premises equipment must make their products and services accessible and usable by individuals with disabilities, where it is readily achievable to do so. Because by U.S. law the term "telecommunications services" applies only to services that facilitate and carry voice communication, other information services such as e-mail and high-speed data transmission are not yet technically covered under Section 255. FCC has asserted the regulatory right to broaden the definition of covered telecommunications services and has indeed created an "adjunct to basic services" category that applies Section 255 to all the features and functions necessary to complete calls. This includes calls used for e-mail, fax, data, and graphics transmission, in addition to activities around traditional voice calls.

Many other researchers have confirmed the elements of the preceding discussion on the merits and deficiencies of distance learning (e.g., Morris et al., 2002; Palloff & Pratt, 2001). While most have not separately addressed the needs of students with disabilities, there is a harmonious voice today that distance learning is not for everyone. Exhibit 8.2 summarizes general advantages and disadvantages to distance learning.

Regardless of the questions still held about this vehicle for learning, distance education is gaining momentum within higher education (Coombs, 1998; Eldredge et al., 1999; Sax, 2002a; Scherer & Sax, in press; Smart, 1999). This medium is well suited to providing access to Internet-based instruction 24 hours a day, thus expanding educational opportunities to those who cannot easily access traditional education because of geographical location, time constraints, work and family responsibilities, or other individual access issues.

As the discussion in this chapter indicates, not all students profit equally from a single instructional approach or method of instructional delivery. As part of the evaluation of Dr. Coombs's two courses, and the evaluation of the ASL course in Maine, we looked at the differences between the most satisfied students and the least satisfied students. This will be discussed later in chapter 11. In general, the dropout rate for online courses runs about 10–20 percentage points higher than for traditional classroom courses (e.g., Council for Higher Education Accreditation, 2002). Psychologists William and Ruth Maki compared students in an introductory general psychology course taught through traditional classroom lectures and online (W. S. Maki & Maki, 2002). They found that, for these students,

EXHIBIT 8.2
Summary of Advantages and Disadvantages of Distance-Learning Courses Compared With Traditional Classroom Instruction

Advantages

- Students who are blind and those who are deaf can participate in the same class equally.
- As with the Maine course, there can be enhanced social interaction among deaf students who are geographically scattered. In Maine, deaf students throughout the state became connected.
- Deaf students often improve their English skills as a result of participation in a distance-learning course.
- Unless students already know one another or have met during a face-to-face orientation to the class, the only things students know about one another are their ideas and thoughts—not whether or not they have a disability or the things that make people shy, aggressive, and so on.
- Electronic conversations, especially when asynchronous, go on with more thought.
- In electronic conversations, everyone gets to participate who wants to. Students who are shy about talking to a group say they feel less self-conscious.
- A student can enter a discussion without worrying about interrupting someone or entering the discussion at an inopportune time.
- The loudest student can no longer take control and distract thoughts that otherwise might lead to some coherence in the presentation of the material.
- Good teaching can get out to more people. Guest Web lecturers can be brought in, and students can be exposed to leaders in the field.
- Distance-learning courses are advantageous for students who are off-campus, who need a flexible schedule, who would not otherwise have access to content specialists in certain subject areas, and who are motivated and have a self-disciplined learning style

Disadvantages

- It can be time consuming for the instructor to read and respond to e-mails, and students may feel they are not getting enough personal attention.
- Distance-learning instructors must be adept at multitasking. The content has to be defined, the presentation style selected to match course objectives, online discussion managed, and so on.
- Faculty can feel increasingly dependent on these technologies and that a course is "more and more a committee enterprise with photographers, computer technicians, and so on."
- Distance-learning courses can be expensive to develop.
- Many students miss seeing other students in face-to-face situations and may feel socially isolated talking only through their computer.
- When the technology does not work optimally, it can result in a frustrating experience for both students and faculty.
- The use of e-mail can mean there are long wait times for responses to students' questions and continued dialogue about an issue, especially when students may be in different time zones.
- Some students may not perceive communication via computer as *interaction* and may feel the communication is too impersonal: "I did not know who was saying what. In a classroom I can see the students' faces, their opinions, etc. You can have a hot discussion in class but [with e-mail] you just sit and face a computer."
- Many students need and prefer the structure of regular classes and the support of peers.

(continued)

EXHIBIT 8.2   *(Continued)*

Recommendations

- Consider arranging for instructional faculty and students to have initial or periodic face-to-face contacts (such as was done in Maine) to achieve the desired level of personal involvement.
- Inform students before they register for a course that it will be offered via computer and that face-to-face contact with faculty and other students will be minimal.
- Course materials should be available very early, and students should be able to access training in the use of the course technologies.
- Pick the right technology for the educational goal. Technology has made it possible to make presentations much more interesting and more visual. It can enliven a dull topic through the use of graphics and can better focus students' attention. But with online presentations, information can be presented too fast and too many graphics can lead to overload. Remember that students need "soak time."

the traditional lecture course was preferred and that those who performed the best in the online course scored high on multimedia comprehension. The researchers suggested changes that closely parallel the recommendations in this chapter. How can we ensure that material taught by distance, over the Web or via computer software, yields information that students want to learn? We discuss this in the next chapter.

9

GETTING GOING ON LEARNING

I've been deaf since I was 3. When watching TV, hearing people had to stop and explain to me what was going on. If someone telephoned me, somebody else took the call. . . . Now I have a fax machine . . . I'm on the Internet . . . I have regular communications with people who are blind, people who are both deaf and blind, and it's all completely accessible to me.

—Dr. Frank Bowe

[T]he moral is, pick the right technology for what you want to accomplish.

—A college faculty member

There are many issues that the disability community faces in this new century. With changing laws and even faster evolving technology, it is important to continually revise and reassess the roles that schools, colleges, and universities play in the educational development of individuals with disabilities. It becomes the schools' responsibility by law and by social contract to maintain a universal education curriculum that will allow all students to access information in barrier-free environments. It is important to maintain a curriculum that is universally designed and uses a variety of media, including videos, PowerPoint presentations, graphics, alternative print formats, and audio sound, not to mention the various ways of inputting, navigating, and getting information from a computer-based curriculum. By using these resources, the teacher can create a welcoming learning space in which to reach and interact with all the students, including those who are blind or deaf.

The real challenge is to transform data into meaningful information, as Phil Bravin, former president and chief executive officer of the National Captioning Institute, stated in the quote in chapter 2. He also said the following:

A person receives data through the sense of vision or hearing, which allows them then to process the data into information. If we don't think of it that way, then we can't individualize the learning environment.

The input is modified to suit the needs and the wishes of the individual, to maximize his or her effectiveness of learning. (Bravin, 1994)

In keeping with Phil Bravin's comments, the input of data is not *information* the individual will determine is worthy of learning until that individual finds it meaningful. Learning objectives need to be written with the student and course content utmost in mind. Then, and only then, should a technology (as merely a means of transmitting content) be selected.

In this chapter, I discuss ways to make the information transmitted by educational technology meaningful for the individual user. This simple-sounding process is rather complex in many situations, and in all cases it is of the utmost importance: Without a convergence of meaning and information, no learning can take place.

Information consists of text and print materials; graphics, pictures, and visual cues. Sound can consist of music, wave forms, amplification, and so forth. When text, graphics, and sound converge, this convergence is called *multimedia*. But it simply exists as converged information until someone finds a way to use it and to make it meaningful. Only then does multimedia become informative and educational.

How do we ensure that media converges into information we want to impart? How can it all come together? For people who are deaf, one way it can all come together is by keeping the end user in mind. As discussed earlier, whether a particular student prefers captioning or interpreting varies by both student and context. Some students may prefer the independence and autonomy afforded by many technologies, whereas others may prefer the "human touch" of an interpreter who can individualize the interpretation. We simply cannot do away with the "human touch factor." People who are deaf often benefit most when both multimedia and an interpreter are available, as the interpreter is needed for discussion and dialogue in the classroom.

Yet, the presence of an interpreter does not negate the need for accessible media in presenting information essential to succeed academically in a class. Captioning needs to be mandated for all media with auditory components in classrooms with deaf students, even when interpreters are present. Multimedia products are simply impossible to interpret simultaneously; not only is it an overload for an interpreter but it usually results in less than full access for deaf students. Too often, teachers assume that the interpreters will make multimedia programs accessible so they do not bother to seek out captioned media in the first place.

Redundancy in information is a point that needs to be emphasized (e.g., Bishop & Cates, 2001; Scherer, 1994a). What will succeed in all of the various learning environments is the best blend of people's common sense and appropriate choices in technologies designed with the learner and that learner's needs and preferences in mind. Examples of such successful media-based efforts for deaf students include the following (Scherer, 1994b):

- A software program for deaf college students offers self-paced instruction with numerous possibilities for branching and inter-action. Other course materials include captioned videotapes, a course test, and a student notebook. A faculty mentor meets with the student to ensure understanding and provide encouragement.
- Deaf students with physical or learning disabilities are provided access to a variety of augmentative communication supports, including low tech (pictures/symbols/print on paper or boards) to high tech (computer based or dedicated communication devices). A communication device has several advantages over paper-and-pencil for these students. For example, a deaf student with cerebral palsy may be functionally literate but unable to write legibly. Nonreaders may need picture-based software to select voice/print output messages to communicate.
- Software is designed to improve the English skills of secondary and postsecondary deaf students. A writing program consists of exercises that address problems common to students whose primary language is ASL, such as article placement, verb tense, proper word choice, and correct word endings. Exercises include short essays or paragraphs with these types of errors, and the student practices identifying the errors and correcting them. Software vocabulary development exercises include multiple meaning words and idioms encountered by students in news-papers and other publications.
- With one virtual reality system, an individual can don a helmet that displays two television sets, one in front of each eye, and a pair of headphones, and a three-dimensional world is created that is quite realistic. The user can point with a special glove to move the objects in the environment. To look down the platform, the person just turns his or her head. Wherever the person looks, he or she sees what is in that direction. Again, by pointing with a glove, the user travels, turns, travels to the other side. Technology has also created realistic three-dimensional environments in sound. A person who is blind tried one of these environments. He donned the system and as he walked around, he was avoiding objects and doorways and other obstacles completely acoustically. With cross-sensory information such as this, someone with paralysis who cannot pick up glassware may be able to manipulate the various items

in a chemistry experiment and carry out the same experiments as their colleagues (Vanderheiden, 1994). Other applications of virtual reality for people who are blind exist or are being developed (e.g., Krueger & Gilden, 2002).

It is also the responsibility of the teacher to help students learn how to organize information and remember it—in other words, teaching students how to learn. Technology can help as the examples above show, but it can also become overdone and get in the way of learning. Trial use of a multimedia tutorial integrating video, captioning, and control for the learning of complex material indicated that complex or new material is not learned well by some students when caption and video are shown simultaneously (Scherer, 1994b). The learning of complex material is maximized with alternating video and caption. Thus, some recommendations would include the following: First, tell the student what is about to be done concurrent to displaying captions. Second, show the task being performed with video only (no captions) so that the student may pay full attention to the video. Third, tell the student what has been done concurrent to displaying the captions. Fourth, provide video controls to allow review of all lesson videos.

Although it is easy to be dazzled by technology, there are many non-technological means by which accessibility can be facilitated, and most of these have not been implemented to the full extent possible. For example, merely speaking all material as one puts it up on an overhead or writes it on a blackboard can make a tremendous difference to the inclusion of students with vision loss.

SIMULTANEOUSLY MEETING THE NEEDS OF STUDENTS WITH VISION LOSS OR HEARING LOSS

Many technologies benefit one group but create barriers for another group. It is ironic that this applies to many disability access features as well. It is possible to increase access of a product for one population that in fact will make it less accessible to people with other disabilities. It is therefore important to support a cross-disciplinary, cross-disability focus to accessibility efforts so that common solutions are developed. Multimedia systems can cause problems and, as we all know, multimedia systems are becoming standard and ubiquitous.

Multimedia products, which offer great promise for providing interactive learning environments for individuals of all ages, have the potential to pose significant accessibility problems, especially for people with sensory disabilities. When information is presented primarily in an audio format, people who are deaf or hard-of-hearing may not be able to access it, and if information is presented primarily in a visual format, people who are blind or have low vision may not be able to access it. Multimedia developers need to address accessibility issues during the design phase of product development rather than as an add-on after a product has been completed (e.g., Bowe, 2000; Vanderheiden, 2001b). And teachers need to be judicious and alert in their selection of products.

In chapter 3, Dr. Frank Bowe (who is deaf) talked about his telephone conversation with Dr. Larry Scadden (who is blind) which became possible because they each "made a movement from people to machines." He explained further what this means to him:

> Larry and I used to rely almost all the time on other people. Today we don't. We rely on machines and we have the machines at home and in our offices. Back in the early 1980s, I hired a full-time interpreter to sit in my office and take care of the phone for me. It was an extraordinary expense but people in business pick up the phone and they call, so somebody had to be there to answer the phone. I don't do that anymore. I have a fax machine at home, I'm on the Internet, and I completely ignore the telephone. If they want me, they use the fax and send me a fax saying "Frank, please call me." I can communicate with people with any disability, and I do. I have regular communications with people who are blind, people who are both deaf and blind, and it's all completely accessible to me with no human interaction at all. Larry, meanwhile, uses the same technology. He can get on Internet and listen to everything I read. If I send information to him, I type it, I send it; he gets it, he listens to it, and neither one of us have to have any human assistance in that communication. (Bowe, 1994)

During a multimedia presentation at, say, a conference both Drs. Bowe and Scadden attend, as Dr. Bowe watches the captions on a videotape, Dr. Scadden listens to a video description. On a videotape, people on the screen move around and do things that are not reflected in the dialogue. In video description, a person speaks a description of that action into a microphone that Dr. Scadden can hear with a special headset. Both captioning and video description are people- and time-intensive and, thus, expensive. According to Dr. Bowe, however:

> Where we're now going with all this is toward a system where the network will do some of these things and it will not be so people-intensive. We're seeing some of this, for example, with voice dialing where you pick up the phone and say something like "Larry Scadden" and a computer picks up the phone and dials it. Larry's phone starts ringing about 5 seconds later. That's an example of speech recognition in the network. (Bowe, 1994)

Today, Dr. Bowe can be in his office, at home, or in a classroom and his students can be anywhere in the world and they can see and hear him.

When he teaches students with and without hearing, with and without eyesight, in a classroom equipped with computers at each desk, he can have an interpreter as well as interact with students by having a live "chat" via computer. Anything his students say or ask will be displayed on his computer screen and vice versa. Later, a complete transcript of these dialogues can be provided. In Dr. Bowe's words:

> The advantages to this are many. The first advantage is that all of the computer hardware, software, compatibility stuff, is in the network. We don't have to know about cable, how to interface, how to make it work. All we do is type. Number two: It will be much, much cheaper than any other alternative. We don't even need a building. We don't need people, coffee breaks, and health plans for them. The third benefit: The technology becomes available to anybody from anywhere. This will be of great benefit to people who became blind in their 50s or 60s, 70s. Two thirds of all people who became deaf became deaf after the age of 50. These people are typically very different from Larry and myself. They don't want special equipment; they don't want special help. If you put this special stuff into the network, you hide it, and you don't force people to use equipment that they don't want other people to see, that makes them look "special" or "different." The technology will, however, have limitations. I can't imagine it doing video description. I can't imagine any software being able to look at a moving image, extract meaningful information from it and speak that out for Larry to listen to. I can't imagine reverse interpreting. (Bowe, 1994)

For such a system to be successful and result in real benefits to deaf students, Dr. Bowe emphasized:

> Deaf people are going to have to read, read very well, read very fast. Captions appear on the screen very fast, for a very short period of time. The same thing is true of much of the information over the computer. The ability to read is going to be the number one thing that will make their lives easier and make it possible to earn a living. (Bowe, 1994)

Much more attention needs to be focused on the role technologies will increasingly be playing in providing instruction to children, youths, and adults who have hearing or vision loss. Emphases need to include (a) practical applications of technologies in a variety of educational settings and (b) better preparation of educational professionals, as they will be expected to minimize the complexities of technology while at the same time use technology to increase student interaction in the traditional classroom. Teacher education students as well as many current teachers need an active introduction to and practice in using a variety of technologies for instruction. They must be encouraged to learn and keep up with new technologies and applications of those technologies, participate in electronic networks of professionals in special education, and stay abreast of the research contributing to this field. They must also be provided regularly with information on the implications of choosing particular technologies and delivery systems for students with disabilities, and this needs to be incorporated in teacher education programs and reinforced through state and professional certification requirements. As an example, Exhibit 9.1 summarizes key considerations for selecting instructional technologies that may be helpful and assist in accomplishing learning goals.

There are two approaches to making information and educational systems accessible. The first approach is by individual modification or retrofit, and the second is by universal design (e.g., Connell et al., 1997; Vanderheiden, 1994, 2001a, 2001b). Both have advantages, and both are necessary. It is not possible to design everything so that everyone can use them. The first approach, individual modification, should be used in those cases in which something in fact is not directly accessible to a particular individual. Often, the most efficient way to establish an effective workstation for an individual, a place where he or she will consistently work, is to actually custom design or modify the setting to enable that person to work as efficiently as possible so that he or she can be productive and competitive in his or her education or employment. However, for public systems and in such environments as classrooms, more emphasis should be placed on universal design, or designing things for which access is built in. This lowers the cost, provides wider access, helps people who are older who have trouble in using or accepting technologies, and actually provides better design for many people. A frequently used example of this is curb cuts, which are used by people with wheelchairs as well as by people who do not have disabilities who use them for strollers and delivery carts.

When you go to a laboratory, a university, or a library, you do not want to have to argue with the librarian about reprogramming the computer to make it accessible. You want it to already be accessible to you. The importance of getting industry to consistently build access directly into their products has already been discussed. Prototypes must be made available for consumers to try in actual situations of use so that industry does not produce a product that has not had widespread consumer usability testing (e.g., Kilgore et al., 2001; Vanderheiden & Tobias, 2002). Cross-disability access must also be evaluated.

TECHNOLOGY IS ONLY AS GOOD AS ITS USEFULNESS FOR ANY PARTICULAR STUDENT

Today technology is used to connect our schools with our homes. From your computer, you can electronically access information about where things are and how to get to places. You can obtain the weather report at any

CURRICULUM DESIGN

Instruction is developed after a thorough analysis of the information and skills to be learned (educational goals), and the content organized into instructional modules. Provide examples and practice activities reflecting the information/skills to be learned, and assess information and skill acquisition after each instructional module. Only at this point think about the *means* of (a) providing instruction, (b) giving examples and practice, and (c) assessing students' learning. A technology or system or multimedia presentation may or may not be beneficial. It is important, when matching a student with a technology, to consider the function and features of that technology in light of the educational goal for that particular student. Below are three areas to consider when choosing a technology-based approach to instruction.

Delivery Systems

Although not every educational technology can be considered a delivery system, it is generally considered to be the physical equipment or the electronic system that serves as the vehicle to the instruction. This may be, for example, a basic computer, a computer with an enlarged display, or one with voice output; or it may be a closed-caption decoder, a teleconferencing system, a large-screen projection system, a videocassette recorder, interactive CD/DVD equipment, a self-correcting workbook, or Web-based instruction.

For the successful use of any delivery system, there are some common and fundamental questions to ask:

- Will use of the delivery system require that more (or less) time be devoted to this educational goal than is appropriate or desirable?
- Do the required supports exist in the environment(s) of use (electrical outlets, lighting, appropriate noise level, available space)?
- Is the system tested and of high quality (reliable, effective, etc.)?
- Can the learner use the system independently and, if not, is the essential support available?
- Do the requisite skills exist for use or does the user require training to develop the skills? If the latter, the preferred format for (one-to-one tutoring, group) and availability of that training need to be determined.

Computer use involves considerations around type of computer (portable note-taker for people who are blind, or handheld) as well as the most appropriate means of input, output, and navigation (see chap. 7). Does the system need to be portable, and is it? Attention also needs to be given to the positioning of the computer and the placement of peripherals so that they are ergonomically correct for the individual user.

Computer software features to consider include the intelligibility of text, sound, and visual information;

- the availability of spelling and grammar checks and a thesaurus;
- enlarged print;
- word prediction;
- auditory, visual, or multisensory feedback;
- variable and adjustable speed of presentation and acceptable response times;
- the degree to which the user possesses the requisite skills (academic, cognitive, physical) to use it optimally and, if not, the type of training most appropriate for the user or student to obtain the skills;
- the ability and age appropriateness of the content and the type and frequency of motivation and reinforcement used.

(continued)

EXHIBIT 9.1 *(Continued)*

Instructional Strategies

These are considerations as to how the delivery system will be used as a learning tool:

- Does the system foster inclusion and participation? If it is for solitary learning, have other participatory educational activities been built into the overall instructional plan?
- In a group situation, is turn-taking facilitated?
- Does the system recognize and build on student strengths and is it motivating?
- Are the learning episodes controlled by the learner, the teacher, or the technology? Can the student review directions? Take a break and have the work be saved? Exit the program independently?
- Is personal choice and "human override" built in?
- Is a multisensory presentation important? If so, does the presentation contain textual, graphic, auditory, and experiential features?
- Is the visual material of high quality and high resolution?
- Is the auditory message clear? Does background sound, such as music, help (by calming and enhancing student mood) or hinder learning?
- Is there an adequate amount and variety of practice material available?
- Is the intent of the instruction consistent with the educational goal—the development of new skills, the improvement of acquired skills, changes in attitude or behavior?
- Is the instruction structured to meet the student's needs—as a drill, tutorial, means of problem-solving or discovery?
- Are the rate and length of the learning episodes appropriate?
- Is the presentation format consistent with the initial cuing?
- Is prompting, feedback, reinforcement, and response/progress tracking handled well?
- What is the plan for monitoring student use of the system as intended, attainment of the instructional goals, the need to revise/upgrade the system?

Subject Content

Below are some guiding questions for determining the appropriateness of the content of the technology (e.g., videotape, software program) under consideration. Their purpose is to assist you in considering areas that can be modified so that the match of student and technology is optimized in light of the educational goal. (Also review considerations under Delivery System for computer software and Instructional Strategies for applicability of those items to the content.)

- Does the actual content being covered conform to your curricular and instructional goals?
- Is the terminology consistent with that used by the teacher or the program?
- Is the language level appropriate?
- Is the presentation of the content appropriate to the maturity, the experience, and the interest level of the student audience?

Reminder. If you are using this exhibit as a checklist during instructional design, the instructional goal and subject content must be determined first, then the most desirable instructional strategies need to be identified, and, last, the delivery system for the instruction selected. At the end of the instruction, it is important to assess how much the student learned and developmentally progressed from this educational experience.

location at any time in a user-friendly fashion. You can find out if somebody in your town is selling a particular model of a car or something you wish to buy, have things delivered to your home, pay bills, do banking, deliver messages that can be received as text or voice output, and receive the latest news on any topic. You can participate in social, religious, and entertainment activities. You can literally get almost any type of information in a straightforward fashion. You have access to libraries, and whether you live in a large city or rural community, you can have access to the same information. Small schools that cannot afford to have physics or chemistry laboratories can access simulations of how certain reactions work. And you have the ability to select the information in a form that is the easiest for you to work with and is compatible with your needs.

In addition, television, electronic books, CDs and DVDs, virtual reality and simulations, computer labs, fax machines, PDAs, video cameras, and digital still cameras are just some of the many technologies used daily in today's schools. Ten years ago this list would have been much shorter; in another 10 years it will likely be longer and different from this one.

When assistive, access, and educational technologies were fairly new, there was not a lot of product choice and it was more acceptable to get by with telling a child, "Sally, you're going to have to learn to like using this because it's all we have. It may not be easy, but it's the best we can do for you right now." Now, because there is so much more choice in products and their features, this is no longer acceptable (Scherer, 2002a; 2002b). Educators and learners alike can exercise a good deal of choice thanks to today's technologies, but these technologies are most effective when they are shaped to meet a student's particular learning needs, not when they are used as a mere enhancement to learning (e.g., Edyburn, Higgins, & Boone, in press; Scherer, 1994a, 2000). Any technology (assistive, instructional, access) that is forced on students and that does not fit with their preferences or ways of doing things has a decreased probability of use, as do technologies that minimize interactions with teachers or interfere with social activities enjoyed by students.

Furthermore, the focus now should be on individual learners with vision or hearing loss. No longer is a student in need of a cure or a special school. Now we help students become all they can be in as inclusive an educational setting as possible. And we are expected to be knowledgeable about all that is available to help us accomplish this and all that is available to the student and his or her family. We are to know the student's needs and preferences, educational goals, and what particular technologies and features are most appropriate and desirable (Scherer, 1990b; Scherer & McKee, 1994b; Scherer, McKee, & Keefe, 1994). What can we select that will benefit the student most and meet the student's needs, educational goals, and preferences?

KEY INFLUENCES ON THE USE OF
TECHNOLOGIES BY STUDENTS

Technology cannot change how people learn. It can only change how they are provided instruction. Technology is part of the teaching and learning arsenal, and it is the job of today's teachers, from preschool through postgraduate and adult education, to assemble the components and make them flow into a meaningful learning experience. As noted by Fradd et al. (1986), teachers must succeed in three broad areas: the illumination of lessons, the establishment and maintenance of rapport, and the acclimatization and socialization of students in classroom environments that are built as much from interactions between student and teacher as from those between student and peers.

Although we may not have had a long history with technologies in education, we have had a long history with teaching and instruction. We have a fairly good idea about what works and what does not. Technology is just another tool, like a blackboard or a pencil. It is not what technology does to education, but how wisely we use it—or choose not to use it. As noted by Hooper and Hannafin (1991) over 10 years ago,

> Emerging instructional technologies have been much heralded, but often for the wrong reasons. The potential of emerging technologies stems not simply from technologically advanced capabilities, but from the ability to vary instructional methods and media systematically. (p. 69)

It can be added that new technologies make it possible to accommodate varied student learning styles and preferences.

We have gone from an orderly, authoritarian, factory model of schooling to one that prepares us to live and work in a world of multitasking. Additionally, teachers today are under unprecedented pressures to be accepting of a wide variation in student intelligence, emotional maturity, and physical characteristics. They are expected to enthuse, teach, and motivate students in spite of vast differences in students' abilities and characteristics. The great hope behind the drive for the use of both educational and assistive technologies is that they will enable the achievement of these goals. As important as educational and assistive technologies can be in helping students with disabilities receive the highest quality education, many barriers exist to the maximum utilization of these technologies. School personnel, families, and students often have (a) little knowledge of available technologies, (b) difficulties accessing and affording technologies, and (c) lack of training in the use of technologies (Scherer, 2002a).

As already noted several times, students do not benefit equally from use nor do they all approach technologies with a positive view of them. To

EXHIBIT 9.2

Educational Goal
- Intended purpose
- Essential instructional content

Environment
- Support from family and peers for use
- Degree it fosters achievement of the educational goal
- Access to the technology

Student
- Learning preferences and style
- Prior exposure to educational technologies
- Desire to achieve educational goal
- Temperament and personal goals

Technology
- Degree of physical comfort in using the technology
- Compatibility of technology use with social activities
- Technology supports varying abilities
- Availability of training/support and upgrading
- Ease of setup and use

what can differential use of and satisfaction with technologies be attributed: the particular learner's characteristics, those of the technology in question, or those of the environment in which the technology is designed to be used? We know that technologies that are forced on students and do not fit with their preferences or ways of doing things have a decreased probability of use. For example, an educational technology that requires discipline, patience, and perseverance and that provides infrequent reinforcement may not appeal to a teenager who likes continual excitement (Scherer & McKee, 1991, 1992, 1994a, 1994b). Moreover, as stated previously, technologies that minimize interactions with teachers or interfere with social activities enjoyed by students are often abandoned. Technologies are most effective when they are shaped to meet a student's particular learning needs, preferences, and temperament. Thus, the use or nonuse of an educational technology is the outcome of a complex constellation of factors, listed in Exhibit 9.2.

The existence of these myriad factors in Exhibit 9.2 indicates the importance of assessing the quality of the match between a student and a technology being proposed for that student's use. A more detailed discussion of these domains is the primary focus of the next chapter.

V

MATCHING LEARNERS
WITH THE MOST
APPROPRIATE
TECHNOLOGIES AND
STRATEGIES FOR THEIR USE

10

INDIVIDUAL LEARNER PREFERENCES AND NEEDS

[Larry Scadden and I] were saying how it's kind of amazing that we made it through the public schools despite the fact that there was no technology to accommodate us. Yet, both of us have continued our education. We both have PhD degrees.

—Dr. Frank Bowe

In chapter 5 I discussed how I had observed Ellen learning braille and listening to her Helen Keller story audiotape as a reward. I saw how Stephen was able to participate in his class's math exercise with the help of his vision teacher. What I did not see was either student having any significant interactions with her or his classmates.

I had not seen this at the New York State School for the Blind, either, even though it must certainly occur. But let us just consider the included students with vision loss I observed in the highly ranked public school system discussed in chapter 5. According to Maslow's hierarchy of needs, one must first satisfy the drive or need for esteem, affiliation, and belonging before intellectual/achievement needs can be satisfied. In today's schools, everyone is keeping such a frenetic pace and multitasking or working on so many academic and skill areas simultaneously that, paradoxically, time for fun and socializing has had to become very highly structured and tightly scheduled. For students with vision and hearing loss, their class time is frequently filled with services that are pulled in to them or they are pushed out to receive services elsewhere. In addition, as described by the college students with hearing loss in chapter 4, there is a need to devote a good deal of one's "leisure time" to homework and studying outside of the class-room—more time than the average student without a hearing or vision loss likely needs to devote. So how connected can these students feel with their peers and the world in which they find themselves approximately 8 hours a day?

At this point in Stephen's life, he should be experiencing, according to Erikson's (1963) fourth stage (Industry vs. Inferiority), success at activities leading to a sense of accomplishment and adequacy. But how can students achieve a sense of accomplishment when they are continuously on the move or having every move they make shadowed by one type of teacher or another, and they are told to work on activities no one else in their class is doing (in a setting where every other student is working together on a common assignment), and then, to add to a feeling of disconnection, have what they are doing become an obstacle to all the rest of the class (as when Ellen's classmates could not drop their homework in the boxes because Ellen was seated in the way). Would Hansell (1974) give Ellen and Stephen a "passing score" on their "essential attachments" to other people, a social role, to the feeling one matters and that one's life is meaningful?

There is no doubt that Ellen and Stephen experience a sense of accomplishment when they master a task and achieve the academic goals set out for them. But these are often different tasks and goals from the ones their school has established for their classmates. When they reach adolescence and confront Erikson's stage of Identity versus Confusion, what is the identity that is formed? That of a student different from everyone else? Or that of a self-confident student secure in making and expressing choices in an inclusive world? How do we make sure it is the latter?

In spite of the fact that technologies have made it possible for many students to attend regular public schools, a good number of special educators are concerned that an increased emphasis on technologies will further separate students with disabilities from their peers and will reinforce the attitude that people with disabilities present difficult problems requiring complicated, expensive, high-tech solutions (e.g., Scherer, 1999). Moreover, there is concern that as technologies are becoming more commonly used, there is a risk of "overequipping" a student (e.g., Scherer, 2000).

Technologies often require a great deal of time to master. The emphasis on computerized devices and computer use keeps growing, and those students with cognitive or information-processing deficits often face frustration and additional obstacles to their sense of accomplishment and adequacy. The use of a combination of assistive and educational technologies can lead to a situation of overload (Scherer, 2000).

For many students with disabilities, however, technology is not a choice. It is necessary to keep them active participants in today's classrooms. Technology enables them to complete tasks that they cannot accomplish alone. Assistive technology (AT) has provided them the means to communicate more effectively, to go where they wish on their own, and to complete assignments more independently (e.g., Craddock & Scherer, 2002; Munk,

2003). These ATs often allow students with disabilities to achieve the same instructional objectives as their nondisabled peers (e.g., Craddock, 2002; Flemming & Flemming, 1995).

Research has long supported the beneficial impact of AT on children and students with disabilities (e.g., Abrahamsen, Romski, & Sevcik, 1989; Behrmann & Lahm, 1984, 1994; Blackhurst & Edyburn, 2000; Bowser & Reed, 1995; Brinker & Lewis, 1982; Craddock, 2002; Craddock & Scherer, 2002; Denham, Bennett, Edyburn, Lahm, & Kleinert, 2001; Edyburn, 2000a, 2000b, 2001; Hutinger, 1987; Hutinger, Johanson, & Stoneburner, 1996; Judge & Parette, 1998; Parette & Van Biervliet, 1991; Zabala, 1995). The number of AT devices in use is lengthy, and the list is growing longer each day. In addition to the technologies already mentioned for students with hearing and vision loss, there are such devices as electronic communication devices that provide speech for nonverbal or hard-to-understand children, and pocket-size spelling devices, electronic schedule reminders, and so on. These examples illustrate how AT is truly assistive in enabling schools to better provide instruction suited to individual needs and support that is less expensive than an aide and more immediate than waiting for an adult to help (Flippo, Inge, & Barcus, 1997; Judge & Parette, 1998; Schiller, 1997). In essence, children with disabilities of both high and low incidence have the potential to benefit from AT when the applications are customized to their individual abilities and needs.

The importance of AT in the lives of students was underscored by Congress with the inclusion of AT in the 1990 Americans With Disabilities Act, the Individuals With Disabilities Education Act (IDEA) Amendments of 1997, the Rehabilitation Act of 1973 (as amended in 1998), and the Technology Related Assistance for Individuals With Disabilities Act (Tech Act), which was reauthorized in 1998 as the Assistive Technology Act. IDEA further supports the use of AT by students with disabilities by stating that schools must provide AT for students, as well as pay for repairs and maintenance if it purchased the AT, if the student's Individualized Education Program (IEP) team determines a need for the technology. The student is free to take the AT home if it is needed for the student to fully benefit from its use. However, when the school district pays for AT it becomes the property of the school. When a student graduates or otherwise leaves the school, he or she has to procure another replacement AT. Within IDEA, additional emphasis is placed on identifying the supplementary supports and services needed to enable the child to be educated in the general education classroom and with the general curriculum. As of July 1, 1998, all IEP teams had to "consider whether the child requires assistive technology devices and services" to receive a free and appropriate public education. The federal definition of assistive technology used in IDEA is essentially the same as that first set forth in the Technology-Related Assistance of Individuals With

Disabilities Act of 1988 (see chap. 2, this volume). Assistive technology service is defined as

> any service that directly assists a child with a disability in the selection, acquisition, or use of an assistive technology device. The term includes:
>
> (a) The evaluation of the needs of a child with a disability, including a functional evaluation of the child in the child's customary environment;
>
> (b) Purchasing, leasing, or otherwise providing for the acquisition of assistive technology devices by children with disabilities;
>
> (c) Selecting, designing, fitting, customizing, adapting, applying, retaining, repairing, or replacing of assistive technology devices;
>
> (d) Coordinating and using other therapies, interventions, or services with assistive technology devices, such as those associated with existing education and rehabilitation plans and programs;
>
> (e) Training or technical assistance for a child with a disability, or if appropriate, that child's family; and
>
> (f) Training or technical assistance for professionals (including individuals providing education or rehabilitation service), employers, or other individuals who provide services to employ, or are otherwise substantially involved in the major life functions of children with disabilities. (Golden, 1998, p. 3)

As the examples in chapter 5 of Betty, the veteran teacher at the New York School for the Blind, and the vision teacher in the public school illustrate, different schools have different mixes of students and, as a result, different educational goals. An educational goal must be specified as clearly as possible to assess the quality of the match where a technology is likely to be involved. The goal may be remedial in nature, it may be curriculum specific, or it may simply be for enrichment. It would usually involve the achievement of one of the following skills:

- a particular cognitive skill such as comparing, classifying, or applying;
- a motor skill such as operating, measuring, adjusting, or assembling;
- a personal/social skill such as increasing attending behavior, resolving conflict, clarifying values, or increasing empathy;
- a study skill or a problem-solving skill such as outlining, following directions, or predicting;
- a skill in a particular content area (mathematics, reading, science, history);
- the resolution of a problem of access to education caused by distance, time, a learning disability, or a physical limitation; or
- the matching of a learning style to the educational goal or providing variety to the learning environment.

A key educational goal for Ellen is to learn to braille. For some students at the New York State School for the Blind, the educational goal is the same even though the teaching methods, instructional strategies, and technologies used to reach that goal are different. For Stephen, it is to be included in a regular fifth-grade math class and get a passing grade. The educational goal for high school students throughout Maine who learned American Sign Language through distance learning approaches was to master the technologies necessary to participate in the course, get a passing grade in the course, and be able to communicate with a person who is deaf (see chap. 8, this volume). For Dr. Norman Coombs at the Rochester Institute of Technology and his counterpart at Gallaudet University, it was to have enrolled students successfully complete two history courses offered via distance learning technologies (see chap. 8, this volume).

Students of diverse ages from distinctly different institutions can share the same educational goals. While there may be shared educational goals across schools, different educational goals exist within any particular school. For example, the vision teacher for Ellen and Stephen is working on very different goals for them.

UNDERSTANDING DIFFERENT LEARNING STYLES

Learning is shaped by our prior knowledge, the frequency and type of social interactions we have, and the methods used to teach us. The most successful learning occurs when numerous strategies are used. In a survey of an average class (elementary, secondary, postsecondary, or adult continuing education), it is said that about 5% of what is heard during a lecture is retained, approximately 30% of what is observed during a demonstration, about 50% of what is learned by participating in a discussion group, and about 90% through practice by doing (Tehama County Department of Education, 2002). Who benefits more from any of the above forms of learning depends to a great deal on one's *learning style*. There are linear or analytic learners (prefer the details) and global learners (prefer the big picture). Teachers also have a tendency to prefer one or the other style in the ways they provide instruction and relate to students. Some examples of how linear/analytic learning and teaching styles match are shown in Table 10.1. Matching global learning and teaching styles are shown in Table 10.2. When a learner's and teacher's styles do not match, there can be dissatisfaction and misunderstandings, even conflict. It is important to an IEP team to make as good a match of student and teacher as possible and to identify mismatches early (e.g. Gregory & Chapman, 2001; Tomlinson, 1999).

Making distinctions between linear/analytic and global learning is just one approach to understanding differences in student preferences and

TABLE 10.1
Matching Personal Learning and Teaching Styles: Linear or Analytic

Area of preference	Students with hearing or vision loss who prefer. . .	Will learn best from teachers who. . .
Classroom structure	Working within parameters, competitive	Organize and structure the class period, enforce rules
Presentation style	Step-by-step instructions, clear and explicit directions, ordered and logically structured lectures with details	Are serious, lecture with an emphasis on details, demonstrate applications
Instructional pace	Slow, stable, predictable instruction	Introduce new ideas in a logical, sequential order
Learning exercises	Independent and autonomous reading, applications, watching a demonstration	Assign independent exercises that build on practical applications
Tests and assignments	Multiple-choice and paper-and-pencil tests, emphasis on the practical, product- and deadline-oriented	Assign homework that focuses on reading and responding with the facts and details, administer standardized tests

TABLE 10.2
Matching Personal Learning and Teaching Styles: Global

Area of preference	Students with hearing or vision loss who prefer. . .	Will learn best from teachers who. . .
Classroom structure	Free, unstructured, nurturing	Emphasize discovery learning, exploration, field trips, prizes as rewards
Presentation style	Multimedia, big picture	Are sensitive, involve students, learning is fun
Instructional pace	Fast, exciting, adaptable	Flexible, dynamic
Learning exercises	Talking about concepts, listening, experimenting, debate and argument	Introduce cooperative team-oriented experiences, games, role-plays, case studies, simulation
Tests and assignments	Open-ended, portfolios, choices and process, resourcefulness	Emphasize broad concepts, philosophical discourse, imagination and creativity

academic performance. Another perspective (e.g., Tobias, 1996) focuses on the differences among visual, auditory, and kinesthetic learners. If using this model, it is important to keep in mind that a student with a moderate hearing loss may very well be an auditory learner, and a student with low vision may be a visual learner. Two people can have identical hearing but may learn and take in and process information differently—further supporting the value of redundancy, multimedia, and universal design for learning. For example, Dr. Larry Scadden, who has been blind since a young age, says:

> I am definitely a kinesthetic learner, but I would have been a visual learner. I'm not an auditory learner despite what most people think about my preferences. Touch, as with braille, is good; but it is the active scanning of braille that makes a huge difference for me. (personal communication, July 20, 2000)

The key is to realize that the way in which particular educational goals are achieved will be unique for each individual student and to present information according to the learner's preferred style, not disability. Some basic ideas for doing this in three sample domains are presented in Table 10.3.

MULTIPLE INTELLIGENCES

Current theories assert that intelligence is multifaceted and not a single, overall, general measure of thinking and information processing. According to Sternberg's triarchic model (e.g., Sternberg, 1998), there are three fundamental intelligences:

- analytic (what has traditionally been measured by IQ tests as an underlying g or general factor) and involves critiquing, judging, comparing, and contrasting;
- creative, which involves imagining, discovery, and inventing; and
- practical, which includes applying, implementing, and using.

But according to Gardner (1983), who has also done extensive research into the various ways students learn, there are seven, even eight, perhaps nine different kinds of "intelligences." A particular learner will typically have a combination of intelligences but will favor one over the others. Thus, Gardener believes, all students can learn, and an appropriate use of technology is to help teachers and students understand the individual learning strengths of each student across the full spectrum of learning. Teachers must then use this knowledge to diversify their approaches to education if they are to successfully reach the many different intelligences that exist in

TABLE 10.3
Gathering and Processing Information According to Three Learning Styles

Style	Learner preferences	For learners with hearing loss	For learners with vision loss
Looking	Reading, watching a demonstration, using illustrated charts, sorting by color.	The more visual information the better. Use color, graphics, photos, and so on.	For low vision, use enlarged visual images in bright colors. For blind students, trace images of objects with super string.
Listening	Discussing ideas in groups, hearing instructions out loud, sorting by sound.	For learners with severe or profound hearing loss, use a loud bass beat to accompany visual information. Conduct group discussion using sign language or pantomime.	Verbalize as much information as possible, have students work in discussion groups, allow music in the background.
Touching, moving	Learning by moving about a room; manipulating, sorting, and organizing objects.	Have them learn by doing and being active.	Encourage blind students to learn braille, work with a computer keyboard, work with objects, participate in a role-play.

Note. Adapted from *The Way They Learn* by Cynthia Ulrich Tobias, published by Focus on the Family. Copyright © 1992, Cynthia Ulrich Tobias, M.Ed. All rights reserved. International copyright secured. Used by permission.

their classrooms. Characteristics associated with Gardner's seven "multiple intelligences" are represented in Table 10.4.

In today's inclusive classroom, there will be a mix of student abilities and learning styles. For example, let us revisit the fifth-grade inclusive math exercise in which Stephen participated that was described in chapter 5. By my count, this exercise drew on at least four different learning styles. After the teacher presented the instruction on the blackboard in a traditional lecture format (Logical–Mathematical), the teacher then asked the students to stand up. He divided them into two halves, with one half being asked to move to the right side of the room and the other half to the left (Body–Kinesthetic). He took one of two piles of papers and distributed the sheets to the students in one half. Then he took the other pile and distributed that to the other group of students. The students in one half had the math questions; the students in the other half had the answers. Their task was to find the student on the other side of the room and obtain enough

TABLE 10.4
Gardner's Seven Intelligences

Type of intelligence	Characteristics and strengths	Ways to activate, profit from it
Verbal–Linguistic (senses of hearing and sight)	Printed or spoken words, reading, writing, verbal recall, visual scanning	Read, listen, and write. Keep a journal. Take notes and create a study guide. Good with mnemonics, Question & Answer flash cards, listen to an audiotape while following along with the text.
Logical–Mathematical ("scientific thinking")	Numbers, facts, sequence, abstract pattern recognition	Create a diagram, compare and contrast, use inductive or deductive reasoning, guided independent study, labs, data/research projects.
Body–Kinesthetic (sense of touch, motion)	Movement, physical tasks	Give hands-on demonstrations, enact a drama, play a physical game, walk, dance, role-play, go on field trips.
Visual–Spatial (orientation is space)	Drawings, visual images	Represent graphically, color code, create a portfolio or scrapbook.
Musical (patterns in sound)	Rhythm and melody	Compose a jingle, sing it, create or study with background music.
Interpersonal (between people)	Communication, cooperation with others	Tell it to a friend out loud, work in a group, mentor/peer tutor, give an oral report.
Intrapersonal (within the person)	Observe and ponder, self-reflection	Keep a journal, personal portfolios, unguided independent study.

Note. An eighth intelligence is "Naturalistic Intelligence." According to Gardner (1983), people with this intelligence have the following abilities: to recognize flora and fauna, and to make other consequential distinctions in the natural world and to use their abilities productively (in hunting, in farming, in biological science). Gardner is also considering adding a ninth intelligence, "Existential Intelligence." From *Frames of Mind: The Theory of Multiple Intelligences*, by H. Gardner, 1983, New York: Basic Books. Copyright 1983 by Basic Books and author. Adapted with permission.

information to match Question with Answer (Body–Kinesthetic and Interpersonal).

The teacher took each matched pair in turn and asked the child with the Question to repeat what was on his or her paper (Verbal–Linguistic). Then he asked anyone in the class for the correct answer.

Visual, auditory, and kinesthetic learners all could benefit and learn from this exercise as it tapped into, at least in part, their preferred learning style. So, too, could linear/analytic and global learners, although the linear/analytic students may have felt more comfortable during the lecture even if they still learned from the exercise that followed it.

Teachers who work with students one-to-one (like Ellen's vision teacher helping her learn and practice braille, and Betty at the New York State School for the Blind who used behavioral shaping or operant conditioning to "shape" more socially desirable behaviors in Jamie) also take into account the student's particular learning needs and preferences. Accurately tuning in to students' learning styles can make a tremendous difference in what they learn and how quickly they learn it.

THE NEED TO MATCH STUDENTS WITH THE MOST APPROPRIATE TECHNOLOGIES FOR THEIR EDUCATIONAL SUCCESS

There are now thousands of assistive, access, and educational technologies and a lot of choice available within any given product line. Achieving the optimal match of student and technology is a complex process. How do we start to narrow down the array of choices to a more manageable number?

The bull's-eye chart in Figure 10.1 is meant to be equally applicable to assistive, access, instructional, and educational technologies. It depicts the complexity of the process of achieving an optimal match of student and technology (or other support) and the individuals' ultimate empowerment and quality of life. The chart begins with an assumption that educational goals have been determined. As noted earlier, an educational goal must be specified as clearly as possible and may be remedial in nature, may be curriculum specific, or may simply be for enrichment. Once educational goals have been specified, a logical place to begin in the matching of student and technology, as mandated by law, is to evaluate and address the unique characteristics and personal resources of that student in line with the educational goals established for that individual.

CONSIDERATIONS IN MULTIPLE DOMAINS FOR HITTING THE BULL'S-EYE AND ACHIEVING A GOOD MATCH OF STUDENT AND TECHNOLOGY

Making distinctions between linear/analytic and global learning and differences among visual, auditory, and kinesthetic learners are important considerations, remembering that a student with a moderate hearing loss

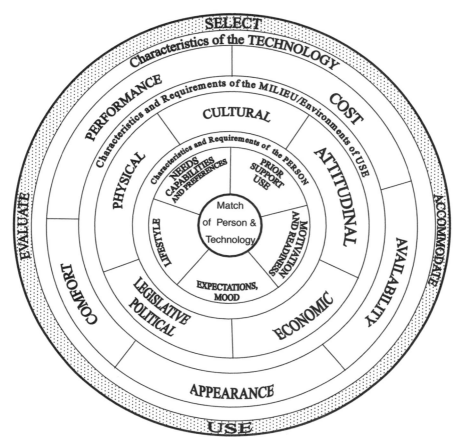

Figure 10.1. Influences to consider when trying to hit the bull's-eye of an optimal match of person and technology. Courtesy of the Institute for Matching Person & Technology, Webster, New York.

may very well be an auditory learner and a student with low vision may be a visual learner. But there are other important factors as well. For example, beyond educational goals, students have dreams and their own personal goals they have established for themselves. These dreams may seem unrealistic to teachers but may be very motivating to that student and keep that student's competitive spirit, perseverance, and enthusiasm for learning strong. However, goals and dreams that put the student under a great deal of stress, cause considerable frustration, and lead to resentment toward and withdrawal from peers are a different matter. In the latter case, the goals and dreams are not helping this student achieve, in Erikson's terms, a sense of industry, identity, and intimacy or, in Maslow's terms, needs for affiliation and achievement. In fact, if this situation is severe, it typically becomes a major indication of the need for a mental health evaluation and intervention.

Getting to know any given student is multifaceted. Sample key considerations within the five domains in the bull's-eye chart regarding the characteristics and resources of the person, or individual student, include the following:

Needs, capabilities, and preferences

- What does the student need to do to succeed academically?
- Can the student participate in the same ways as other students? If not, what strategies, supports, or technologies would help? In other words, what needs to be substituted, added, or adapted?
- Is the student in agreement that the proposed technology or other support will result in a gain?
- What are the student's strengths, interests, and learning style?
- Does the student prefer to do things alone and experiment?
- Does the student prefer to have someone else help him or her because he or she desires that interpersonal contact?
- Does the student have the essential requisite skills to use the technology to maximum advantage? For example, does the student have keyboard skills? The requisite ability to read?

Prior exposure to and experiences with technologies (and other supports)

- What is that student's receptivity or predisposition to the use of a technology?
- What is the student using or doing now?
- What has worked well for this student?
- What has not worked well?

Motivation and readiness to achieve goals

- What are the student's dreams and goals?
- Does the student view technology (or other support) use as a helpful and desirable means of achieving these dreams and goals?
- Does the student perceive a discrepancy between the current and desired situation?

Expectations, mood, and temperament

- What does the student expect to happen educationally, socially?
- Is the student generally happy and composed? Or sad and anxious?
- What is the blend of autonomy and support from others that this student wants to achieve?

- What is the student's receptivity or predisposition to the use of a technology?
- Is there an appropriate mix of assertiveness and self-determination versus compliance and reliance on support or interdependence?
- Does the student have appropriate trust in and respect for those who will be helping in support selection?
- What is the student's energy level? A student who is fatigued, or one who is tense and anxious, is not in a state of mind or mood conducive to effective learning.

Lifestyle

- What are the typical routines of the student at school and home?
- What is the peer group doing? And the family and their activities?

Moving outward from the center of the circle and beyond the characteristics and resources of the person, considerations related to the characteristics and requirements of the environments/milieu of use and their impact on the individual learner become key. The word *milieu* is used because it connotes the fact that a person's environment is not just a built one consisting of physical objects and electrical outlets and lights, but a place comprised of people who have a variety of attitudes and values. For example, there is a value-rich "hidden curriculum" in every school that underlies the actions of administrators and teachers and determines what and the ways in which students are taught and how they are socialized (e.g., Margolis, 2001).

We have seen a shift in what is going on politically and economically in our schools because of the IDEA Amendments of 1997 where AT consideration and parental involvement are mandated. Also, we are seeing a movement away from an entirely medical model where the focus is on individuals' limitations and the things they cannot do and the goal is to try to find a technology that will compensate or overcome limited capabilities. Now thinking focuses on a student's abilities, how we can strengthen those abilities, and how a technology can enhance functioning, academic performance, and social participation. What can we do in the physical or built environment to help this student function better, and then what can we do to help that person develop a sense of belonging and connection?

A factor that needs to be considered when evaluating technology preferences is the increasing diversity of cultures, languages, and lifestyles in the United States (e.g., Hourcade, Parette, & Huer, 1997). Changes in the traditional family structure, in the cultural backgrounds, and in the linguistic heritages of families necessitate the need for educators to develop skills in working with families from diverse backgrounds and understanding their perspectives regarding the selection and use of technology (e.g., Parette, 1998).

For example, the same day I visited Ellen and observed her learning braille in the public school, I met with a young deaf boy who had just recently arrived from the Ukraine. His parents had planned the trip for many months, but his father died a couple of months prior to the scheduled departure. His mother moved him and his six siblings here anyway. Now, this student has to learn English and an entirely new alphabet, but he cannot hear. He was provided with hearing aids, but his lip-reading skills, as well as his own speech muscles, are trained to understand Ukrainian, not English. He has to learn everything new.

Sample key considerations regarding the characteristics and requirements of the milieu/environments include the following:

Cultural

- Within the student's familial culture, what have been his or her experiences and opportunities?
- Will the family encourage and support use? Sometimes parents are as much primary users of these technologies as the students. It is also important to assess their perspectives as well as those of the students.
- Within this particular educational culture, will peers encourage and support use?
- Is there tension between parents who are assertive and the teachers and administrators involved in decision making for the student?

Attitudinal

- Do parents have expectations and desires for the student different from those of teachers/administrators who have to work with limited time and dollar resources?
- What are the predispositions of relevant teachers to using a technology with this particular student?
- Is the peer group going to be accepting, even supportive of this student's use of the planned technology? Or is technology use apt to set the student apart from peers?
- Is there a "hidden curriculum" that will not support this student's use of technology?
- Have additional supports and assistance been considered and are they available if needed?

Physical

- Are all of the necessary architectural supports in place for this student to access and use the planned technology?
- If assistance is required for student training and use of the technology, is it available?
- Do classroom settings need to be reorganized?
  - Is adequate space available in the room?
  - Is the lighting sufficient?
  - Will the student need to be near an electrical outlet?
  - Will the student require extra table/desk space for a device?
  - Will the student have clear access within the classroom and be able to have an unobstructed and clear view of the teacher, blackboard, and so on?
- Will the student have physical access to all work, library, cafeteria, auditorium, athletic, and lavatory facilities?

Legislative/Political

- Is the school or university familiar with all of the relevant legislation related to technology use in education?
- Have additional supportive resources in the community been identified?

Economic

- What are the repair record and maintenance requirements of the technology, and how much do they cost?
- Will the vendor come in and provide services? At what cost?
- How often are upgrades available and how much do they cost?
- Has school or university planned a budget to appropriately provide technology or other support for all students who could benefit from them?
- Does an inventory exist of who has which technology or support?
- Is a plan in place to recycle technologies no longer needed by particular students?

Characteristics of the particular technology (or other support) being considered is the next circle as we move outward from the bull's-eye. As discussed earlier in this book, technology devices and technology services are two halves of a whole. There are many aspects of a technology to consider when beginning the process of narrowing down the available choices. Sample key considerations regarding the characteristics of the technology include the following:

Availability

- How available is it? Can it be obtained in a timely fashion?
- Will it need adjustment or setup?

Appearance

- How age-appropriate is the technology, and is it compatible with participation in social activities and extracurricular activities?
- Does the student feel self-conscious using it?

Comfort

- Does using the technology cause fatigue, strain, or pain?
- Is the technology easy for the student to use, transport, and set up?

Performance

- Does the technology support the student's varying abilities?
- Does the technology require considerable maintenance?
- How easily and quickly can servicing and repairs be done?
- For those with rapid developmental changes, how easily and quickly can upgrades be obtained?
- What is the impact of climate on this technology? Humidity, heat, cold?
- If the technology needs to be portable, is it?
- How durable is it, and can it withstand a lot of wear and tear in going from room to room or home to school?
- How compatible is it with other equipment being used at school and at home?
- Is the student already using a device or number of devices, and will it interface well? Is a point of overload being reached?
- How accurate and fast is the device?
- Is training needed in order for the student to use this device? How much training? Who will provide the training?
- Will using this device be distracting to other students? For example, frequent beeping or loud clicking from information entry or output.

Cost

- What is the balance of value and cost? Some options besides the school purchasing AT for students 3 to 21 years of age are the following:
  - Private health insurance (also serves people of all ages with no upper age limit);

- The Equipment Loan Fund (also serves people of all ages with no upper age limit);
- Medicaid and the Medicaid Long-Term Home Health Care Program (also serves peoples of all ages with no upper age limit);
- Vocational rehabilitation services (also for people up to age 65) if vocationally related; and
- Commission for the Blind and Visually Impaired if vocationally related.

In all the above examples with the exception of the Equipment Loan Fund, the AT is the property of the user. An excellent resource on funding options for AT is Appendix D, "Finding and Funding Assistive Technologies," as well as the article by Kemp, Hourcade, and Parette (2000).

- What are the relative advantages to purchasing, leasing, or renting the technology?
- Are there effective alternatives that cost less?
- Is the cost reasonable in light of the device's performance and the expected gains?
- Are warranties and guarantees available?
- Can it be serviced locally or must it be shipped elsewhere?
- Is ongoing training and support built into the cost? An upgrade?

At this point, one product should emerge as more desirable than others. Now it needs to be obtained and resources supporting its use put in place. The following list of 10 questions is helpful to have on hand when beginning to consider the incorporation of the technology into the student's and school's accustomed routines and structure.

1. What needs to be done?
2. For whom?
3. Who will do it?
4. By when?
5. Where?
6. How will it be done?
7. What resources are needed?
8. From whom?
9. What specific questions do vendors, therapists, or others need to answer?
10. Are you certain the outcome will be user empowerment, goal achievement, and an enhanced quality of life?

The outermost ring in the bull's-eye comes after a technology has been chosen and now is being evaluated for its *usability* for the particular student in all appropriate environments. *Usability* is actually the one word that captures the essence, the sum total, of each preceding ring and element discussed earlier.

The first and last steps in achieving a good match of person and technology is to conduct a thorough assessment of student, milieu/ environments, and technology features. After a trial period of use, after training, and once the student uses the technology in actual situations and natural settings, feedback should be sought on how well the technology is performing for that student and how the student has changed in capability and academic performance. This is being *evidence-based* and *measuring outcomes* of the technology as an intervention. IDEA mandates outcomes in the documentation of educational performance.

Such findings may reveal that a student has stopped using a device when all it may require to become useful again is some small adjustment or modification or an upgrade to match the student's developmental advancement (e.g., Scherer, 2000). Consideration might be given to selecting a peripheral, additional, or ancillary device, making the necessary adjustments and upgrades and so on until the student finds the device usable again. Sample key considerations regarding usability include the following:

Accommodations

- Has trial use occurred in the settings of use?
- Does the technology require customizing or other adaptations to the student?
- Are accommodations needed in the environments of use?

Use

- Has the technology been assembled correctly?
- Is the technology being used as intended?
- Does the student have changing needs that should be evaluated?
- Have there been changes in the settings of use?
- Will the student be transferring to another school (or out of school) and is a plan in place for that transition?

Selecting the technology or other support

- What will best suit this student's needs and preferences? Additional technology features? Personal assistance? A combination?
- What is the most cost-effective choice?
- What is the most empowering choice for this student?
- Have the options been prioritized and has it been documented why one product or feature is preferable to another?

Ideally, this is a continuous cycle in order to keep pace with the uses' developmental progress. One may think that a particular device is perfect for a given student, only to find out later that the student stopped using it altogether, avoided use from the beginning, or uses it only in limited situations. If the student is supposed to use the device 50% of the day but only uses it 25% of the day, then that needs to be addressed. Why is that happening?

On the basis of earlier research (e.g., Scherer, 2000), when the use of a device interferes with other activities or need satisfaction, it may be viewed as ineffective and then becomes abandoned. Consumers themselves may be unwilling to request training or other assistance. While many remain uninformed about the options available to them, others are not accustomed to being assertive and may hesitate to ask for the assistance to which they are entitled. As was found in Cushman and Scherer (1996), when the device itself was satisfactory, survey respondents often reported changed priorities or needs that led to the need to begin the process again, with the evaluation of the characteristics and resources of the person, the characteristics and requirements of the milieu/environments, the characteristics of the technology, and the technology selection, accommodation, and usability.

When discussing a complex process, it is always useful to provide an example of how it can be applied and how it translates into meaningful information and practical outcomes. Here is an example of a college student with low vision who is beginning to become frustrated with the amount of time he spends doing coursework. Jeffrey has 20/200 uncorrected vision, 20/80 corrected vision, and impaired peripheral vision. Functionally, when looking at a person's face, he can focus on the eyes or the mouth, but his field of vision is not large enough to see both at the same time.

Jeffrey, as a college freshman, has been receiving services from the Commission for the Blind and Visually Impaired for several years and receives mobility training to improve his ability to get around more easily on the college campus. He uses a cane to detect obstructions and changes in terrain as well as to identify himself as a person with a vision loss.

Jeffrey has not learned braille and thus has not used any of the existing braille technologies. He has tried numerous computer-related technologies but rejected them because the more portable ones that he could take into classrooms were too expensive for what he said he gained from their use. He does use closed circuit television (CCTV) in the campus library, but says he experiences eye strain when using it for extended periods of time. CCTV is also the only means of access he has to the information he needs on the campus. Because he does not own a CCTV, he must travel to the library.

For short periods of reading, Jeffrey uses various handheld magnifiers that are portable and inexpensive. He finds them awkward to use because they have to be manually moved across the page, which makes it difficult for him to keep track of which line he is reading. Often, he needs to read the same line several times.

Jeffrey tried a handheld telescope to help him see the blackboard in the classroom but said he could not focus and read fast enough to keep up with the professor. He also found that it prevented him from being able to take notes in class, and it called attention to him in the classroom. For taking notes, he uses a tape recorder that records at a variable speed so that more information will fit on a single cassette. This allows him to review his audio notes without having to gain access to the library's CCTV. His ingenuity also led him to purchase a campfire lighter, which is large and is activated by squeezing a trigger, to light the burners in his chemistry lab.

Jeffrey realizes he needs to have equal access to the information that is necessary to complete his college education and has several unobtrusive, portable, and low-tech devices that he uses, preferably those that are familiar to others and found in commercial stores. His priorities and preferences are to use portable devices so that he is not tied to a particular place or workspace. He has not used more sophisticated technologies and does not know braille, so his options are further restricted. Nor does he appear motivated or ready to use these products. He lives on campus, so his lifestyle has not yet made it worth his while to invest in them. Additionally, his level of maturity and self-esteem places a priority on not standing out in his classes and with his peers. Until the desire or need to make modifications presents itself, this is likely not to change.

The physical characteristics of his environment/milieu led him to use a cane for safety and mobility. He had also stated that most technologies available to students on campus were usually in disrepair or were inaccessible to him because of location and inconvenience. Identified environmental factors that create or magnify problems for students with disabilities need to be brought to the attention of the Disability Support Office and other campus officials. However, Jeffrey has not self-advocated and has not done this.

The high costs of many devices from which he could potentially benefit are a barrier to Jeffrey. He believes the degree of effort conserved by using current high-cost devices does not outweigh their price. They are not likely to be viewed by him as comfortable to use (physically or personally/socially) or affordable unless he believes they are adding significantly to his safety, they are essential to perform a task, they reduce the effort necessary to perform an activity, or they reduce inconvenience and dependence on another person.

In summary, Jeffrey could benefit from a link to the Disability Support Office (which he did not know existed on his campus), which can discuss with him such services such as notetaking, classroom and testing accommodations, and alternative ways of accomplishing tasks without attracting attention to himself. Environmental barriers need to be identified and rectified. As far as the introduction of any new technology, considerations for portability, psychological comfort, performance, and cost all have to be given priority in Jeffrey's case. Because Jeffrey is only a freshman and both college life and the campus are new to him, he should be engaged in a dialogue about his social activities and friendships to ensure he is developing a sense of fitting in and belonging. If his social life seems lacking, then he might benefit from support in identifying appropriate social clubs, sports activities, and other social settings that would bring him into contact with peers. Ideally, these might initially center around a group task.

Jeffrey's example began with a focus on his academic life. By using the domains in the bull's-eye to identify the most salient issues for Jeffrey, it became clear that exploring his needs for affiliation and belonging, his social participation on campus, could benefit from attention to this aspect of college life. This example illustrates that human performance and participation cannot be reduced into various and separate features of an individual. Nor is it possible or desirable to separate a person's characteristics from the context, environments, and situations in which the person performs and participates. A person's optimal technology use and benefit will best develop when all the elements in the bull's-eye chart and their interaction have been considered.

It is undeniable that the use of a comprehensive assessment process yields a lot of information to digest, organize, and consolidate into a strategy for intervention or support. As in Jeffrey's example, the payoff for devoting upfront time to a comprehensive assessment can be significant as the outcomes can provide valuable information and ideas for next steps, approaches and alternatives, and strategies for obtaining desired supports. The assessment and evaluation process is explored in more depth in chapter 11. In addition, Appendix A and Appendix C contain forms that help throughout the process depicted in the bull's-eye chart. Appendix B shows how information from these forms can be organized into a "statement of need," describing the student's match with technologies and other supports determined to be important to academic participation and success.

11

THE MATCHING PERSON AND TECHNOLOGY MODEL

[The STATEMENT project] identified the problem areas that I might have not just with the academic side of things but also the environmental side of college life. . . . [The STATEMENT assessment provides] a written account of your needs [which] backs up your claim for AT.
—A student in Ireland

During a meeting I attended at a public secondary school, there was a big flip chart in the front of the room with office notes stuck all over, several on top of one another, in a seemingly scattered, unorganized, and random way. Under a heading labeled "Individual Needs of the Student" were numerous Post-it notes naming people to contact, things to do, meetings that needed to be set up. And that was just one ring in the bull's-eye chart discussed in chapter 10 (see Figure 10.1). Those Post-it notes serve as a good example of just what it often feels like to obtain the desired services for students at the present time—scattered and unorganized. There is so much to know about the students, the available technologies, where the students will use the technology and whether everything is in place that needs to be, and who will look into the details, make the accommodations, conduct follow-up evaluations, and make the decisions. How is it possible to organize all this, make sense of it, and put it together so that the process moves forward in a timely way instead of getting mired in a scattered array of seemingly disconnected tasks? In this chapter I discuss one model as an effective way to put together all the assessment tasks required for matching assistive educational technologies with student users. I then give three examples of the model's uses.

THE NEED FOR A PROCESS FOR
MATCHING PERSON AND TECHNOLOGY

Frameworks have been developed to help school districts improve the assistive technology (AT) services they provide. One such framework is the Educational Tech Points (Bowser & Reed, 1995), in which each Tech Point represents a point in the process of referral, evaluation, and development of the Individualized Education Program. A packet developed by the Wisconsin Assistive Technology Initiative is organized around functional categories with a continuum of devices to consider (Reed & Walser, 2000).

Another resource, the SETT Framework (Zabala, 1995), is designed as a team-driven aid to gather and organize data on the student, environment, and tasks associated with assistive technology tools. Additional tools for planning AT and AT assessments include *Quality Indicators for Assistive Technology (QIAT) Services* in school settings (QIAT, 2003) and *Essential Elements of an Assistive Technology Assessment and Assessment Report*, also specific to school settings (Case & Lahm, 2003).

While these excellent resources are responsive to unmet needs in schools, they are primarily frameworks and means of organizing and planning information to be gathered. They are not assessments. The availability of a systematic, comprehensive, and structured assessment process for matching students with the most appropriate assistive and educational technologies for their use is being viewed as increasingly fundamental to the provision of quality services. In fact, a special issue of the journal *Technology & Disability* was recently published that is devoted to the topic of "The Assessment of Assistive Technology Outcomes, Effects and Costs" (Gelderblom & de Witte, 2002). The special issue editors stated in their introduction that they selected eight instruments "specifically designed to measure outcomes of AT and with demonstrated soundness" and "to stimulate the use of standardized instruments" (p. 93) in the field. The eight instruments included are as follows, in alphabetical order according to the primary author's last name:

- The Siva Cost Analysis Instrument, or SCAI: measuring costs of individual AT programs (Andrich, 2002);
- The Quebec User Evaluation of Satisfaction with assistive Technology (QUEST 2.0): an overview and recent progress (Demers, Weiss-Lambrou, & Ska, 1996, 2002);
- Psychosocial Impact of Assistive Devices Scale (PIADS; Jutai & Day, 2002);
- The LIFE-H: Assessment of the quality of social participation (Noreau, Fougeyrollas, & Vincent, 2002);

- **Development**
Who developed it and for what purpose? Was it developed by someone
trained in tests and measures, scale construction, scoring, and so on? Does
its purpose match your use of it? Is there a manual with clear guidelines for
use, administration, and scoring?

- **Pilot Testing**
Has the assessment instrument been adequately tested in the field, and have
the bugs been worked out? Read all the questions and items on the form to
make sure the wording is clear, items are not offensive, and that they ask for
information that you want.

- **Validation**
Has the assessment instrument been tested with populations relevant to your
users? For example, a form developed for use with children usually cannot be
used with adults. Have others obtained reliable and useful information through
the use of the assessment measure?

- **Ongoing Evaluation**
Is the assessment continually being tested, validated, and, if necessary, revised? Do the items reflect today's thinking and phrasing?

- **Dissemination**
Is the assessment easily obtainable and affordable? Is there ongoing support
provided for users of the assessment?

Note. From Scherer (1995d).

- Preference-based assessment of the quality of life of people with disabilities (Persson et al., 2002);
- Matching Person and Technology (MPT) assessment process (Scherer & Craddock, 2002);
- OTFACT: Multilevel performance-oriented software with an assistive technology outcomes assessment protocol (Smith, 2002); and
- Individually Prioritized Problem Assessment (IPPA; Wessels et al., 2002).

The focus of this chapter is on the Matching Person and Technology, or MPT, model and accompanying assessment process (Scherer, 1998), although the measures mentioned above should be examined, as well as many other available measures and assessment processes, as they may be more appropriate for a given evaluation need. When selecting a measure for use, however, be certain that it meets the criteria of high quality. Some questions to ask of every assessment or measure used or test purchased are listed in Exhibit 11.1.

Regardless of which assessment is chosen, it will require time to administer, score, interpret, and translate into action, but it will be time well spent. As in purchasing cars and houses, selecting a college, or searching for the "perfect first job," the investment of an hour early in a decision-making process can save time, money, and frustration later on.

MATCHING PERSON AND TECHNOLOGY
MODEL AND ASSESSMENT PROCESS

The MPT process assesses the elements of the bull's-eye chart in chapter 10. It consists of a series of instruments developed to address and organize the many influences that affect the use of assistive, access, instructional, and educational technologies, including psychological and social factors. The MPT process has been designed to apply to students in secondary, postsecondary, and lifelong learning (a separate version exists for young students); its use, as we saw with Jeffrey in chapter 10, has resulted in high satisfaction with options that match not only the individual's strengths and needs but also their preferences, level of motivation and readiness, expectations and mood, and lifestyle factors. This information is then balanced with the characteristics of the milieu/environments in which the technology will be used, along with the features and functions of the technology itself. The MPT is a practical and research resource to identify the most appropriate technology for a person in light of the user's needs and goals, barriers that may exist to optimal technology use, areas to target for training for optimal use, and the type of additional support that may enhance use. It has been designed to organize information efficiently and thoroughly while achieving an optimal match of student and technology. Ideally, it is used for multiple or complex technologies and where a choice is available. After the person has received the most appropriate technology for his or her use, the MPT forms are administered at one or more times post AT acquisition to assess changes in perceived capabilities, subjective quality of life (QOL), and psychosocial factors such as self-esteem, mood, self-determination, and social participation and support. As discussed in chapter 10, evidence-based practice is required in IDEA. It is used in preschool, K–12, postsecondary, and vocational education. The MPT process contributes to evidence-based practice by promoting G.O.O.D. practice:

- Get the information.
- Organize the information.
- Operationalize and implement the steps in the process of matching the person with desired supports.
- Document, revisit, and update the effects of the supports.

It is important to always keep in mind that the MPT process and forms are not intended to evaluate teacher performance, but to foster and evaluate technology users' development, achievement, and satisfaction.

The MPT process is both a personal and collaborative (user and provider working together) assessment, and the paper-and-pencil measures can also be used as interview guides. A range of assessments are offered from a quick screen to specialized evaluations (which can be completed in approximately 15 minutes) to a comprehensive assessment (which can be completed in 45 minutes by someone trained and experienced in using the forms). The MPT process is applicable across a variety of users and settings. The process is depicted in Figure 11.1, and the forms used for assessment are briefly described below. Samples of the actual user forms can be found in Appendix A (the companion provider/professional forms have not been included).

Form 1. Initial Worksheet for the Matching Person and Technology Process

This form is organized by areas in which people may experience loss of function (e.g., speech/communication, mobility, hearing, and eyesight) or have important strengths. It is designed to be used by professionals working together with students to identify areas to strengthen through the use of a technology (or other support/strategy) or environmental accommodation.

It is important to note strengths and difficulties, as well as goals and beginning strategies for goal achievement. It may involve a technology or a change in the environment or both. When a new technology is being introduced to a student, it is better to work from an area of strength. Each item should be addressed, regardless of whether a professional believes it is relevant for this student or not. As with the lifeline interview technique (discussed in chap. 1, this volume), one never knows what connection will be triggered or what observations will be recollected that will affect later decision making. For example, when one focuses on communication and is about to recommend a device that requires very good vision, and that aspect has not been assessed, there may be problems if the student does have significant vision loss. For young children, ideally, this form is completed in collaboration with the parent, although a separate version of the MPT forms for children has been created (Matching Assistive Technology and CHild, or MATCH).

Form 2. History of Support Use

This form inquires into what has been tried in the past and why a new type of technology is better than the alternatives. It is organized according to

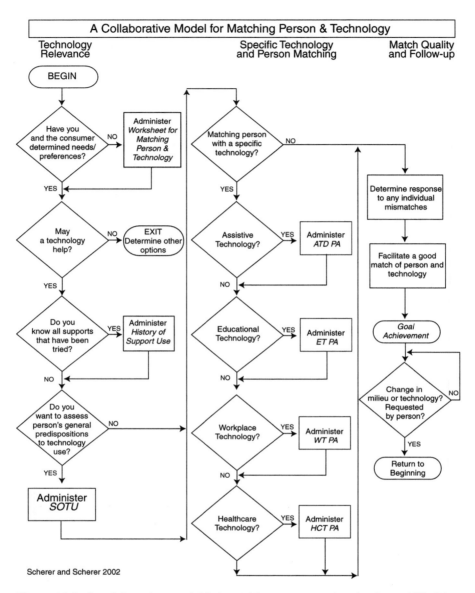

Figure 11.1. A collaborative model for matching person and technology. ATD PA = Assistive Technology Device Predisposition Assessment; ET PA = Educational Technology Device Predisposition Assessment; WT PA = Workplace Technology Device Predisposition Assessment; HCT PA = Health Care Technology Device Predisposition Assessment; SOTU = Survey of Technology Use.

the same areas of functioning as the initial worksheet for the MPT process, and for each area there is a place to list three technologies (or supports/strategies) that have been tried.

Although Forms 1 and 2 do focus on the "separate parts" of the student and it is believed that each key area is addressed, obstacles to optimal technology use may still be missed. The goal, however, is to emphasize and do a comprehensive assessment considering the whole student, the environments of technology use, and so on, but to achieve this by considering in turn the many parts that constitute the whole and their relationship to one another.

Form 3. Survey of Technology Use

When a technology is determined to be an option, the student is asked to complete the Survey of Technology Use (SOTU), a 29-item checklist that inquires into the respondent's present experiences and feelings toward technologies. The questions on this form ask students to list all of the different technologies they use and feel comfortable using, the idea being that the introduction of a new technology should build on and capitalize on existing comfort and skill. Students are also asked to provide information about areas regarding their general mood, preferences, and social involvement that have been found in research to have a favorable predisposition toward technology use.

The professional version is identical to the students' version. Both forms were designed to be used as a set so that different perspectives of teacher/professional (or parent) and student become evident and, thus, can be addressed.

Form 4. Assistive Technology Device Predisposition Assessment

The Assistive Technology Device Predisposition Assessment (ATD PA) inquires into consumers' subjective satisfaction with current achievements in a variety of functional areas (9 items), asks consumers to prioritize aspects of their lives in which they desire the most positive change (12 items), profiles consumers' psychosocial characteristics (33 items), and asks for consumers' views of their opinions and expectations regarding the use of a particular type of assistive device (12 items). Sample items in each of these areas are shown in Appendix A. Subscales include view of capabilities, subjective QOL, self-determination, mood and self-esteem, and reliance on therapists. The ATD PA (professional form) allows the professional to determine and evaluate incentives and disincentives to the use of the device by a particular consumer.

Form 5. Educational Technology Device Predisposition Assessment

The Educational Technology Device Predisposition Assessment (ET PA) is a 43-item self-report checklist developed to assist professionals and teachers in compiling comprehensive prelearning and postlearning profiles of the individual they are planning to equip with an educational technology so that the use of the technology will result in an enhanced educational experience. Such profiles can help provide the rationale for funding and training, demonstrate improvement in skills over time, and organize information about the needs of a particular student population. The form is designed to assess student perspectives (a companion teacher/educator version is available to identify areas in which perspectives agree or not) in four key areas:

- characteristics of the educational goal and the educational need that a teacher is attempting to address through the use of a specific technology;
- characteristics of the particular educational technology under consideration;
- characteristics of the psychosocial environments in which the technology will be used, such as supportive family, peers, or teachers; and
- characteristics of the student that may influence technology use, including learning style and preferences.

The profiles derived from the above forms and measures can help provide the rationale for funding and training, demonstrate improvement in skills over time, organize information about the needs of a particular student, and provide insights into those factors that contribute to (or detract from) the use of the desired technology. With such insights, the teacher can diagnose and intervene in potential or existing problem areas and, thus, better ensure that the use of the technology will enhance a student's educational experience. Information is obtained to write a summary statement about what needs to be done, for whom, by whom, by when, necessary resources, and questions for vendors.

The MPT model/theory emerged from a grounded theory research study (Scherer, 2000). To operationalize the model and theory, I developed an assessment process consisting of several instruments from the experiences of technology users and nonusers obtained through participatory action research. Items emerged from characteristics differentiating the actual experiences of users and nonusers, and they have held up well in additional research studies. Thus, on the basis of the results of measurement standards applied to date, the MPT assessments have been determined to have reasonable interrater reliability and validity.

Reliability and Validity of the MPT Assessments

Development and validation of the MPT assessments followed the recommended steps for test and measure construction listed in Exhibit 11.1: (a) concept definition and clarification, (b) draft of items and response scales, (c) pilot testing, and (d) determination of measure quality and usefulness (Scherer, 1995d). Studies related to the psychometric properties of the ATD PA and ET PA, which are of most relevance to the content of this book, include the following.

Interrater Reliability

Thirty rehabilitation professionals or graduate students rated videotaped interviews, supplemented with written information, of individuals' responses on the ATD PA and TPA. Item modes were calculated, and the differences between the mode and individual rater responses were computed. The items related to the technology itself and its use within the family or workplace received the highest consistency in ratings. Items concerned with user characteristics and whether each was an incentive or disincentive to technology use had less consistent agreement (Scherer & McKee, 1992).

Item analyses were conducted on the ATD PA scale hypothesized to assess QOL to determine *internal consistency*. Initially, each item was correlated with the total score for QOL (with the item removed). All items were retained in the analysis, and coefficient alpha for the QOL subset was .80, which is high. In Ireland, the QOL scale also has been determined to have high internal consistency with a coefficient alpha above .80. The Ireland assessment combined items from the SOTU, ATD PA, and ET PA. In the Ireland assessment, their study of technology needs and preferences of students with disabilities (including many with hearing or eyesight loss) transitioning from secondary education to employment or university, a scale to measure learner self-esteem and autonomy has been found to have high internal consistency with a coefficient alpha above .80 (Scherer & Craddock, 2002). Data on the validity of the MPT process and assessments in a consumer and peer provider partnership approach to technology selection, training, and outcomes are an ongoing focus of the pioneering model of service delivery being used now in Ireland (Craddock, 2002; Craddock & McCormack, 2002). A similar model with peer mentors in a New York State Tech Act project used the MPT assessments to help consumers identify the best technologies for their use (Heerkens, Briggs, & Weider, 1997).

Validity

Scherer and Cushman (2001) studied 20 people with newly acquired spinal cord injury (10 men and 10 women) who completed items from (a)

Section B of the ATD PA hypothesized to assess QOL, (b) the Satisfaction With Life Scale (SWLS), and (c) the Brief Symptom Inventory (BSI) while in acute rehabilitation. One month postdischarge, participants rated their AT satisfaction. *Concurrent validity* of the ATD PA's QOL scale with the SWLS and *construct validity* with the BSI depression subscale was assessed using Spearman correlations. All items on both the SWLS and QOL subset correlated negatively with the BSI depression subscale. The QOL scale total score and SWLS total score correlated highly (.89, $p < .01$), which suggests that they measure the same construct, in this case QOL.

Fourteen consumers provided data on their AT satisfaction at 1-month postacute rehabilitation. Nine (64.3%) of the respondents indicated they were *satisfied* with their AT, and 5 (35.7%) reported being *not satisfied* with their AT. An independent-sample *t* test was used to evaluate the hypothesis that the QOL scale of the ATD PA would better discriminate (*predictive validity*) between the two groups than the SWLS. The Depression subscale of the BSI was not tested because of its low correlation with AT satisfaction (–.04). People who were not satisfied with their AT ($M = 23.20$, $SD = 7.59$) on average scored lower on the QOL scale than those who were satisfied with their AT ($M = 34.56$, $SD = 9.27$). The effect size was estimated with the eta-square index (.34) indicating a large effect size. (An alternative way of presenting this statistic is to say that 34% of the variance in the modified QOL subset was accounted for by whether a person was satisfied or not satisfied with their AT 1-month postdischarge.)

Criterion-related validity. Older adults (mean age 65) with normal hearing and comparably aged users of assistive listening devices (ALDs) completed the following measures: (a) Hearing Handicap Inventory for the Elderly, (b) the Communication Profile for the Hearing Impaired (CPHI), and (c) the ATD PA. Parts of the CPHI and the ATD PA produced significant mean differences between ALD users and nonusers, suggesting the value of assessing personality and psychosocial factors involved in technology use. Users in general attribute more value to ALDs, have higher psychological readiness for adopting technical assistance, and perceive fewer difficulties with technology use around family, friends, at work, or at school than do nonusers. Then, behavioral and audiological data were obtained from 40 participants 61 to 81 years of age. Group A included 20 participants with normal audiological thresholds. Group B included 20 participants with mild-to-moderate degrees of high-frequency hearing loss. Each participant completed a hearing loss screening survey, the ATD PA, and the Profile of Hearing Aid Performance (PHAP). The PHAP and hearing loss screening survey were adequate assessments of self-reported hearing loss, as was the subjective rating of hearing section of the ATD PA. People with high-frequency marginal hearing loss reported less satisfaction with their independence, reduced emotional well-being, and more limitation from their hearing loss than those with normal hearing. Discriminant analyses showed that the ATD PA was the best predictor of membership in Group A or Group B, correctly classifying 85% of the participants and providing psychosocial markers associated with awareness of and adaptation to hearing loss (Scherer & Frisina, 1994, 1998).

Predictive validity. To determine the usefulness of the ATD PA in determining reasons for device nonuse or abandonment, 47 patients with mixed diagnoses discharged from an acute inpatient rehabilitation unit completed the instrument at the time of discharge and at 3-month postdischarge. Their occupational and physical therapists completed the professional form of the ATD PA. Among all participants, 128 devices were prescribed; of these, 86 were still used at 3-month follow-up. For those abandoned, the most frequent reason given was that the device was no longer needed, although functional improvement (as measured by the Functional Independence Measure [FIM]) corresponded with device nonuse for just half the devices. Chi-square comparisons of consumer- and therapist-completed forms showed the following: (a) Consumers view some ATs more positively than others, the least positive in this study being walkers; (b) consumers and therapists have different views of the benefits of an AT; and (c) the adaptations required for use of an AT are not well recognized by consumers. The results from the ATD PA indicated that consumers have positive expectations of devices, and if actual performance falls short of expectations, the response may be to discard use of the device; this may be prevented by longer trial periods with devices in a variety of situations (Cushman & Scherer, 1996).

Additional Studies

A study conducted in Montreal, Quebec, Canada (Vincent & Morin, 1999) showed that items from the ATD PA "focus well on the pertinent factors" (p. 100) related to individuals' decisions to use or not use an AT. Another study focused on adolescents who used functional electrical stimulation to stand and who were administered the ATD PA and several other measures. The results supported the use of the ATD PA and highlighted the need to consider psychosocial aspects of matching person and technology (Brown, 1996; Brown & Merbitz, 1995).

To assess the effectiveness of a college course on adapted computer use, Goodman, Tiene, and Luft (2002) asked 14 college students with disabilities (more than half having complete or partial eyesight loss) to identify factors that influenced them to adopt or reject a device for computer access. The results provide evidence of the usefulness of the MPT model and ATD PA items as applied to computer access technology for college students.

The *World Health Organization – Disability Assessment Schedule* (World Health Organization, 2001) has been revised as WHODAS II, a psychometric measure (36-item, interviewer administered) which provides a profile of functioning across six activity domains ("*Understanding and communicating,*" "*Getting around,*" "*Self care,*" "*Getting along with people,*" "*Life activities,*" and "*Participation in society*") as well as a general disability score. Respondents are asked to state the level of difficulty experienced, while taking into consideration how they usually do the activity, including the use of any AT and/or help from a person. While performing, on behalf of the WHO, a standardization of WHODAS II on a university student population, an investigation was conducted into the personal factors affecting the selection, use, and outcomes of technology use as well as coping strategies students with disabilities adopt in university environments (Federici et al., in press). Correlation coefficients between WHODAS II scores and SOTU scores were computed:

- *task*-oriented coping strategies are positively related to a positive evaluation of use of technologies (SOTU), and negatively related to disinterest in or indifference toward the use of technologies (SOTU) and to cognitive concentrating and communicating abilities (WHODAS II);
- *emotion*-oriented coping strategies are positively related to a positive evaluation of experiences with technologies (SOTU) and to a negative evaluation of *personal characteristics* (SOTU), and negatively related to disinterest in or indifference toward the use of technologies (SOTU);

The authors conclude that the dimensions of the WHODAS II, as a tool assessing different dimensions of personal disability, are related and that they might predict individual coping strategies and personal predispositions to technology use, thus demonstrating the concurrent validity of the WHODAS II and the SOTU.

Educational researchers have found that for students in secondary or elementary school, the ET PA is useful when preselecting person characteristics relevant to the use of educational technologies (Albaugh & Fayne, 1996; Albaugh, Piazza, & Scholsser, 1997). Other authors have used the MPT model as the theoretical foundation for concept articles or the development of companion assessments (e.g., Beigel, 2000; Demers et al., 1996, 2002; Zapf & Rough, 2002).

In summary, on the basis of the results of research studies conducted to date by this author and others, the SOTU, ATD PA, and ET PA have been shown to have good reliability and validity; thus, it can be concluded that they are useful measures both practically and in outcomes research. The testing of the MPT model has determined that the model adequately

TABLE 11.1
References for the Psychometric Properties of the Matching
Person and Technology (MPT) Assessments

Reference	MPT form	Interrater reliability	Internal consis- tency	Criterion- related validity	Concur- rent and construct validity	Predic- tive validity
Scherer and McKee (1992)	ATD PA ET PA	✓	✓	✓	✓	
Goodman, Tiene, and Luft (2002); Scherer and Cushman (2001); Vincent and Morin (1999)	ATD PA		✓	✓	✓	✓
Scherer and Craddock (2002)	ATD PA ET PA SOTU		✓	✓	✓	✓
Albaugh and Fayne (1996); Albaugh, Piazza, and Scholsser (1997)	ET PA		✓	✓	✓	✓
D. L. Brown and Merbitz (1995); D. R. Brown (1996)	ATD PA			✓	✓	
Cushman and Scherer (1996)	ATD PA				✓	✓
Scherer and Frisina (1994, 1998)	ATD PA		✓	✓		
Federici et al. (in press)	ATD PA			✓	✓	

Note. ATD PA = Assistive Technology Device Predisposition Assessment; ET PA = Educational Technology Device Predisposition Assessment; SOTU = Survey of Technology Use.

represents the relevant influences on technology use and nonuse. Table 11.1 summarizes this evaluation of the psychometric properties of the MPT assessment.

MPT users have said that they require more training in how to maximize benefit from the MPT process and measures, and they would like the forms to be scored and interpreted, with a particular focus on next steps and strategies to pursue with consumers. Currently, a beta prototype exists of (a) computerized scoring with interpretations of ATD PA results and (b) a CD interactive program that trains users in the comprehensive MPT process (Scherer & Cushman, 2002). Updated information about these resources, as well as general developments with the MPT assessments, can be obtained from the homepage of the Institute for Matching Person & Technology (http://members.aol.com/IMPT97/MPT.html).

STUDENTS' TECHNOLOGY USE: WHICH STUDENTS BLOSSOM AND WHICH WILT?

When we discuss students with hearing or vision loss, there is a tremendous overlap among assistive, access, instructional, and educational technologies. For these students, technology use has some clear advantages, such as being able to receive instruction otherwise not available, being able to communicate with students from other schools, and to interact with faculty. However, for students with disabilities who are struggling with their identity and both affiliation and achievement needs, failure to master or succeed with a technology can lead to frustration, reduced self-esteem, and reduced motivation to succeed in school. How can one identify such possibilities early enough to intervene and prevent such unfavorable outcomes? What steps can be taken to ensure students meet with success in using technologies and have their technology experiences result in positive outcomes? In this section, I present three examples of the use of AT with different student populations and what was learned about matching each population with the appropriate technology.

An Example of Distance Learning in Secondary Education: Characteristics of Learners in Maine Studying American Sign Language

In chapter 8, it was noted that before the high school students in Maine began learning American Sign Language (ASL) via distance learning, they participated in a summer institute where they had an opportunity to meet one another and receive an orientation to the course technologies. They were also there for another reason: to complete paper-and-pencil tests on their learning styles, self-concept, and predispositions to educational technology use. Students were asked to complete the following instruments focusing on their current feelings and attitudes:

1. The Learning Styles Inventory, which is a 30-item assessment that categorizes students according to how social or independent they are and how applied or conceptual they are in their learning preferences.

2. The Tennessee Self-Concept Scale, which is a 100-item inventory assessing family, personal, social, and ethical self, as well as identity, self-satisfaction, and behavior.
3. The following two MPT assessments:
   a. SOTU and
   b. ET PA.

In our analyses of the results of the course (Keefe, Scherer, & McKee, 1996), successful completion of ASL was defined as a final grade of B+ or better. Analyses were done to determine which of the results from the four assessment instruments were most related to course grades and their proficiency and satisfaction with the course technologies as rated by their teachers. The results showed that 15 variables were associated with successful completion. Five of these variables were from the ET PA and 4 were from the SOTU; 83% of the ASL course grades are accounted for by the ET PA and SOTU variables. No variables associated with successful completion of ASL were from the Tennessee Self-Concept Scale, and only 2 variables were from the Learning Styles Inventory. The students' degrees of hearing loss, expected grade, measure of learning disability, and whether they had a deaf family member were also influences.

The profile derived from this study of the successful ASL student is a person who has a deaf family member or who is deaf but does not have a learning disability. This student is a good student in general and typically expects a grade of A (Learning Styles Inventory). The student is motivated, somewhat impatient, is positive in outlook, and seeks fresh, new activities (SOTU). The student understands and is confident that the educational goal will be achieved, is not easily distracted, does not prefer to work alone, and does not have a strong desire to control his or her own learning pace (ET PA).

Variables associated with continuing ASL study were entirely from the ET PA and SOTU. The variables discriminating continuing and noncontinuing students from the ET PA were the following:

- a preference for watching a demonstration versus experimenting on one's own,
- being curious and excited about new things,
- desiring to control one's own learning pace,
- a preference for frequent feedback/reinforcement,
- the view that technology did not interfere with social activities, and
- being motivated to learn.

Variables discriminating continuing and noncontinuing students from the SOTU were the following:

- prior exposure to technologies in education and
- use versus anxiety with equipment having been reinforced.

The students who continued with ASL were "doers" as opposed to "watchers," had more exposure to technologies in education, and had their use of technologies reinforced more than those students not continuing with ASL.

The next analysis looked at the characteristics of those students who successfully completed ASL II and the variables most predictive of success. Once again, the ET PA and SOTU were the strongest predictors of ASL II grade.

Another criterion of success in the course was students' proficiency and satisfaction with the technologies used in the delivery of the ASL instruction. At the end of ASL II, teachers were asked to rate their students' proficiency and satisfaction with four technologies: fax, camcorder, computer, and interactive TV. The ratings were on a 3-point scale (1 = *not very*, 2 = *average*, and 3 = *very*), and the teachers' ratings were averaged across the technologies for each student. The variables most predictive of student proficiency and satisfaction, as rated by their teachers, were seven variables from the ET PA and eight from the SOTU, many of which are the same as those associated with final ASL II course grade, suggesting that course grade and teacher-rated technology proficiency/satisfaction are related. Finally, the overlap among the SOTU, ET PA, Learning Style Inventory, and Tennessee Self-Concept Scale indicates convergence on the constructs of learning style and self-esteem.

Example of MPT Use for Students Transitioning From Secondary School to University, Technical College, or Employment

The Irish "STATEMENT" project (Systematic Template for Assessing Technology Enabling Mainstream Education—National Trial), first discussed in chapter 7, was funded to develop a model of good practice in identifying the AT and training needs of students through the provision of a formal Statement of Assistive Technology Need prior to students moving from second-level education (high school) to third-level education (college), employment, or vocational training. The total number of students who applied to the project was 86, and the breakdown by disability type is shown in Table 11.2.

Roulstone (1998) identified ineffective assessment services for AT as being those in which (a) the primary focus is on the technology provider, (b) the needs of the provider override those of the person with a disability, and (c) the assessor or provider focuses on disability rather than ability. The STATEMENT project adapted the MPT assessments as a means of addressing these issues while taking into account the broader factors that

TABLE 11.2
Disability Profile of Student Applicants

Disability	N	%
People with hearing impairment	21	25
People with visual disabilities	6	7
People with physical disabilities	39	45
People with learning disabilities	13	15
People with mental illness	1	1
People with multiple disabilities	6	7
Total	86	100

Note. From "Applying the Matching Person and Technology Evaluation Process," by M. Scherer and G. Craddock, 2001, *Library Hi Tech News, 18*(1), p. 41. Copyright 2001 by Emerald. Adapted with permission.

lead to a request for assistance and that will likely impact their use or nonuse of technology. Whereas the MPT model was developed and evaluated in the United States, the STATEMENT project was the first time in which the model was adapted for use in the Irish context.

Through the research, development, and piloting of the MPT model, the STATEMENT project introduced an innovative tool and process to support evaluation teams in providing effective evaluations to students with disabilities. The MPT provided the mechanism for achieving a client-focused evaluation service that was viewed positively by participating students (STATEMENT Pilot Programme, 2000, p. iii). Overall, the experiences of the STATEMENT project have added significantly to the development of effective assessment tools, to the understanding of the issues affecting the use of technology by students, and to the structures, resource requirement, and challenges inherent in creating client-centered, cost-effective evaluation services, which ensure the maximum benefit and utilization of technology by people with disabilities.

An Example of Distance Learning in Postsecondary Education: Characteristics of Learners in the National Technical Institute for the Deaf and Gallaudet History Courses

As part of the evaluation of the two pilot telecourses discussed in chapter 8, differences between the most satisfied students and the least satisfied students were assessed by relating their degree of satisfaction with the course to differences in their (a) learning styles or preferences and (b) their predispositions to and experiences with teleconferencing and e-mail (McKee & Scherer, 1994; Scherer & McKee, 1994b). At the end of the course, a sample of 10 students completed the "learner characteristics" portion of the ET PA. Interview data from several questions about the instructional delivery system served to identify the students who were either satisfied or dissatisfied with it.

The ET PA data provided by these two groups of students were then examined to get a view of criteria that distinguish satisfied and dissatisfied students. Overall, these college history students divided themselves into two basic groups: (a) those who were not satisfied and stated they had no intention of enrolling in another such course and (b) those who enjoyed and were satisfied with the delivery system and stated they would be happy to enroll in another teleconferencing course.

Students who were not satisfied said they prefer face-to-face discussions in which they can watch facial expressions. The students from each institution who had the least satisfaction said that they are intimidated by computers, that they believe computer use interferes with their social activities, and that they did not have the background skills for the course. None of the most satisfied students reported intimidation or social interference, and all but one said that they had the background skills for the course. The dissatisfied students self-reported more need for feedback and less adaptability. They also said they did not view themselves as studious and as working carefully, and that they believe they think too much about their limitations.

When one examines the data from the above three evaluations (high school ASL students, Irish students transitioning from high school, and college history students), it is clear that not all students report benefiting equally from any given assistive, educational, or instructional technology. As discussed extensively in chapter 10, there are many influences on the perceived quality of the match of student and technology, which is why it is so important to assess the student's learning needs and preferences and compare those with the features of the technology prior to beginning the actual learning experience.

The MPT assessments are one available means to identify potential mismatches of student and technology. In keeping with the theories of Maslow, Erikson, Hansell, and Gardner, educational and assistive technologies are most helpful in fostering achievement and affiliation when educators keep the following in mind:

1. A technology can encourage or can be a barrier to classroom interaction and assimilation. Students have not only had varying social experiences but have also had varying exposures to technology.
2. Equal instructional time will result in unequal outcomes. One strategy involves the assignment of increasing one-on-one teaching responsibility to computers. However, this will not be beneficial to all students. Some students will benefit more

from peer tutoring, one-on-one sessions with an adult tutor, or well-structured independent assignments.

3. Technology can enhance social skill development by having students work together in teams. For example, AT users and nondisabled students can work as pairs on a computer project. Student "computer experts" with disabilities can serve as mentors to novice students. In this way, nondisabled students can experience the student with a disability as competent and capable and, for both, the positive interaction can be used to build on positive relationships more broadly in the classroom. This strategy has also worked well for children who are quiet and withdrawn. The assumption is that computers are so socially acceptable that common computer interests can be used to help bring students together.

4. The home environment affects what each student will do in the classroom and vice versa, and a high priority at school may be a low priority at home (and, also, vice versa).

5. Hands-on experience with assistive and educational technologies in actual in-use situations should be required before a commitment is made to their purchase or adoption.

6. For teachers hesitant to learn about technology, or who feel uncomfortable about using it, the same strategies useful for students apply (see 2 and 3 above). One approach is to have a school-based computer coordinator, much as schools have art and music specialists.

The importance of ensuring a client-centered approach and a relevant assessment process to match person and technology is clearly highlighted in the examples provided in this chapter as well as in the increasing corpus of research on technology use, which highlights the fact that consumers are less likely to use recommended devices when their needs are neither fully addressed nor understood during the technology selection process (Cook & Hussey, 2002). Educators and other professionals who partner with consumers in the technology assessment and selection process will have preserved the highly valued "personal touch" as well as having helped more learners experience the excitement that accompanies success in accessing information (Lahm & Sizemore, 2002). Bringing together and connecting all of the elements that have been discussed in the preceding chapters—individual needs and preferences, environments for learning, and technologies—is the focus of the next and final chapter.

VI

CONNECTING TO LEARN

12

BRINGING IT ALL TOGETHER
FOR THE INDIVIDUAL USER

Technology doesn't change teaching or learning, people do. Technology [can] help students to reach their goals in a new way. . . . It [can] change how we as teachers instruct them. It is a tool that allows us to go in new directions.

—College teacher in instructional technology

Computers can be used for work, school, and leisure. For a person with vision or hearing loss, computers can provide a vital connection to the outside world through e-mail, the Internet, and the World Wide Web. As a result of the widespread availability, miniaturization, and capacity of personal computers, it is possible to have real-time chats with friends, write with one's voice, have written text and visual information spoken, shop, play games and music, control the environment, watch television dialogue as text captions and actions as audio descriptions, make telephone calls with a TTD or relay service operator, take college courses from a university a thousand miles away, run a business, and so on.

The role of technology in education for students with hearing or vision loss currently has two foci: (a) assistive technologies (ATs) with their strong individual as well as social implications and (b) access, instructional, and educational technologies with both academic and social implications. While technologies are a tool to enhance learning and expand educational opportunities, the interactivity and interconnectivity they offer make them a new resource in the teaching and learning arsenal. Thus, more information on the implications of choosing particular technologies and delivery systems for students with disabilities needs to be available. As discussed in previous chapters, there are as many varieties of student needs, preferences, and learning styles as there are different ways of presenting information. With expanded options have come different features, bells, and whistles, which, on the positive side, have made choices possible but, on the less positive side, have made product selection complex. Educators need an active introduction to the available options and practice in using them.

In elementary and secondary education, the use of the matching person and technology (MPT) assessment process can guide information gathering for the Individualized Education Plan (IEP), ensuring that input are from a variety of sources and that key issues are addressed. To match a student with the most appropriate technology,

- determine the bull's-eye, the goal;
- consider an array of devices;
- narrow down choices;
- arrange trial use in relevant and natural environments;
- plan integration into student's (and family's, classrooms') customary routines;
- identify who will do what training, maintenance, ongoing support, and where; and
- document evaluation procedures and results.

Exhibit 12.1 lists IEP steps and how the MPT assessment forms can inform each as well as the full IEP process.

Regarding the last step in Exhibit 12.1, it is important to regularly review the following with IEP team members, teachers, the student, and family: (a) how well the student is performing academically and socially; (b) the progress in achieving the goals with the technology; and (c) the need and desirability of considering any additional technologies, accommodations, or supports for the student.

DEVELOPING SUCCESSFUL LEARNERS

Who is a successful learner? Pick up any educational psychology text and you will find general agreement on many chief attributes. Successful learners are curious, flexible, motivated, persistent, and resourceful. They show a great deal of initiative and are good problem solvers. They easily transfer and apply new skills or knowledge. They have self-confidence and are self-determining. They work beyond their potential and capabilities and try to capitalize on their strengths and improve their weaknesses. They manage their time well and lead lives balanced with academic and social activities and participate in the world around them. From this list of attributes, it is easy to see that vision or hearing loss, or a disability of any type, has no direct bearing on any of them.

EXHIBIT 12.1
How the Individualized Education Plan (IEP) Steps and the Matching Person and Technology (MPT) Assessment Process Work Together

Assistive technology (AT) assessment focusing on the user of the AT	Assistive Technology Device Predisposition Assessment (ATD PA; Form 4-1, Person) and/or Educational Technology Predisposition Assessment (ET PA; Form 5)
Consideration of a continuum of AT devices or an educational technology (ET) with trials in customary environments	ATD PA (Form 4-1, Device) and/or ET PA (Form 5)
Selection of AT and/or ET and development of plan for its integration • designate who will do what and where • training needs • device maintenance, support, etc.	Data from ATD PA/ET PA
Documentation of evaluation procedure • specify needs and preferences of the user and their importance • describe how the student's disability interferes with important academic activities and goals • note what is presently being used and what has been tried • describe the features of the selected AT or ET, describe why it is better than alternatives and why it will meet the needs.	Sum of information from completed MPT assessment forms
Regular review • goals and achievements • device needs • necessary environmental accommodations	Readminister forms and use posttechnology matching to assess outcomes of the process. For the ATD PA, Use Forms 4-2, Person and 4-2, Device as they have been specifically designed as follow-up measures.

How can we create successful learners? Some important conditions for a successful learning experience include a supportive learning climate, an appropriate level of challenge, and content and information that are judged relevant. Essential considerations for helping an individual become a successful learner are assessing and addressing the characteristics, needs, and preferences of that learner; the barriers and supports in the milieu/environments for successful learning; and the need for support, alternative strategies, accommodations, and technologies. Skills for self-advocacy and self-determination are very important. The form in Appendix A is a tool created by an Independent Living Center that puts the elements together to foster personal advocacy and autonomy in selecting and incorporating technology into their strategies for achieving short- and long-term goals.

Technology remains simply a means of receiving and delivering information. Unless information has meaning for the student, even the best match of student and technology achieves only a partial victory. Although it is beyond the scope of this book to discuss inclusive curricula, instructional design, and effective instructional practices, many excellent texts and resources exist in these areas (e.g.., Fisher, Frey, & Sax, 1999; Fisher, Sax, & Pumpian, 1999; Kearsley, 2001). Some important considerations for students in general, followed by accommodations for people with vision or hearing loss in particular, follow. They have been adapted from material in the MPT model manual (Scherer, 1998), as well as theories of learning (Scherer, 1994a, 1995a, 1995b, 1995c) and principles of instructional design (Scherer, 1990a).

Subject Content

The following are some guiding questions for determining the appropriateness of the content of the instructional or educational technology under consideration:

- Does the actual content being covered conform to your curricular and instructional goals?
- Is the terminology consistent with that used by the teacher or the program so that it will be understandable by students?
- Is the language level appropriate for the students?
- Is the presentation of the content appropriate to the maturity, the experience, and the interest level of the student audience?

Instructional Strategies

Following are questions to consider when determining how the delivery system will be used as a tool:

- Is the intent of the instruction consistent with the educational goal—the development of new skills; the practice, improvement, or generalization of acquired skills; the ability to see relationships, similarities and patterns, or differences and distinctions?
- Is the instruction structured to meet the student's needs—as a drill, a simulation, a tutorial, a means of discovery?
- Does it support a student's creativity and problem-solving ability?
- Are the rate and length of the learning episodes appropriate, and are they well structured?

- For hierarchical learning, is a new learning element or module introduced only when the student has mastered the previous one? At the end, is it evident to the student how the modules are linked and integrated into a whole?
- Are directions repeated when the student begins a new learning module?
- Are advance organizers, prompting, reinforcement, summarization, quizzing, and feedback designed to facilitate movement through the learning modules and lead to success?
- Are the examples used age and gender appropriate and interesting to students with a variety of experiences and interests?
- Is turn-taking facilitated in a small group or classroom situation?
- Are the learning episodes controlled by the learner, the teacher, or the technology?
- Is the presentation format consistent with the initial cuing?
- Does the presentation contain textual, graphic, auditory, and experiential features in keeping with the principles for universal design for learning?
- Are there unessential elements that are used as gimmicks and can possibly be distracting?
- Is the visual material of high quality and high resolution? For students with vision loss, are there text or audio descriptions of pictures, streaming video, and so on?
- Is the auditory message clear? For students who have hearing loss, are text captions or other text presentations of visual images and information provided?
- Is there an adequate amount and variety of practice material available?
- If the student gets stuck, are help menus, dictionaries, and assistance from the teacher available?

Delivery Systems

Although not every educational technology can be considered a delivery system, it is generally considered to be the physical equipment or the electronic system that serves as the vehicle to the instruction. This may be, for example, a basic computer, a computer with a raised keyboard, one with magnified text, or one with voice output; or it may be a closed-caption decoder, a teleconferencing satellite system, a large-screen projection system, a videocassette recorder, a self-correcting workbook, or an electronic questioning device. Exhibit 12.2 summarizes, in keeping with the discussion in this chapter, the characteristics of a good match of student and educational technology.

EXHIBIT 12.2
IT MATCHES

Instructional goals and the material to be learned are suited to the medium of the technology

Technology options, functions, and features match the learner's needs, learning style, interests, and preferences

Motivation of the student for the learning experience is built into an appealing design, use of appropriate language level, and active involvement of the learner in the learning

Ability to hold the student's attention is facilitated by the relevant and dynamic use of visual, audio, and graphic elements

Touching on many senses through a multimodal presentation of information has been given priority in the design (e.g., asks student to draw a concept map, compose a song about the learning)

Collecting and organizing information about what the student already knows and has learned is built in

Habituating the student to success through reinforcement/rewards for completing components is accomplished

Engagement of the learner through examples and experiences makes concepts more concrete (and vice versa)

Synthesis of information and conceptual connections are achieved through questioning, reflection, testing, and application

ACCOMMODATIONS FOR PEOPLE WITH VISION OR HEARING LOSS

It is crucial to remember that the student with vision or hearing loss is one of many students in an inclusive setting, all of whom have their unique learning needs and preferences. In a learning environment that taps into "multiple intelligences" and learning styles, that uses the concept of universal design for learning in which information is presented in multiple ways and uses as many senses as possible, all students will benefit. Students with disabilities are much more like their peers than they are different from them. Thus, they should also follow the same expectations for codes of behaviors.

There is no acceptable reason for not including students with disabilities in all school activities—learning, social, recreational, and so on. While they may benefit from various accommodations (e.g., advance copies of materials to the vision teacher or to be produced in alternative formats, additional time to complete assignments and tests, audiotaping responses to test questions) and assistive, access, and instructional technologies, they should be expected to accomplish the same quality of work as their non-disabled peers. Below are some relatively easy accommodations to help students with hearing or vision loss match the level of academic achievement of their colleagues.

For students who have hearing loss. Students with hearing loss rely more heavily on information that is presented visually. Try to avoid "visual clutter" so that the student can focus on the key points. Also try to use a variety of visual materials (line drawings, computer-generated graphics, real objects). When using written text, try to use a variety of reading levels. For software programs, include supplemental materials in a variety of reading levels and incorporate advance organizers. Provide captions or a sign language version for all audio in a program. Be sure that the lighting is adequate and not too bright (e.g., a computer screen facing a window and reflecting sunlight). For cooperative learning situations, groups should be kept small (four students is a good number, but working in pairs is better).

For students who have vision loss. As described in chapter 5, Stephen was included in the math exercise with the rest of the class, even though he required support from the vision teacher. Because of his lack of eyesight, a smile of approval, a hand signal, or a head nod from the teacher or other students would not be as well perceived as verbal acknowledgment. The vision teacher would describe any such nonverbal behaviors to Stephen. As with Ellen (also chap. 5, this volume), a goal was to have her move about the classroom as much as possible. This helps the person with vision loss feel a part of and comfortable in the setting he or she is in.

A distracting environment is detrimental to learning for everyone. But for people with vision loss, background conversations and other noises can interfere with concentration. To allow students with vision loss to benefit the most from desired sound, encourage them to place themselves as close to the source of sound as is appropriate.

For print materials, there are technologies to magnify text and graphics and other devices to scan and produce braille or audio versions of the information. For students with low vision, matte finishes on paper are preferred as they reduce glare. To establish high contrast and make the text appear as legible as possible, white or light yellow letters on a black background are most readable. For handwritten materials, a thick- or medium-point black felt tip pen produces the boldest letters. When written on yellow paper, or when yellow acetate is used to overlay white paper, a good contrast is achieved. While 14-point type is the legal font size for large print text, others recommend at least a 16- or 18-point size.

For visual information presented during a class lecture, the teacher's notes of the graphic materials presented in narrative form or notes taken by another student will be helpful. An audio description, or the method used at the New York State School for the Blind of taking glue string and outlining diagrams with it to raise the surface of the graphic information (described in chap. 5, this volume), will help the student to better understand graphic information.

In summary, every match of person and technology requires careful consideration. The question today is not whether to use or not to use technology in education but how best to do it in a way that meets the needs of and fosters academic success for every student, regardless of whether the student has a disability. This means we must get to know the student and use a reliable and valid assessment to obtain and organize relevant information. Then we must make sure that information is used, a plan is developed and followed, and the information is updated as the student matures and moves ahead academically and socially. An assessment process is important for the following reasons:

- There is a lot of information to assess and obtain to make a good match of technology and user. A good assessment from the beginning saves time and money in the long run.
- An assessment process will result in an outcome that is student centered and that will lead toward optimal use of a technology and academic achievement as well as personal satisfaction and social participation.
- Getting desired services for students often seems scattered and unorganized. Documented needs will help ensure devices and services are more frequently obtained.
- "Quality assurance" and "evidence-based practice" require the assessment and documentation of outcomes, which are also crucial for funding technology and making future plans with the student.

Undeniably, as this book has indicated, there is a lot of information to obtain. But the process is revealing and rewarding and will surely result in an outcome that is not only student centered but that will lead toward optimal use of a technology and that user's enhanced learning and success.

DEVELOPING SUCCESSFUL EDUCATORS

In Figure 12.1, the complementary relationship of the educational and learning processes is conveyed in the form of a simple, $1 + 1 = 2$ formula.

What constitutes good teaching? Who is a successful educator or teacher? Like Betty at the New York State School for the Blind and the vision teacher at the "good public school" (discussed in chap. 5, this volume), educators and teachers share the same characteristics we have been discussing about learners. They have their own needs, capabilities, and preferences; lifestyle; expectations and mood; motivation and readiness; and prior use

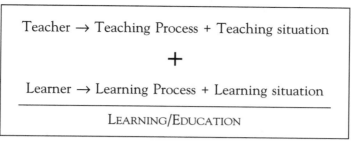

Figure 12.1. The complementary relationship between teaching and learning.

of support that they bring with them to the teaching process and situation. They teach in environments defined to a great extent by legislative and political mandates and economic assets and deficits. Their teaching environments have attitudinal, cultural, and physical attributes that determine the composition of the student body and determine the students they will teach as well as the manifest and "hidden curricula." When wanting to purchase a particular technology for instruction, they, too, need to weigh availability, cost, and performance factors. Effective educators meet and beat the challenge and are not daunted or defeated by it. They are, or make sure they become, comfortable with technology and creatively adapt it to support their teaching. They project enthusiasm and know how to motivate students (Lang, 1996).

The learning/educational process is multifaceted, interactive, and dynamic. Technology clearly has a role to play in the process. But technology by itself cannot teach students. Students require skilled and caring teachers who view technology as a tool, not a replacement, for teaching. But teachers must receive training at both the preservice and inservice levels regarding the choices in technology available (Edyburn & Gardner, 1999), how to choose and use the right technology for a specific educational goal, and how to best incorporate technology into the curriculum.

However, in schools today, most efforts have been devoted to learning about computers and technology and not how to teach and socialize with them. Some strategies educators can adopt in using technology to reach all students, regardless of whether they have a vision or hearing loss, are listed in Exhibit 12.3. Additionally, the resources listed in Appendix E should prove useful.

Effective teachers know how to make information meaningful by linking it to students' prior knowledge and using multimodal instructional strategies. They monitor students' level of understanding, reinforce new learning,

EXHIBIT 12.3
Eleven Steps to Ensuring Success When Incorporating Technology in the Curriculum

1. Technologies have to actually get into the classrooms and other environments (rural and poorer areas need additional assistance).
2. To maximize each learner's success, educators need to individualize learning environments.
3. Educators need support in their efforts to match students with educational technologies, and funds and resources need to be allocated to ensure the students receive training in the best uses and operations of technologies.
4. Educators need to involve parents so that there is more use of technologies in the home.
5. There is a need for more attention to evaluating student readiness/skills and to identifying, understanding, and building on existing learning strategies.
6. Text-based software needs to be tailored to the student's reading skills (speed and vocabulary).
7. Before making a commitment to a technology, educators need to arrange for the student to have a period of trial use.
8. Do not introduce too much technology to the student all at once.
9. Allow students the freedom to explore—and fail.
10. Use real-life and practical activities.
11. Know thyself and develop or strengthen self-advocacy and self-determination skills. Educators should develop this in students with their technology use.

and summarize that learning before moving on to the next lesson or module. In short, the most effective teachers keep the learning needs of students utmost in their minds.

MAKING THE TRANSITION FROM SECONDARY TO POSTSECONDARY EDUCATION

The HEATH Resource Center (1999) indicated that approximately 1 in 11, or 9%, of entering freshmen are students who self-identify as having one or more disabilities. Both the National Center for Education Statistics (1999) and the National Council on Disability (2000) have reported that during the 1997–1998 academic year, approximately 428,000 students with disabilities were pursuing higher education in either a 2-year or 4-year institution.

Students who have been educated in inclusive secondary and postsecondary schools most often choose to attend inclusive colleges or universities as opposed to specialized schools such as the National Technical Institute for the Deaf (NTID). Those students transitioning from high school to adult life in college or work often require assistance in making the transition. Legislation related to students with disabilities has emphasized the importance of the provision of transition services to students with disabilities (it is a required part of the IEP), and many special educators have adopted this as an area of specialization. Yet, many students qualified for college or university confront barriers that result in their lack of participation in higher education. Data from the National Longitudinal Transition Study of Special Education Students (SRI International, 1993) have documented poor outcomes for students with disabilities, with only 20% being independent in work and social activities by the time they have been out of school 3 to 5 years (Sax & Thoma, 2002). This situation of students "falling between the cracks" exists in the United States even though we have had more than 20 years of inclusive education through the Individuals With Disabilities Education Act and its predecessor legislation. In other countries, the situation is much the same. What is particularly missing in many cases is information about and the actual technology students need to make the transition from secondary school to higher education, employment, or independent living. This is troublesome in light of Section 508 of the 1998 Rehabilitation Act, which mandates equal access to information necessary to succeed in various transition environments.

In the Republic of Ireland, the STATEMENT program (discussed in chaps. 7 and 11, this volume) developed a "Statement of Need" that was completed toward the end of a student's secondary career. The student could take this Statement of Need to university personnel or employers to inform them of the technologies and other supports that have been assessed and determined to be supportive of his or her academic or vocational success. Thus, with a Statement of Need in hand, the student is empowered with knowledge regarding his or her strengths and needs, as well as a plan to support self-advocacy for services and accommodations. A copy of one student's Statement of Need is in Appendix B. From a review of Appendix B, it will become apparent that the Irish model can be easily adapted for use in the United States as well as in many other countries.

Everyone's job is made much easier when students come to the campus with a Statement of Need outlining the supports and strategies necessary to help them participate equally in college life and succeed academically and socially, when they are knowledgeable about their rights and are informed of available services, and when they are able to self-advocate for their inclusion. Ideally, this would initially occur during a new student orientation or pre-enrollment visit (e.g., Bondi-Wolcott & Scherer, 1988).

However, students who pursue higher education often experience frustration, disconnection, failure, and even eventual withdrawal. One can glean or hear this directly in the comments made by NTID students in earlier chapters when they discussed their college and distance-learning experiences; it is also commonly heard from students with disabilities in general (e.g., Holloway, 2001). Disability support offices exist in most U.S. colleges and universities, but they also exist internationally. These offices often have to

- coordinate notetaking services;
- develop alternative formats for course materials (enlarged print, braille, audiotape);
- arrange tutoring and mentoring;
- advocate and arrange testing accommodations (additional time, adapted materials, readers and notetakers, physical adaptations);
- advise and train students in learning and study skills (writing and research techniques, spelling, and time management) as well as self-determination and self-advocacy skills;
- assist in technology selection and training for use;
- arrange a mobility orientation of the college/university prior to the start of term (essential for students who are blind or with very low vision, like Jeffrey in chap. 10, this volume); and
- provide a liaison service between faculty and students.

Craig, Michaels, Prezant, and Morabito (2002) conducted a survey with approximately half of the eligible membership (N = 488) of the Association for Higher Education and Disabilities (AHEAD). The membership of AHEAD consists primarily of individuals who coordinate or provide direct services to college students with disabilities. Approximately 80% of the respondents were women, and 25% reported that they had a disability. The majority, 89%, had a master's degree or higher. On average, the respondents reported having three full-time and three part-time staff members and served a mean of 276 students with disabilities, 57% of whom were classified as students with learning disabilities or attention deficit disorder (57%). Sixty-seven percent reported serving 4-year institutions. The most frequently available AT devices on the campuses include scanners (83% of campuses); TTY/TDD (78% of campuses), screen or text reading software and screen magnification devices (78% of campuses), and specialized tape recorders (74% of campuses). However, the researchers found that the actual achievement of AT access, training, awareness, and usage is not consistent with its perceived importance. They also found that disability support services (DSS) providers tend to be most involved on their campuses in issues related to campus library accessibility and least involved in representing or advocating for the technology issues and concerns of students with disabilities in the university or college. Their data also showed that the factors having the greatest potential to facilitate the provision of AT services were the expertise of DSS staff on AT issues, the awareness and knowledge of AT among students with disabilities (such as is accomplished with the

Statement of Need discussed previously), and administrative support and funding for the purchase of AT. Appendix E provides a list of Web sites that will help enhance knowledge of current technologies legislation, and other resources. Researchers in Australia made many similar recommendations (Leung et al., 1999), not the least of which is the need to assess students with disabilities in relation to their AT needs by appropriate educational authorities before enrollment in postsecondary institutions.

Faculty and DSS providers need to (a) have access to initial and ongoing training on AT, (b) have the ongoing programmatic and fiscal support of college administration to increase awareness and knowledge of ATs in general and of specific AT products, and (c) collaborate in AT trainings and strategy development to support student needs. In addition, the President's Commission on Excellence in Special Education (2002) report, "A New Era: Revitalizing Special Education for Children and Their Families," acknowledges the need to more effectively help students with disabilities complete a high-quality postsecondary education.

When one support service at the Rochester Institute of Technology was evaluated (Scherer & Binder, 1992), it was found that for a DSS office to be helpful to students, its services must be individualized around student goals and personalized. The availability of the services must repeatedly be made known to students, faculty, and other offices and personnel in the university. Some students who knew about the services did not see the value in them until they were older. Other students found out about the services only when they were experiencing difficulty or failure, by which point they were vulnerable to dropping out of college. In both cases, the recommended means of remedying this was to sponsor social activities for students where they could receive information about the value of the services in a nonpatronizing way from other "seasoned" students. This also kept student expectations of the services realistic and helped them early on to develop a sense of fitting in and belonging, which was discovered in another research study to be a primary reason for student withdrawal (Stinson, Scherer, & Walter, 1988). This cannot be emphasized enough, as it is easier to focus on technologies than to derive successful strategies for helping students achieve a sense of belonging. It was also recommended that students be involved in the design and provision of some of the support services so that they would have a sense of ownership, belonging, and empowerment.

Another recommended strategy was to appoint "innovative" faculty viewed as leaders by their peers to a disability services advisory committee, as well as other key personnel (e.g., campus security, financial aid staff), so that they would diffuse information about the services throughout their departments. Disability support staff were encouraged to arrange frequent meetings with faculty to address their needs and concerns as well as to educate them about available accommodations, technologies, and other services.

Although this evaluation was conducted a number of years ago, all recommendations were implemented. In 2001, the support service received a Presidential Award for Excellence in Science, Mathematics, and Engineering Mentoring from the National Science Foundation (Rochester Institute of Technology, 2002).

FROM POSTSECONDARY EDUCATION TO WORK AND LIFELONG LEARNING

The technologies, accommodations, and supports discussed throughout this book, the characteristics of successful learners and effective teachers, the instructional strategies recommended for elementary and secondary students with vision or hearing loss, and the need for transitional services and ongoing support all apply to and benefit people with other disabilities as well as those without disabilities. For students in higher education and beyond, the level of maturity and commitment will be different, the materials to be learned more complex, and many of the technologies more sophisticated, but by and large everything discussed up to now applies to them as well.

For example, adults are especially willing to participate in the learning process and benefit from learning that has a direct application to their lives and careers and that uses examples based on their life experiences (e.g., Scherer & McKee, 1994b). Adults are typically more independent learners, but this depends on the particular individual's preferred learning style as to whether they would select hands-on experiences, lectures, demonstrations, or independent study. While technologies are similar if not identical to those used by younger students, what is viewed as appropriate educational software will differ. The rationale for software use needs to be clear, problems should be relevant and help the learner solve a problem of his or her own, the pace should be in the control of the learner, and there should be multiple opportunities for feedback and practice (Scherer & McKee, 1994b).

Adults in the workplace, too, require individualized accommodations depending on job responsibilities, organizational characteristics, and the individual's skills and preferences (e.g., de Jonge, Rodger, & Fitzgibbon, 2001). Most of the information presented in the tables in chapters 1 and 2 applies here. Employees can request workplace accessibility and job accommodations (which may require technologies of many forms) under the Americans With Disabilities Act (ADA). This legislation has enhanced opportunities for people with disabilities in the workplace by requiring the consideration of "accommodations," which includes, for example, acquiring equipment or ATs to enable individual employees to perform jobs for which they are qualified, providing such support services as interpreters, and making necessary adjustments in workstations, examinations, or training materials.

As is true with students at all levels, and in spite of the increasing availability of ATs for people with hearing or vision loss, both employers and employees differ in their knowledge of available ATs and the value they ascribe to them. The following are examples of questions employers have regarding the provision of devices and systems for employees:

- Will the use of the technology result in a significant increase in the employee's productivity? Will this offset the costs of the technology?
- How can we be sure that our limited funds for technologies will result in "the most bang for the buck"—that is, that technologies go to those people who will optimally use them?
- Will a technology for one person establish a barrier for another (e.g., a system relying on auditory output for a person with low vision that cannot be accessed by a person who is hard of hearing)?
- After questions of cost, employers most want to know this: Where can we get technical assistance and more information regarding technologies and ADA compliance?

Curtis Chong, a past president of the National Federation of the Blind in Computer Science, has articulated the difficulties blind people have in performing "the average job in the average place of business" with the current state of technology (Chong, 1997). Inconsistencies between the technologies one is trained on and those confronted on the job are legion. The proliferation of choices in hardware, operating systems, application software, access technologies, screen-reading, and magnification systems and their compatibility (or lack thereof) makes the matching of person with the most appropriate technology complex. Adding to the complexity is the need to build in flexibility to accommodate changes in screen formats, software upgrades, and so on and the ever-growing move away from text-based programming tools. Chong (1997) ended his essay with the following:

> It would seem that the average blind person today, in order to obtain and retain the average job in the average place of business, [must confront formidable and real technological challenges]. Unless they are overcome, it will be even more difficult for the blind to secure employment in the offices of tomorrow. (p. 123)

This book began with the examples of adults who shared their personal experiences with either vision or hearing loss and their frustrations at work, in the home, and in their day-to-day activities. What follows are a few comments from adults with hearing or vision loss about their experiences as employees. It will become apparent that many frustrations as well as obstacles exist to this day.

I find where I work that there are always new bosses and managers and that in each new situation you are still Christopher Columbus. Sometimes I have to go back and start again, educating the new manager or new boss. It doesn't carry down through policy or experience because it might be the new person's first time working with a person with a disability.

At one point my hearing loss made me very, very angry. As a result of that anger, my demands were quite unreasonable. If the employer perceives it as unreasonable, I don't think they should be responding to it completely. When I was very angry, I was asking for attention more than . . . because in that anger I was not coping so that the devices that could have been provided would not have been of real use. It's a state of crisis where a person is not coping and if an employer starts providing everything a person is demanding, then they're not responding to the real problem.

My supervisor is great in providing me with what I need in situations, but other people in the organization really don't seem to be aware of the needs. There are instances where you are invited to meetings in other places and you go to the meeting and they don't seem to know what to do for you. The whole organization really needs to be educated.

Although employers may not always know what to do, they do seem to be open to employees' ideas. This puts responsibility on the employee for being aware of one's needs, openly communicating those needs to the employer, having realistic and reasonable expectations, and being educated about alternatives—just as the people quoted in this section have indicated. Experiences have shown that when that occurs, employers have been ready to listen and to assist the employee in getting what is needed for the employee to succeed on the job.

AT THE END OF THE DAY . . .

There are many challenges to address to create a more workable partnership of technology and education and to help ensure that 21st-century teachers face classrooms of myriad faces, personalities, and capabilities and achieve a truly equal education for all students.

Technology ideally is used to unlock and enhance individuals' abilities throughout life and in many different learning environments. Too often, however, it is used as a mere "gee whiz" and possible distraction to learning, instead of a resource to enhance learning and performance. Thus, a significant number of people avoid, abandon, and report not benefiting from technologies.

Technologies that are forced on students and do not fit with their preferences or ways of doing things have a decreased probability of use. As noted earlier, a technology that requires discipline, patience, and persever-ance and that provides infrequent reinforcement may not appeal to a teenager who likes continual excitement. Moreover, technologies that minimize inter-actions with teachers or interfere with social activities enjoyed by students often go unused. Exhibit 12.4 summarizes the influences on variable degrees of educational technology use discussed throughout this book. All technolog-ies are most effective when they are shaped to meet a student's particular learning needs, not when they are used as a mere enhancement to learning (Scherer, 1996a, 1996b, 2001). As we have also seen, the choices available today in computer functions and features have both benefits and pitfalls. Although consumers can exercise more choice and select functions and features they believe are most suitable to their needs, the complexity of matching a person with the most appropriate technology is often frustrating and can be time consuming unless a well-structured process is followed and an appropriate assessment is conducted at the very beginning.

Whether the theme in this book is technologies and systems for instructional delivery, technologies for access to information and instruc-tion, or technologies to enhance individual functioning, the overarching goal is to make learning accessible, information meaningful, and achieve-ment possible. Today, a student with a disability can use many of the same educational and information technologies as students without disabilities when universal design and multimodal principles are followed. By removing unnecessary barriers to technology use and access to information, student self-reliance and independence, self-determination, and empowerment are enhanced.

The use of ATs in school, the home, the workplace, and the community has enhanced the available opportunities for people with disabilities to participate in all major life activities. Advances in AT will continue to evolve as will surgically implanted devices. With the tight budgets faced by schools and the need to help so many students, inappropriate matches of student and technology and technology nonuse are luxuries we can ill afford. We must reduce this abandonment and nonuse rate, increase the literacy of all students, and help those with additional needs succeed in participating in the larger society.

The list of disabilities in chapter 5 includes a definition for *serious emotional disturbance*. The individuals who have shared their life stories in this book—regardless of age or whether they were teacher or student—have described times in which they fit this definition. Their lack of connec-tion, sense of belongingness, and attachment to the world around them indicates that many challenges remain in preparing the youth of today for participation in all desired activities and environments. Although it may be tempting to blame the system, the budget, the constraints of time, and so on, technology does offer promise in helping individuals to connect to

EXHIBIT 12.4

The Matching Person and Technology (MPT) Model: Influences on Various Person and Technology Match Outcomes

	Milieu	Personality	Technology
Use			
Optimal	Support from family/peers/teacher	Self-determined	Goal achieved with no pain, fatigue, or inconvenience
	Realistic expectations of family/ teacher/employer	Motivated	Compatible with/enhances other supports
	Settings/environments fully support and reward use	Cooperative	Is safe, reliable, easy to use, set up, and maintain
	Received necessary training for use	Optimistic	Has the desired transportability
	Convenient access to support, computer lab, classroom	Good coping skills	No better options currently available
	Appropriate training available	Patient	Supports lifestyle and social activities
		Self-disciplined	Available upgrades
		Generally positive life experiences	
		Has the skills to use the technology	
		Perceived discrepancy between goal and current situation	
		Is not self-conscious about using device	
		Positive history of technology use	
Partial/Reluctant/ Inappropriate	Pressure for use from either family/ peers/teacher	Self-conscious when using the technology	Goal not fully achieved or with discomfort/inconvenience
	Assistance often not available	Unmotivated	Requires a lot of setup
	Some environments/settings discourage use, make use awkward	Impatient/impulsive	Interferes somewhat with other support use
	Inadequate training received	Unrealistic expectations	Technology is inefficient
		Low self-esteem	Other options to device use preferred
		Somewhat intimidated by technology	Incompatible with some social activities
		Technology partially or occasionally fits with goals	
		Deficits in skills needed for use	

Nonuse

Avoidance	Lack of support from either family/peers/teacher Unrealistic expectations of others Assistance not available Setting/environment disallows or prevents use Training not available	Person does not accept goal Person does not want the device Depressed Unmotivated Uncooperative Withdrawn Intimidated by technology Many changes required in habits and lifestyle Does not have skills for use	Perceived lack of goal achievement or too much discomfort/inconvenience in use Requires a lot of setup Perceived or determined to be incompatible with other supports or lifestyle Preferred device too expensive Long delay for delivery Other options preferred Viewed as socially undesirable
Abandonment	Lack of support from either family/peers/teacher Setting/environment discourages or makes use awkward Requires assistance that is not available Training not adequate	Self-conscious using the technology Depressed Low self-esteem Hostile/angry Withdrawn Resistant Prefers human touch Poor adjustment skills Many changes in lifestyle with use Lacks skills to use device and training not available Perceives no benefit in use	Goal not achieved and/or with discomfort/inconvenience Is incompatible with the use of other technologies Has been outgrown Too difficult to use Technology is inefficient Repairs/service not timely or affordable Better/preferred options became available Incompatible with social activities

one another and to participate fully in the larger society. To make the most of this promise, it falls upon us all to ensure that technology is appropriately selected and matched to its users; that users are empowered to exploit the advantages of technology to enhance their performance, achievement, and personal well-being and accomplishment; that technology liberates and makes available exciting and rewarding opportunities. The role of technology is to foster connections: make learning—and life—accessible and fuller, not to isolate and limit its users.

APPENDIX A

Matching Person and Technology Process and Samples of the Assessment Forms

---

The Matching Person and Technology Assessment Process and Instruments

---

Step 1: Initial Worksheet for the Matching Person and Technology (MPT) model is used to determine initial goals that the professional and the user have established, including possible alternative goals. Second, potential interventions supportive of these goals are written in the space provided on the form. Third, any technologies needed to support the attainment of the goals are recorded. (See sample in this Appendix.)

Step 2: History of Support Use is used to identify technologies used in the past, satisfaction with those technologies, and those that are desired and needed but not yet available to the consumer. The professional and consumer complete this form collaboratively. (See sample in this Appendix.)

Step 3: The consumer is asked to complete his or her version of the appropriate form depending on the type of technology under consideration: general, assistive (see sample in this Appendix), educational (see sample in this Appendix), workplace, or health care. The user form may serve as a guide for an oral interview, if that seems more appropriate for the situation. The professional completes the professional version of the same form and identifies any discrepancies in perspective between the professional's and the consumer's responses. These discrepancies then become a topic for discussion and negotiation.

Step 4: The professional discusses with the user those factors that may indicate problems with his or her acceptance or appropriate use of the technology.

Step 5: After problem areas have been noted, the professional and consumer work to identify specific intervention strategies and devise an action plan to address the problems.

Step 6: The strategies and action plans are committed to writing, for experience has shown that plans that are merely verbalized are not implemented as frequently as written plans. Written plans also serve as documentation and can provide the justification for any subsequent actions, such as requests for funding or release time for training.

Note. There is a complete manual describing the administration and scoring of each measure, interpretation and use of the results, as well as the reliability and validity of the measures. More information is available at http://members.aol.com/IMPT97/MPT.html

Sample Portion of the MPT Survey Forms
(Includes less than 50% of the items from original form)

INITIAL WORKSHEET FOR THE MATCHING PERSON AND TECHNOLOGY PROCESS

In which of the following does the individual experience a limitation or have a particular strength (check all that apply)? For each area, indicate goals as well as potentially desirable technologies, environmental accommodations, and other interventions for this person.

Domain	Limitations	Strengths	Goals	Interventions	Examples of technologies/ Environmental accommodations
___ Speech/ communication	1.	1.	1.	1.	Electronic communication device, manual board
	2.	2.	2.	2.	
	3.	3.	3.	3.	Communication skill training for key others
___ Mobility	1.	1.	1.	1.	Wheelchair, walker, adapted driving devices, ramps, appropriate surfaces
	2.	2.	2.	2.	
	3.	3.	3.	3.	
___ Dexterity, hand control	1.	1.	1.	1.	Adapted computer keyboard and mouse, grooming aids
	2.	2.	2.	2.	Automatic door openers, touch screen bank terminals
	3.	3.	3.	3.	

_____ Eyesight

1.
2.
3.

1.
2.
3.

1. Magnification devices, reading machines
2.
3. Appropriate lighting, tactile labeling/signage

_____ Hearing

1.
2.
3.

1.
2.
3.

1. Phone amplifier, personal FM system, signaling devices
2.
3. Noise reduction, captioned programs

_____ Reading/writing

1.
2.
3.

1.
2.
3.

1. Books on tape, computer with speech output
2.
3. Trained readers/notetakers, testing accommodations

HISTORY OF SUPPORT USE: TECHNOLOGIES, SPECIAL PURPOSE DEVICES, AND PERSONAL ASSISTANCE

In which areas does the person (a) use, (b) have past use, and (c) need a technology or other support? Write the name of the support in each relevant domain and then record the information requested under the one most appropriate column.

Domain	Name of Support	SUPPORT CURRENTLY USED			SUPPORT USED IN THE PAST (not listed under *currently* used)				SUPPORT NEEDED		
		Months Used	Percent of Day Used	Satisfaction with support (1 = very dissatisfied, 3 = neutral, 5 = very satisfied)	Months Used	Percent of Day Used	Satisfaction with support (1 = very dissatisfied, 3 = neutral, 5 = very satisfied)	Reason for No Longer Using	Need and Want, but Do Not Have	Need, but Do Not Want	Reason
Speech/ Communication	1. 2. 3.										
Mobility	1. 2. 3.										
Dexterity, hand control	1. 2. 3.										
Eyesight	1. 2. 3.										

Hearing 1.			
2.			
3.			
Reading/Writing 1.			
2.			
3.			

Copyright 2003, Institute for Matching Person & Technology, Inc.

<table>
<tr><td>Initial</td><td>**Assistive Technology Device Predisposition Assessment**
(Includes less than 50% of the items from original form)</td><td>Form 4-1
Person</td></tr>
</table>

Name _____ Date of Birth _____

Primary Goals (6 months): _____ Today's Date _____

Primary Goals (1 year+): _____ Form completed by _____

A. How are your capabilities *today* in the following areas *with* AT (or other support)? Circle the best response for each and write in the name of the primary device or support you use where relevant. Then, put a plus [+] for any device or support needs that you believe will *increase* over the next 12 months. Put a minus [–] for any that you believe will *decrease* over the next 12 months.

	Poor	Average	Excellent	Name of Support	Need increase [+] or decrease [–]
1. Eyesight	1	2 3	4 5	_____	_____
2. Hearing	1	2 3	4 5	_____	_____
3. Speech	1	2 3	4 5	_____	_____
4. Understanding, remembering	1	2 3	4 5	_____	_____
7. Grasping and use of fingers	1	2 3	4 5	_____	_____

B. How satisfied are you currently in the following areas? Circle your response to each. Then, circle the number of the item(s) you most want to see improve over time. If more than one is circled, indicate under the column labeled *Importance*, the item that is #1 in importance, #2, etc. For circled items, indicate if the primary obstacle you face is due to environmental barriers [E] or to your disability [D].

	Not Satisfied	Satisfied	Very Satisfied	Importance	Primary Obstacle [E], [D]
14. Participation in desired activities	1 2	3	4 5	_____	_____
15. Educational attainment	1 2	3	4 5	_____	_____
18. Close, intimate relationships	1 2	3	4 5	_____	_____
19. Autonomy and self-determination	1 2	3	4 5	_____	_____
20. Fitting in, belonging, feeling connected	1 2	3	4 5	_____	_____

C. Please circle all the statements below that describe you.

22. I have the support I want from family
23. I have the support I want from friends
24. I feel encouraged by therapists, caregivers
25. I feel the general public accepts me
26. I aspire to go to school or work
27. I'm often frustrated or overwhelmed
28. I'm curious & excited about new things

33. I'm usually calm and patient
34. My life has purpose, meaning
35. I'm self-disciplined
36. I'm often angry
37. I'm often depressed
41. I like having a challenge
42. I'm responsible & reliable

44. I find technology interesting
45. I'm cooperative
46. I prefer a quiet lifestyle
47. I often feel isolated & alone
48. I accomplish what I set out to do
52. I often feel insecure
53. I feel as if I have little privacy

COMMENTS:

Copyright 2003 M.J. Scherer

| Initial | **Assistive Technology Device Predisposition Assessment**
(Includes less than 50% of the items from original form) | FORM 4-1
Device |

Name _____   Date of Birth _____

Primary AT Goals _____   Today's Date _____

_____   Form completed by _____

DIRECTIONS: Write the name of each device being considered in the boxes under "DEVICE." Then, read each of the twelve items below (A–L) and circle the letter of the *three* that are most important to you. Rate each device for the twelve items (A–L) according to the following scale and then write the numbers in the appropriate boxes:

> **5** = All the time
> **4** = Often
> **3** = Half the time, neutral or not applicable
> **2** = Sometimes
> **1** = Not at all

A. The assistance and accommodations exist for successful use of this device.
D. I am confident I know how to use this device and its various features.
F. This device will fit well with my accustomed routine.
G. This device will benefit me and improve my quality of life.
J. I will feel comfortable (and *not* self conscious) using this device around friends.
K. I will feel comfortable (and *not* self conscious) using this device at school or work.

DEVICE	A	B	C	D	E	F	G	H	I	J	K	L	Total (add A-L)

Review each **total score** above. In general, the device with the highest total score is the one most preferred (maximum number of points=60). However, when total scores are close, more weight should be given to the three items circled as being *most important*.

DEVICE SELECTED FOR TRIAL USE:

Vendor _____   Contact Person _____   Phone _____ Fax _____

Manufacturer _____   Style _____   Delivery Date: _____

Cost: _____ Payer: _____   Funding request notes:

How long device is expected to meet person's needs _____ (Years) _____ (Months) _____ (Weeks)

Educational Technology Predisposition Assessment Student Form
(Includes less than 50% of the items from original form)

Student's Name		Date	

Technology		Educational Goal	

A. GOAL

1. Do you understand the goal that is written above?

1	2	3	4	5
no		somewhat		yes

4. How much do you *want* to achieve this goal?

1	2	3	4	5
not much		somewhat		yes

B. (EDUCATIONAL) TECHNOLOGY

1. Have you ever experienced this type of technology or this method?

1	2	3	4	5
never		some		often

3. Have you observed others using this technology/method?

1	2	3	4	5
never		some		often

C. MILIEU/ENVIRONMENT

1. Do you prefer to learn from listening to a teacher's lecture or by reading a textbook?

1	2	3	4	5
listening		both		reading

3. Do you prefer to watch a demonstration or experiment on your own?

1	2	3	4	5
no		somewhat		yes

5. Do you think your friends/peers would be supportive of you doing this?

1	2	3	4	5
no		somewhat		yes

D. THE PERSON

Circle all the statements below that describe you.

1. I am curious & excited about new things.
3. I receive criticism well.
4. I move from task to task easily.
6. I often want to work slower/faster than others.
7. I work carefully.
8. I have the background skills and knowledge for what I need to learn.
10. I want to control my own learning pace.

13. I like to try new things.
15. My physical dexterity is good.
16. I would describe myself as studious.
18. I am sometimes critical.
19. I can perform the series of steps required to operate this technology.
20. I like using a computer.
22. I sometimes need frequent feedback.

25. I am often easily bored.
27. I feel often anxious.
28. I have a cooperative attitude.
30. I work with precision.
31. I prefer getting feedback from a computer than from my teacher.
32. I am motivated to learn.
34. Use of this technology will interfere with my social activities.

Please list other characteristics that describe you as a learner.

35. _____ 36. _____ 37. _____

APPENDIX B
Copy of Statement of Need Form

STATEMENT OF NEED

Date of Report: 30th September

Student's Name: Student

Address:

Institution Enrolled:

Place of Study:

Course: LLB Law

Disability/Condition: Visual Impairment, Osteoporosis, Raynaud's Disease

Medical or Other Evidence Submitted: Doctor's Letters

INTRODUCTION

Student was referred to me by the University of XXX, for an assessment of her academic and IT requirements to enable me to recommend appropriate provisions and to support her claim for the XXX allowances. I assessed her on 15th September, 1999.

Student has partial sight in both eyes and experiences floating objects in her field of vision. She wears glasses to correct her vision to some degree, but they only bring about a slight improvement and Student reported that she has difficulties reading, operating a computer, and with mobility. Her mobility is also affected by osteoporosis and she commented that she has difficulty getting around, especially in poor weather. Additionally, Student has Raynaud's Disease, which causes tingling and aching in both hands with the result that she finds it difficult to write for extended periods, to manipulate textbooks etc. or carry objects.

It is clear that whilst Student is undertaking a course of study she will experience difficulties in notetaking, producing written assignments, and writing answers in examinations. Every effort should be made, therefore, to bring about a situation whereby she can study independently and efficiently.

Resulting from my evaluation of Student's disability, I have recommended a package of aid that will support her and enable her to derive the greatest benefit from her course. In presenting my recommendations, I have taken full account of the student's existing learning strategies and preferred study methods.

Within this report are recommendations to the student, the University, and the funding agency. As follows:

TO THE STUDENT

1. Tape recordings of lectures and seminars should be used as your primary means of notetaking.
2. Request copies of typed lecture notes and OHP's from the teaching staff before the start of lectures, preferably in a size 32 Times New Roman font (bold).
3. When necessary, obtain and photocopy fellow students' notes to supplement your tape-recorded notes. When photocopying them you should have them enlarged to a size that is more comfortable to read.

*If this method of notetaking proves to be unsatisfactory, you may wish to employ the services of a notetaker. If this is the case you should contact XXX for advice.

4. Written lecture notes, tape-recorded notes, handouts, OHP's and other students' notes should be typed up into a comprehensive set of notes at the earliest opportunity.
5. You should request that staff provide you with a more focused reading list, so that you might spend less time reading material only peripheral to the subject.
6. You should contact staff at the Student Services/DLO Office to enquire about the University's extended library loan facility, and assistance in obtaining and photocopying reading materials.
7. When reading books and other textual materials, you should use an illuminated magnifier.
8. To improve your posture when reading and writing, you should make use of a book holder and writing slope.
9. You should contact the XXX student library with regard to borrowing books on cassette, by telephoning their Customer Services department on XXX.
10. Books may be accessed electronically or obtained on tape and computer disk from the following organisations which you may wish to contact for further information:

   - http://www.net.library.com

   - Recording for the Blind & Dyslexic in the USA:
     20 Roszel Road
     Princeton, NJ 08540
     USA

     Tel: (609) 452-0606
     Fax: (609) 987-8116
     Internet: http://www.rfbd.org

11. I recommend that you undertake as much work as possible at home using a word processor and screen magnification software. This will reduce the number of journeys you have to make to campus, particularly when the weather is poor.
12. You should make use of an Internet connection to access the University's Library Catalogue, as well of a host of other research information such as the Lexis legal data services, Law Commission documents, etc., with the aid of screen magnification software.
13. As you experience difficulty in seeing a standard computer display, I recommend that you use ZoomText Extra Level 2 for Windows, a screen magnification program. You should experiment with levels of magnification and colour settings until you find a combination that is optimal for your reading.
14. To reduce the amount of time you spend typing up copies of OHP's, handouts and textbook references you should use a flat-bed scanner in conjunction with an OCR package to scan these items into your computer.
15. To reduce the discomfort you experience when operating a computer, you should use an ergonomically designed trackball and wrist supports.
16. I would strongly advise you to obtain some formal mobility training to increase your level of independence, specifically for your journey to and from university, and around the campus. Such training can be obtained from the NCBI, contact XXX.
17. You should travel to and from the university campus by taxi as much as possible. You should ask your XXX to reimburse you for the cost of these journeys.

TO THE UNIVERSITY

Notetaking

1. Staff should permit Student to tape-record lectures and seminars, as this will be her primary means of notetaking. Additionally, detailed verbal descriptions of information displayed on chalkboards and OHP's should be given in order that they may be captured on tape.
2. During lectures, when answering questions from the floor, it is essential to repeat the question for the benefit of the tape recorder.
3. Wherever possible, staff should provide Student with copies of their typed lecture notes and OHP's a week in advance of each class, preferably in a size 32 Times New Roman font (Bold).
4. If not already done so, staff should asterisk essential texts in reading lists, to provide a more focused list, leading to a reduction in time spent reading material only peripheral to the subject.

5. If not already available on the University's computer facilities, the University should consider investing in a copy of ZoomText Extra Level 2 screen magnification software. In addition to enlarging a computer's display, it also offers a screen reading feature using synthesized speech output. Further information may be obtained from:

> Sight & Sound Technology
> Quantel House
> Anglia Way
> Moulten Park
> Northampton, NN3 6JA
> United Kingdom
> Tel: 01604 798070

Course Work

6. Requests for time extensions to assignment submission dates should be viewed sympathetically, but only when it is clear that compliance with deadlines will disadvantage the student, and will not lead to a situation where providing an extension will compound the situation.

Examinations

7. At the present time, Student has expressed the desire to write her examinations in the normal manner. She should be permitted 15 minutes per hour extra time so that she can take breaks to rest her hand and spend time reviewing the question paper and her own work.
8. The examination paper should be printed in a 32 point Times New Roman font (Bold) and Student should be permitted to take in her own hand held magnifier. Student should also be provided with an A2 writing slope or similar to facilitate a comfortable posture when reading or writing.

TO FUNDING AGENCY

It is clear that Student's condition will place her at a significant disadvantage relative to other students. She should, therefore, be provided with funds from the Disabled Student's Allowances to enable her to purchase the aids and services that are essential to place her on an equal footing. As follows:

Specialist Equipment Allowance

1. Tape-recorder, footswitch, and cassette tapes. This will be Student's primary means of taking notes in lectures and seminars.

2. A desktop computer, including Office package, a modem, and a printer. This will permit the following:

- The typing up of tape-recorded lecture notes;
- The production of course work assignments with the aid of screen magnification software;
- The scanning of textual materials;
- Access to research materials on the Internet with the aid of screen magnification software.

3. A flat-bed scanner and an OCR package will enable the scanning of textual materials so that they be brought up on screen and reviewed with the aid of screen magnification.

4. ZoomText Extra Level 2. This application enlarges the on-screen display so that a visually impaired person can see it more easily.

5. A screen filter. This will assist Student by eliminating much of the glare from her computer monitor, thereby reducing eyestrain and enabling her to work for longer periods.

6. An Internet account. This is to enable Student to access essential course materials and information resources on the World Wide Web, such as the Lexis legal data services, Law Commission documents, etc., with the aid of screen magnification software. Additionally she may exchange information with staff via e-mail, and search for titles available in the catalogue of talking books at the Recording for the Blind & Dyslexic in the USA's Web site.

7. An A2 Posturite writing slope with bookholder, a portable bookholder, and an illuminated magnifier. These will enable the positioning of books and documents at eye level, avoiding the need for unnecessary bending to read such materials on a flat desk surface.

8. An ergonomic mouse and wrist rests. These will enable Student to operate a computer with minimum discomfort to her wrists and arms.

9. Funds for insurance cover of computer equipment, software, and peripherals. The student should enquire as to whether these items would be adequately covered against theft and damage on her home contents insurance. If this is not the case, the student should be provided with funds to cover the cost of providing additional insurance cover.

10. Funds for photocopying. These are necessary to enable the copying of a range of library materials, which will need to be copied and retained. This is essential as a large number of books are only available from the library on short-loan and other materials, such as journals and study packs, cannot be borrowed.

11. The student should be reimbursed for the cost of computer consumables (e.g., paper and ink cartridges) and fat pens or pen grips upon production of the appropriate receipts to the Authority.

Nonmedical Helper's Allowance

1. Setup configuration and testing of the student's computer system, peripherals, and software.
2. One day's training in the use of specialist software.
3. Professional fees for undertaking an assessment of the student's course-related needs, and the production of this report.

Travel Costs

Student should be reimbursed for the cost of travel to and from the university campus by taxi.

A comprehensive list of assistive technological aids, including prices and suppliers is provided below. The computer hardware and software described is compatible with the University's systems. Furthermore, on the basis of my present knowledge, I consider that this equipment will suffice for the duration of the student's course.

The range of computers and printers now available is considerable. We recommend a basic specification but it is recognized that some students may wish to improve this for themselves. We hope XXX will be willing to agree to this provided students are prepared to pay any differences in cost from their own funds.

From time to time, XXX or students contact us to say that they have found equipment that they consider to be better value for money. Experience has shown us that on further investigation of these claims, such packages usually turn out to be less comprehensive or of an inferior quality. XXX chooses its suppliers from a short list of organizations it has worked with regularly and knows to be reputable and who provide a reliable after sales service. All equipment, hardware and software recommended has been tested by XXX and has been found to be compatible and reliable. If students or XXX choose to alter the specifications of any equipment or its supplier, XXX will not be held responsible for any lack of functionality, compatibility, or reliability of such items.

If you require any further information or need to discuss the contents of this report, please do not hesitate in contacting me.

Joe Bloggs
AT Advisor

Supplier/Order Information

Item	Price	VAT	Total	Supplier
Desktop PII/400 PC with 128 MB SDRAM, Intel BX chipset, 6.0GB hard disk, 3.5″ floppy drive, 32 speed CD Drive, PCI 64 voice wave table sound card, 8MB ATI Xpert98 AGP graphics, 17″ Multi-media Monitor, Windows '98, Midi Tower case, 3 Years On-site warranty. Please quote order reference: DART/ULH/P400				
Add Modem				
Epson Stylus 440 ink-jet printer (including cable), Code 0E1287.				
HP 5200C flat-bed scanner. Order code: 0G5723				
Caera OmniPage Pro v 9.0 Competitive Upgrade. Code: OH7797				
2 × 50 Maxell 3.5″ HD disks IBM formatted. Code: 2 x 044532				
Microsoft Office 2000 – Student Licence Pack. Code: 075935				
TOTAL (including VAT @ 21%)				

Item	Price	VAT	Total	Supplier
APH Handy Cassette recorder package				
Battery charger				
Footswitch				
Lapel microphone				
25 Cassettes (C90)				
Delivery				
TOTAL (including VAT @ 21%)				

Item	Price	VAT	Total	Supplier
ZoomText Xtra Plus level 2 Version 7.02				
Delivery				
TOTAL (including VAT @ 21%)				

Item	Price	VAT	Total	Supplier
Luxo Fluorescent magnifier Lamp. Code: LFM101A				
Additional 2x lens for Luxo Magnifier Lamp. Code: LFM8D				
TOTAL (including VAT @ 21%)				

Item	Price	VAT	Total	Supplier
Logitech Trackman Marble Plus. Code: LOG/TMPL				
Voltfree Screen Filter for 17″ monitor. Code: VF17P				
Ergorest Mouse Pad (shallow clamp). Code: EMOUSE1S				
Ergorest wrist support (shallow clamp). Code: EREST1S				
Mini Posturite writing slope. Code: PPOS/2				
Posturite Bookholder. Code: POS/PBH				
Carriage				
TOTAL (including VAT @ 21%)				

Item	Price	VAT	Total	Supplier
BookChair portable book-holder				
Carriage				
TOTAL (including VAT @ 21%)				

Item	Price	VAT	Total	Supplier
Karoo Extra ISP subscription. Yearly subscription @ £15 per month (includes VAT).				
TOTAL (including VAT @ 21%)				

Item	Price	VAT	Total	Supplier
3 year's insurance (of computer equipment & software) @ 9% of total value of computer equipment, software, and peripherals (if required).				
TOTAL (including VAT @ 21%)				

Item	Price	VAT	Total	Supplier
Computer consumables (paper, ink cartridges, etc.)				
TOTAL (including VAT @ 21%)			£0.00	

Item	Price	VAT	Total	Supplier
6 photocopy cards				
TOTAL (including VAT @ 21%)				

Item	Price	VAT	Total	Supplier
One day's training in the use of specialist software.				
Setup and configuration of PC				
Professional fees for undertaking the assessment of course-related needs.				
TOTAL (including VAT @ 21%)				

APPENDIX C
Checklists for Educational Technology Evaluation and Selection

These samples are from the Matching Person and Technology (MPT) model and self-assessment tools (http://members.aol.com/IMPT97/MPT. html). They have been designed to help potential users of educational technologies examine their preferences and expectations.

Responses to the items in the MPT assessments assist the learner and teacher (and for young learners, parents, and Individualized Education Program [IEP] team members) in making choices best suited to the learner's needs. In many cases, appropriate choices help avoid the frustration caused by technology that is not compatible with the learner's preferences, personality, and learning style.

As a learner and potential educational technology user, important questions need to be answered in order to obtain the educational technology that will really further your abilities. Knowing who you are, what you need, and why will qualify you to control your learning experience. You can explain your preferences and needs to others more easily and effectively. A better sense of self allows you to look outward with confidence to find choices. Choice is power. This power directs you to move forward and plan strategies based on those available choices and your expectations. Purposely setting goals keeps you moving forward rather than focusing on weaknesses and fears.

It is important to think about the resources you already have and identify what resources you still need. It will be helpful to do some self-examination of your goals, then your ideas for ways to achieve those goals. **The forms in Appendix A will help in this process. The first form in the MPT assessment process is called "Initial Worksheet for the Matching Person and Technology Process" and it is one you should refer to now.** As you use this form, it is important that you focus on your *current strengths as well as barriers*. Fill out the form in two steps:

1. Write down your initial goals and include possible alternative goals.
2. Determine what would help you reach these goals.

Once this is done, you will be ready to identify an action plan to address your goals and proposed interventions. You should commit to writing out and developing your strategies and action plans. Experience has shown that plans that are only talked about are not carried out as often as written plans. Written plans also can provide a reason for further actions such as funding or training, etc.

On the next two pages are charts for short-term and long-term goals, attempts toward achieving the goals, and results. Transfer the ideas you write here to the *Initial Worksheet for Matching Person and Technology Process* under "Goals" and "Interventions."

SHORT-TERM GOALS

DATE NOW	WHAT YOU WANT TO ACCOMPLISH	BY WHEN	HOW YOU CAN ACCOMPLISH IT	DATE DONE

LONG-TERM GOALS				
DATE NOW	WHAT YOU WANT TO ACCOMPLISH	BY WHEN	HOW YOU CAN ACCOMPLISH IT	DATE DONE

SELECTING ASSISTIVE AND EDUCATIONAL TECHNOLOGIES
(INCLUDING SOFTWARE)

For people about to use a particular assistive or educational technology or software program for the first time, and for those who are going to be using an upgrade or something new, a great deal of effort and time is often required to find the most appropriate match with the user's learning style and preferences. Your responses to the questions that follow will assist both you (as learner and technology user) and the provider, teacher, or IEP team in making choices best suited to your needs. In many cases, correct choices help avoid the frustration caused by technology that is not compatible with your preferences.

Because it can be difficult to figure out what questions to ask, and it can be easy to forget what to ask, here are some questions to help you get started. The questions are divided into two sections as examples for you to have handy when you are talking to providers, teachers, or the IEP team. The answers to these questions can also serve as important information to share as you work toward narrowing your product choices.

The checklists are divided into the following two sections:

1. Questions to ask during the assessment or evaluation process.
2. Questions to ask when a specific product is recommended.

Because not every question will be relevant to your situation, each question has two boxes. The first box is used to indicate how important this particular question is for you or for this product. The other box is to rank how well this question is addressed. You can use check marks, or a 1–5 scale, or any rating system you prefer. A question mark can indicate those questions where more information is needed. Finally, there are places to write in your own questions and jot down notes of key things to remember.

QUESTIONS TO ASK
DURING THE ASSESSMENT OR EVALUATION PROCESS

Importance *Rating*

☐ ☐ Am I being treated with courtesy and respect?

☐ ☐ Is it clear I will be involved in selecting the technology and features I will use?

☐ ☐ Are the preferences I'm expressing being heard?

☐ ☐ Do I detect impatience with my questions?

☐ ☐ Am I being clear about what my expectations and needs are?

☐ ☐ Is there a duplication in services or products with any of my choices?

☐ ☐ Will services and technologies be adapted to my changing needs?

☐ ☐ Is the assessment provider or team knowledgeable, credentialed, and skilled?

☐ ☐ Does the assessment provider or team keep up with the latest developments, approaches, and products?

☐ ☐ Will there be an adequate range of services and technologies to meet my needs?

Additional questions I want to keep in mind or have addressed:

☐ ☐ _____

☐ ☐ _____

☐ ☐ _____

☐ ☐ _____

Important things I learned from this meeting or discussion:

_____

_____

_____

_____

QUESTIONS TO ASK
WHEN A SPECIFIC PRODUCT IS RECOMMENDED

Importance   *Rating*

☐   ☐   Does this product do everything I want it to do?

☐   ☐   Have I seen it demonstrated?

☐   ☐   Does it require some skills or capabilities I don't have?

☐   ☐   Will I receive adequate training in how to use this product from a knowledgeable source?

☐   ☐   Is the size and weight of the device manageable for me?

☐   ☐   Can I use the product without assistance or is the assistance I need readily available?

☐   ☐   Can I answer honestly that I am comfortable about using this technology?

☐   ☐   Will I actually use the technology, or is it apt to go unused?

☐   ☐   Have I considered all the other alternatives?

☐   ☐   Will this technology meet my needs in various situations and environments?

☐   ☐   Do I need special features because of the weather conditions or physical features of my area?

☐   ☐   Does the device have the stability I need in a variety of situations and environments?

☐   ☐   Does the device have the durability I need in a variety of situations and environments?

☐   ☐   Do I need to make changes in my environments to accommodate my use of this device?

☐   ☐   Can this product be adapted if there are changes in my functional abilities, activities, and/or size?

☐   ☐   Is it comfortable to use?

☐   ☐   Are the knobs, switches, straps, etc. accessible and easy for me to use?

☐   ☐   Are there extra features I should consider to make the product more versatile?

☐   ☐   Are there extra features that I'll never use?

☐   ☐   Are adaptations or additional parts necessary for this device?

☐   ☐   Do I adequately understand the technical assistance for the product?

☐   ☐   Will I have access to and information about repair and maintenance of the device?

☐   ☐   Can I maintain the device myself?

QUESTIONS TO ASK
WHEN A SPECIFIC PRODUCT IS RECOMMENDED, continued

Importance   Rating

☐   ☐   Do I understand the maintenance schedule of the device?

☐   ☐   Is the average turnaround time for repairs acceptable?

☐   ☐   Is a loan available if doing without is a problem?

☐   ☐   If the device needs assembly, is there someone who will do it?

Additional questions I want to keep in mind or have addressed:

☐   ☐   _____

☐   ☐   _____

☐   ☐   _____

☐   ☐   _____

Important things to remember about using this technology:

_____

_____

_____

_____

APPENDIX D

Finding and Funding Assistive Technologies
(Assistive Technology Law Center, Ithaca, NY)

Public school districts are required by law to provide assistive technologies (ATs) necessary for the achievement of students' educational goals and are written into the Individualized Education Program (IEP). But budgets are limited, and not all desirable technologies may be able to be obtained (such as a notebook or palm computer). Devices considered to be "medical treatment" are not expected to be paid for by school districts.

Under President Bush's New Freedom Initiative, emphasis is placed on the development and deployment of ATs. The focus includes major commitments to an expansion of resources available for AT loans to individuals with disabilities under the Alternative Financing Program (AFP) of Title III of the Assistive Technology Act, and commitments to a number of innovative programs, such as the use of technology to develop home-based entrepreneurship and employment opportunities, and the importance of technology in the implementation of the Olmstead decision.

While individuals obtain funding to pay for their devices from a variety of public and private sources, the majority of funding comes from the following:

1. **Private insurance plans,** which include medical insurance (e.g., Blue Cross/Blue Shield) or accident insurance (e.g., automobile, home), will cover many devices needed to maintain the student's health and independence.

2. **Federal and state programs** beyond what is available in public school districts may provide funding for devices when private insurance is not available or is no longer adequate.

   a. Vocational rehabilitation serves people with disabilities who have the potential for work. Federal/state vocational rehabilitation programs define the potential for work very broadly to include many types of activities beyond full-time competitive employment such as part-time, sheltered, and supported employment as well as homemaking. Vocational rehabilitation services may assist people to transition from secondary education or pursue postsecondary programs or vocational training. If a device is determined to be necessary for employment, or becoming employable, then vocational rehabilitation services will pay for it. If a person is not seeking employment, and a device is necessary for a person's independence, the person may receive assistance from an independent living program or center.

b. Medicare, Part B serves people 65 and older as well as those who have been receiving social security disability insurance benefits for a period of 24 months and people with disabilities whose parents are disabled, retired, or deceased. Medicare, Part B covers durable medical equipment and prosthetic devices that are determined to be "medically necessary."

c. Medicaid may pay for devices not covered by private insurance for those who meet financial criteria. As with Medicare, the device must be "medically necessary." Under Medicaid Amendments for Special Education Related Services of 1988 (Pub. L. 100-360), the student must be Medicaid-eligible, the device must be considered "durable medical equipment (DME)," and it must be in the student's IEP.

3. **Charitable sources** can assist people with particular disabilities who work through organizations by or for people with that disability (e.g., the United Cerebral Palsy Associations) to obtain equipment. Private organizations such as the Lion's Club, Kiwanis, and so on may support the cause of a student who needs devices. The Foundation for the Junior Blind (FJB) in Los Angeles sponsors "Angel Grants," whose benefactor is anonymous, for the purchase of AT to visually impaired individuals up to $10,000 per person, at several sites around the country (which are not publicized). The manager of development at FJB is in charge of coordinating the program. A biography and list of needed AT are submitted for consideration by the unknown committee. If approved, the candidate is given the equipment after writing a letter of appreciation and signing an agreement that the equipment will never be sold or given to a third party, and if the equipment ever becomes unneeded, it is to be given back to the benefactors through FJB. For more information, contact FJB through their website at: www.fjb.org.

Community medical equipment and home health care dealers/providers are often very knowledgeable about payors for particular kinds of devices, and many have an individual on staff who assists people in applying for funding. Also, each state presently has a Tech Act project that has been funded through the Assistive Technology Act. The state projects serve as information and referral sources. To locate any particular state project, contact the U.S. Department of Education in Washington, DC.

APPENDIX E
Resources

This appendix provides a representative, but not comprehensive, list of key resources for obtaining further information on the topics in this book. Web sites were chosen on the basis of the probability that they would routinely be updated and that the URL would not change.

U.S. Organizations With a Focus on Children and Adults With Disabilities

Council for Exceptional Children (CEC): The CEC is the largest international professional organization dedicated to improving educational outcomes for individuals with exceptionalities, students with disabilities, and the gifted. The organization provides a number of services, including professional development resources, journals and newsletters on new research findings, classroom and information services. http://www.cec.sped.org

American Psychological Association (APA): The APA is a scientific and professional organization that represents psychology in the United States. With more than 155,000 members, APA is the largest association of psychologists worldwide: http://www.apa.org. Division 22— Rehabilitation Psychology has Special Interest Groups on Assistive Technology, Deafness, and Pediatrics and a bibliography on a wide range of rehabilitation topics: http://www.apa.org/divisions/div22. There are also APA Divisions on Evaluation, Measurement, and Statistics; Applied Experimental and Engineering Psychology; and Educational Psychology among many others: http://www.apa.org/about/division.html

U.S. Organizations Focused on Assistive Technology

Alliance for Technology Access (ATA): The ATA is a network of community-based resource centers, developers, vendors, and associates dedicated to providing information and support services to children and adults with disabilities, and to increasing their use of standard, assistive, and information technologies. http://www.ataccess.org

RESNA (Rehabilitation Engineering and Assistive Technology Society of North America): RESNA is an interdisciplinary association of people with a common interest in technology and disability. Membership is open to all

interested individuals and includes such professionals as rehabilitation technology researchers, rehabilitation engineers, occupational therapists, physical therapists, speech language pathologists/audiologists, orthotists and prosthetists, educators, suppliers and manufacturers, end-users and advocates, policy specialists, and a variety of other rehabilitation and health professionals.
http://www.resna.org

European counterpart: *Association for the Advancement of Assistive Technology in Europe (AAATE)*, http://www.fernuni-hagen.de/FTB/aaate.htm

Australian counterpart: *The Australian Rehabilitation and Assistive Technology Association (AAATE)*, http://www.e-bility.com/arata/index.shtml

Special Interest Group, *Human Perspectives of Technology (HPT)*. Focuses on provision of the most appropriate and desired interventions that have the greatest likelihood of success, consumer use, and consumer satisfaction of the user's technology preferences, including:

- how well the technology meets the user's goals, needs, and lifestyle
- the user's perpective on different types of technology
- how to promote effective use of technology

http://www.e-bility.com/arata/sigs—humanperspectives.shtml

Web Sites Focused on Assistive Technology

Tech Connections is a resource for information on assistive technology designed to accommodate people with disabilities in the workplace and in everyday life activities.
http://www.techconnections.org

ABLEDATA is the premier source for information on assistive technology products and resources featuring an online product catalog. It is sponsored by the National Institute on Disability and Rehabilitation Research, U.S. Department of Education.
http://www.abledata.com

AT Network is dedicated to expanding the accessibility of assistive technology (AT) tools, resources, and technology that will help increase independence, improve personal productivity, and enhance quality of life. Information and links to sites are organized by function, group, and topic, and an online journal is published twice a month.
http://www.atnet.org/news/index.html

California State University Northridge (CSUN) Center on Disabilities sponsors an annual International Conference on Technology and Persons with Disabilities. The Proceedings from the conferences are online: http://www.csun.edu/cod/conf/index.htm

Closing The Gap provides practical up-to-date information on assistive technology products, procedures, and best practices. They sponsor an annual conference and publish a newspaper: http://www.closingthegap.com

Web Sites on Key Legislation

Individuals With Disabilities Education Act Amendments (IDEA) of 1997: The IDEA, passed in 1975, changed the lives of children with disabilities by legislating for inclusive education measures, giving all children an equal opportunity to excel academically. This 1997 Act strengthens academic expectations and accountability for the nation's 5.8 million children with disabilities and bridges the gap that has too often existed between what children with disabilities learn and what is required in regular curricula. IDEA is due to be reauthorized in 2003 and the following Web site will have the new legislation: http://www.ed.gov/offices/OSERS/IDEA

Assistive Technology Act of 1998. The full text of this legislation to support programs or grants to states to address the assistive technology needs of individuals with disabilities can be accessed through the National Center for the Dissemination of Disability Research (NCDDR) Web site: http://www.ncddr.org/relativeact/statetech/ata98.html

Section 508 of the Rehabilitation Act of 1973. The public can access resources for understanding and implementing the requirements of Section 508 through this Web site: http://www.section508.gov

No Child Left Behind Act of 2001 (Pub. L. 107-110). Known in short as NCLB, this Act is the Reauthorization of the Elementary and Secondary Education Act of 1965. The full text of NCLB can be accessed at: http://www.ed.gov/legislation/ESEA02. The NCLB Web site is: http://www.nclb.gov.

A general index of U.S. legislation related to education can be accessed at: http://www.ed.gov/legislation/

Disabilityinfo.gov is a comprehensive Federal Web site of disability-related government resources: http://www.disabilityinfo.gov

Web Sites Focused on Topics in This Book

AbleNet offers practical products and creative solutions for teaching children with disabilities.
http://www.ablenetinc.com

CPB/WGBH National Center for Accessible Media is a research and development facility dedicated to the issues of media and information technology for people with disabilities in their homes, schools, workplaces, and communities.
http://www.wgbh.org/ncam

Equal Access to Software and Information (EASI) is the premiere provider of online training on accessible information technology for people with disabilities.
http://www.rit.edu/~easi

HalfthePlanet provides access to services and products, peer support, and disability-related news and information.
http://www.halftheplanet.com

ICan Website is an online disability community with more than 10,000 pages of mostly original content. It continues to expand its influence with news, columns, and services not found elsewhere.
www.iCan.com

InfoUse uses information, technology, and participatory research to improve community equity, access, and outcomes. Planning work in disability, employment, independent living, and health empowers people to make personal and systems changes.
http://www.infouse.com

Job Accommodation Network (JAN) is a free consulting service of the U.S. Department of Labor, Office of Disability Employment Policy, that provides information about job accommodations, the Americans With Disabilities Act (ADA), and the employability of people with disabilities.
http://janweb.icdi.wvu.edu/

National Center for the Dissemination of Disability Research (NCDDR) in the U.S. Department of Education funds a variety of high-level research and knowledge dissemination projects to advance knowledge related to disability issues.
http://www.ncddr.org/index.html

National Council on Disability (NCD) is an independent federal agency making recommendations to the President and Congress on issues affecting Americans with disabilities.
http://www.ncd.gov/

National Information Center for Children and Youth With Disabilities (NICHCY) provides information on disabilities and disability-related issues with a special focus on children and youth (birth to age 22). Anyone can use

their services—families, educators, administrators, journalists, students.
http://www.nichcy.org/

National Rehabilitation Information Center (NARIC) collects and disseminates the results of federally funded research projects. NARIC's literature collection, which also includes commercially published books, journal articles, and audiovisuals, averages around 200 new documents per month. NARIC is funded by the National Institute on Disability and Rehabilitation Research (NIDRR) to serve anyone, professional or layperson, who is interested in disability and rehabilitation, including consumers, family members, health professionals, educators, rehabilitation counselors, students, librarians, administrators, and researchers.
http://www.naric.com

Office of Special Education and Rehabilitative Services (OSERS), U.S. Department of Education provides a wide array of supports to parents and individuals, school districts, and states in three main areas: special education, vocational rehabilitation, and research.
http://www.ed.gov/offices/OSERS/index.html

The Trace Research & Development Center is a part of the College of Engineering, University of Wisconsin–Madison. Founded in 1971, Trace has been a pioneer in the field of technology and disability. The Trace Center is currently working on ways to make standard information technologies and telecommunications systems more accessible and usable by people with disabilities. This work is primarily funded by the National Institute on Disability and Rehabilitation Research (NIDRR) (U.S. Department of Education).
http://trace.wisc.edu

U.S. Library of Congress, National Library Service for the Blind and Physically Handicapped (NLS): Through a national network of cooperating libraries, NLS administers a free library program of braille and audio materials circulated to eligible borrowers throughout the United States.
http://www.loc.gov/nls/

Untangling the Web is a compendium of hundreds of disability-related Web sites in 19 different categories, including "Visual Disability," "Hearing Disability," "Information Technology," and "Assistive Technology."
http://www.icdi.wvu.edu/others.htm

World Wide Web Consortium's Web Accessibility Initiative (WAI) pursues accessibility of the Web through five primary areas of work: technology, guidelines, tools, education and outreach, and research and development:
http://www.w3.org/WAI

Measurement and Assessment

Assistive Technology Outcomes is dedicated to the development, evaluation, and application of valid, reliable, and sensitive outcome measures to enable assistive technology practitioners to determine the cost-effectiveness of their services, to gauge the value of providing assistive technologies, and to select the best technology from an array of choices. http://www.utoronto.ca/atrc/reference/atoutcomes/index.html

Institute for Matching Person & Technology. Homepage for information about the Institute as well as the Matching Person and Technology assessment process and accompanying instruments. http://members.aol.com/IMPT97/MPT.html

Quality Indicators for Assistive Technology (QIAT) is a nationwide grassroots group that includes hundreds of individuals who provide input into the ongoing process of identifying, disseminating, and implementing a set of widely applicable Quality Indicators for Assistive Technology Services in School Settings. http://www.qiat.org

STATEMENT Project, Client Technical Services, Central Remedial Clinic, Ireland. An innovative project devoted to student involvement in the identification of their assistive technology needs and preferences. The outcome is a "Statement of Need" that students take to their college/university or place of employment to secure the most appropriate assistive technology for their participation and success. http://www.crc.ie/services/technology/projects.htm#statement

Student, Environment, Tasks, Tools (SETT) framework is a guideline for gathering data to make effective assistive technology decisions. http://www2.edc.org/NCIP/workshops/sett/SETT_home.html

Wisconsin Assistive Technology Initiative (WATI) is a statewide project funded by the Wisconsin Department of Public Instruction to help all school districts develop or improve their assistive technology services. WATI also works with Birth to 3 programs through a grant from the Wisconsin Birth to 3 Program. http://www.wati.org/

ERIC Databases

ERIC is the Educational Resources Information Center (ERIC), a federally funded national information system that provides, through its 16 subject-specific clearinghouses, associated adjunct clearinghouses, support components, and a variety of services and products on a broad range of education-related issues. The general Web site is http://www.eric.ed.gov

http://www.askeric.org/AskERIC is a personalized Internet-based service providing education information to teachers, librarians, counselors, administrators, parents, and anyone interested in education throughout the United States and the world.

http://www.ericec.org (ERIC Clearinghouse on Disabilities and Gifted Education)

http://www.ericsp.org (ERIC Clearinghouse on Teaching and Teacher Education)

http://www.eriche.org (ERIC Clearinghouse on Higher Education)

http://ericae.net (ERIC Clearinghouse on Assessment and Evaluation)

Web Site Search Engines for Finding Other Resources and International Sites

www.altavista.com

www.google.com

GLOSSARY

Activities of Daily Living (ADL): Various routine activities that are performed day to day, such as putting on clothes, preparing meals, household chores, working at a job, going to school, using transportation to get from one place to another, and so on.

Advocacy/Self-Advocacy: Actively representing and supporting your own or another person's interests in obtaining access to needed services and supports.

Alerting Device: An accommodation for people who are deaf or with hearing loss that emits visual or tactile signals.

American Sign Language (ASL): A manual means of communicating used by people who are deaf. It is a language with its own grammatical structure and is often used to fulfill foreign language requirements.

Americans With Disabilities Act (ADA): A federal civil rights law prohibiting discrimination on the basis of disability in (a) employment; (b) programs, services, and activities of state and local government agencies; and (3) goods, services, facilities, advantages, privileges, and accessibility of places of public accommodation.

Amplification: Increases the loudness of sounds.

Assistive Listening Devices (ALDs): Supplementary electronic devices to help people with hearing loss (and/or learning disabilities) to hear more directly lecturers, ringing phones and door bells, television and radio. Can be worn with or without hearing aids. Includes induction loop, infra-red, and FM amplifications systems.

Assistive Technology Act (ATA) of 1998: A federal law enacted in 1998 providing financial assistance to states. The ATA of 1998 replaces the Technology Related Assistance for Individuals With Disabilities Act. It is scheduled to sunset in 2004.

Assistive Technology Device: Assistive technologies are designed to improve the functional capacity of students with disabilities. Legally, they have been defined as any item, piece of equipment, or product system, whether obtained commercially off the shelf, modified, or customized, that is used to increase, maintain, or improve functional capabilities of individuals with disabilities.

Assistive Technology Service: Any service that directly assists an individual with a disability in the selection, acquisition, or use of an assistive technology device.

Augmentative and Alternative Communication Device (AAC): Electronic, mechanical, and manual devices used by individuals with speech disabilities to communicate.

Braille: A tactile system consisting of raised dots that enables people who are blind to read written materials.

Captioning: The overlaying of text on a TV, movie, or computer screen that puts spoken language into written form. Used by people who are deaf, have learning disabilities, and to achieve multimodal and redundant information presentation. Captions can be open (visible to all viewers) or closed (requiring a special decoding device).

Closed Circuit Television (CCTV): Magnifies images in a text by projecting it onto a monitor.

Descriptive Video Services: Verbal descriptions of actions and movements in movies, plays, and TV programs.

Early Intervention Services: A program of activities and services, including assistive technology, required by the Individuals With Disabilities Education Act (IDEA) for children from birth through age 2. Emphasizes cognitive, communication, motor, and social skills.

Essential Functions of the Job: The term used in the Americans With Disabilities Act (ADA) to mean fundamental tasks that an employee is required to perform. Generally, job descriptions specify the necessary and fundamental duties of the employment position. These tasks are contrasted from marginal duties that are not necessary to the position and are designated in the job description as "other duties assigned."

Free and Appropriate Public Education (FAPE): The requirement under the Individuals With Disabilities Education Act (IDEA) entitling children with disabilities ages 3–21 to an individualized public education at no cost to parents.

High Tech: Primarily refers to computerized or sophisticated electronic devices.

Individualized Education Plan (IEP): A written plan specifying supports, including assistive and educational technologies, determined to be necessary for the student to succeed in an inclusive education setting.

Individualized Transition Plan (ITP): Among other things, a document that identifies assistive and educational technologies determined to be necessary for the student to succeed beyond secondary education and in postsecondary education or employment. In Ireland, it is called a "Statement of Need."

Independent Living Services: A wide variety of services designed to enhance the abilities of individuals with significant disabilities to live independently, either in the community or with their families, and, if appropriate, to secure and maintain employment.

Individual Education Program (IEP): A legal document developed by a team containing a special education student's present levels of educational performance along with goals and objectives, special education and related services, and placement for each school year.

Individualized Plan for Employment: A written document stating the employment outcome of a vocational rehabilitation client and the specific vocational rehabilitation services the Department of Rehabilitation shall provide to the client.

Individuals With Disabilities Education Act (IDEA): Federal law that authorizes special education and related services including assistive technology. Reauthorization is due to occur in 2003.

Instructional Technology: Designed to improve the functional capacity of instructors (i.e., to enhance the instruction of students).

Least Restrictive Environment: The term used in the Individuals With Disabilities Education Act (IDEA) stating the requirement that, to the maximum extent appropriate, children with disabilities, including children in public or private institutions or other care facilities, are educated with nondisabled children; and that special classes, separate schooling, or other removal of children with disabilities from the regular educational environment occurs only when the nature or severity of the disability is such that education in regular classes with the use of supplementary aids and services cannot be achieved satisfactorily. 34 C.F.R. § 300.550(b)(1) & (2)

Low Tech: Typically refers to low cost and nonelectronic devices.

Multimedia: The simultaneous use of sound, text, music, color, graphics, video, and/or animation and their integration.

Office of Special Education Programs (OSEP): A division of the U.S. Department of Education administering the Individuals With Disabilities Education Act. From time to time, the OSEP issues policy letters clarifying the Department's position on various special education topics.

On-Screen Keyboard: A keyboard appears on a computer monitor through special software. The keyboard is accessed with a mouse or with an alternative means of pointing.

Optical Character Recognition (OCR): Translates scanned text into a file that can be edited.

Opticon: An older device that converts visual or text information into raised pins forming an exact replica.

Personal Devices: Under the Americans With Disabilities Act (ADA), equipment, aids, and supplies used by an individual with a disability primarily for meeting personal needs unrelated to the activities and programs covered by the ADA.

Reasonable Accommodations: Under the Americans With Disabilities Act (ADA), reasonable adjustments, modifications, or provision of services and equipment necessary to enable an individual with a disability to enjoy equal opportunities in employment. The term is routinely used to include accommodations needed under other circumstances such as attending public programs and participating in community activities.

Rehabilitation Act: Federal law entitling individuals with disabilities to vocational rehabilitation and independent living services. This law also prohibits discrimination on the basis of disability by various entities including the federal government, recipients of federal financial assistance, and federal contractors. Section 504 mandates the provision of a free appropriate public education (FAPE) to students with disabilities.

Related Services: A range of supports and services that are necessary for a child with a disability to receive a free and appropriate public education. Related services include assistive technology devices and services.

Screen Magnification Program: A computer program that enlarges the size of text and graphic information displayed on a monitor.

Screen Reader: Software that reads computer text and "speaks" it through voice output.

Self-Advocacy: The awareness, motivation, and ability of an individual to represent and communicate his or her own interests, to exercise personal choice, and to exert control over his or her environment.

Self-Determination: Refers to the freedom to make choices, decisions, and mistakes; to express one's opinions and preferences. Support is based on the skills, experiences, and goals of the person being supported and is determined individually and in partnership with people providing support.

Special Education: A program of services and activities required by the Individuals With Disabilities Education Act to provide a free and appropriate public education to children with disabilities.

Speech Synthesis/Speech Synthesizer: Produces voice output from a computer.

Statement of Need: Used in the Republic of Ireland to identify assistive and educational technologies determined to be necessary for the student to succeed beyond secondary education and in postsecondary education or employment (see Individualized Transition Plan [ITP]).

Sticky Keys: Allows people with limited hand or finger control to type multiple keystrokes with one finger.

Supplemental Aid or Service: A range of services and devices that are necessary for a child to be educated in the least restrictive environment.

Supplemental Security Income (SSI): A need-based program through the Social Security Administration for low-income people with disabilities or people over the age of 65 that provides a cash grant to meet basic food, clothing, and shelter needs.

Tech Act: Technology Related Assistance for Individuals With Disabilities Act of 1988. A federal law enacted in 1988 and expired in 1998 that provided grants to states for the purpose of carrying out a coordinated program for systemic change to promote access to assistive technology. Reauthorized in 1998 as the Assistive Technology Act.

Telecommunications Device for the Deaf (TDD), also known as Text Telephone (TT): Allows people who are deaf to communicate over the telephone by typing and reading text messages. A TTD or TT device consists of a phone coupler, keyboard, text display, and a printer.

Vocational Rehabilitation Service: A range of vocational services including training, counseling, job placement, and assistive technology provided by the Department of Rehabilitation for the purpose of maximizing the employability of individuals with disabilities.

Word Prediction: A program that displays probable words after the user inputs a couple of letters. The user selects the desired word or continues to type.

REFERENCES

Abouserie, R., Moss, D., & Barasi, S. (1992). Cognitive style, gender, attitude toward computer-assisted learning and academic achievement. *Educational Studies, 18,* 151–160.

Abrahamsen, A. A., Romski, M. A., & Sevcik, R. A. (1989). Change and the causes of change. *American Journal of Mental Retardation, 93,* 506–520.

Aguayo, M. O., & Coady, N. E. (2001). The experience of deafened adults: Implications for rehabilitation services. *Health and Social Work, 26,* 269–276.

Albaugh, P. R., & Fayne, H. (1996). The ET PA for predicting technology success with learning disabled students: Lessons from a multimedia study. *Technology and Disability, 5,* 313–318.

Albaugh, P. R., Piazza, L., & Scholsser, K. (1997). Using a CD-ROM encyclopedia: Interaction of teachers, middle school students, library media specialists, and the technology. *Research in Middle Level Education Quarterly, 20*(3), 43–55.

American Foundation for the Blind. (2002a). *Education: An overview.* Retrieved March 11, 2002, from http://www.afb.org/info_document_view.asp?document id=1372

American Foundation for the Blind. (2002b, April). *What is braille?* New York: Author. Retrieved April 28, 2003, from http://www.afb.org/braillebug/braille_ technology.asp

Americans With Disabilities Act of 1990, Pub. L. No. 101-336.

Andrich, R. (2002). The SCAI instrument: Measuring costs of individual assistive technology programmes. *Technology and Disability, 14,* 95–99.

Arkow, P. (1989). *Pet therapy: A study and resource guide for the use of companion animals in selected therapies* (5th ed.). Colorado Springs: The Human Society of the Pikes Peak Region.

Barker, B. O., & Burnett, K. R. (1991, October). *Distance learning in Hawaii: Establishment and evaluation of a rural teacher inservice training program.* Paper presented at the annual conference of the National Rural Education Association, Jackson, MS. (ERIC Document Reproduction Service No. ED 338 473)

Barker, R. G., Wright, B. A., Meyerson, L., & Gonick, M. R. (1953). *Adjustment to physical handicap and illness: Survey of the social psychology of physique and disability* (2nd ed.). New York: Social Research Council.

Barry, E. K., & Barry, S. J. (2002). Personality type and perceived hearing aid benefit revisited. *Hearing Journal, 55*(8), 44–45.

Barry, E. K., & McCarthy, P. (2001). The relationship between personality type and perceived hearing aid benefit. *Hearing Journal, 54*(9), 41–46.

Behrmann, M. M. & Lahm, E.A. (1984). Babies and robots: Technology to assist learning of young multiple disabled children. *Rehabilitation Literature, 45,* 194–201.

Behrmann, M. M. & Lahm, E. A. (1994). Computer applications in early childhood special education. In J. L. Wright & D. D. Shade (Eds.), *Young Children: Active Learners in a Technological Age* (105–120). Washington, DC: NAEYC.

Beigel, A. R. (2000). Assistive technology assessment: More than the device. *Intervention in School and Clinic, 35,* 237–243.

Bishop, M. J., & Cates, W. M. (2001). Theoretical foundations for sound's use in multimedia instruction to enhance learning. *Educational Technology Research and Development, 49*(3), 5–22.

Blackhurst, A. E., & Edyburn, D. L. (2000). A brief history of special education technology. *Special Education Technology Practice, 2*(1), 21–35.

Blasch, B. B., Wiener, W. R., & Welsh, R. L. (Eds.). (1997). *Foundations of orientation and mobility* (2nd ed.). New York: American Foundation for the Blind.

Bondi-Wolcott, J., & Scherer, M. (1988). The Explore Your Future program for hearing-impaired students: Some deaf students have it easy in their transition from high school to college. *Journal of Rehabilitation, 54,* 15–17.

Bowe, F. (1994, July). *Technologies and systems for instructional delivery.* Presented at the National Symposium on Educational Applications of Technology for Persons With Sensory Disabilities, Rochester, NY.

Bowe, F. G. (2000). *Universal design in education.* Westport, CT: Bergin & Garvey.

Bowser, G., & Reed, P. (1995). Education tech points for assistive technology planning. *Journal of Special Education Technology, 12,* 325–338.

Bravin, P. (1994, July). *Learner characteristics and preferences.* Presented at the National Symposium on Educational Applications of Technology for Persons With Sensory Disabilities, Rochester, NY.

Brewster, S. (2002). Visualization tools for blind people using multiple modalities. *Disability and Rehabilitation, 24,* 613–621.

Brinker, R. & Lewis, M. (1982). Making the world work with microcomputers: A learning prosthesis. *Exceptional Children, 49,* 163–70.

Brown, D. L., & Merbitz, C. (1995). Comparison of technology match between two types of functional electrical stimulation hand grasp systems. In *Proceedings of the RESNA '95 annual conference* (pp. 381–383). Arlington, VA: RESNA Press.

Brown, D. R. (1996). Personal implications of functional electrical stimulation standing for older adolescents with spinal cord injuries. *Technology and Disability, 5,* 295–311.

Buckleitner, W. W., Orr, A. C., & Wolock, E. L. (1998). *Young kids and computers: A parent's survival guide.* Flemington, NJ: Children's Software Revue.

Cagle, S. J., & Cagle, K. M. (1991). *Ga and Sk etiquette: Guidelines for telecommunications in the deaf community.* Bowling Green, OH: Bowling Green Press.

Case, D., & Lahm, E. A. (2003, March 19). The essential elements of an assistive technology assessment and assessment report. *2003 Proceedings of the Technology and Persons With Disabilities Conference.* Retrieved April 28, 2003 from http://www.csun.edu/cod/conf/2003/proceedings/28.htm

Castellano, C., & Kosman, D. (1997). *The bridge to braille: Reading and school success for the young blind child*. Baltimore: National Federation of the Blind.

Chong, C. (1997, February). Performing the average job: A question of technology. *The Braille Monitor*, 122–123.

Connell, B. R., Jones, M., Mace, R., Mueller, J., Mullick, A., Ostroff, E., et al. (1997). *The principles of universal design*. Raleigh: North Carolina State University, Center for Universal Design. Retrieved April 28, 2003, from http://www.design.ncsu.edu/cud/univ_design/princ_overview.htm

Cook, A. M., & Hussey, S. M. (2002). *Assistive technologies: Principles and practice* (2nd ed.). St. Louis, MO: Mosby.

Coombs, N. (1998). Bridging the disability gap with distance learning. *Technology and Disability*, 8, 149–152.

Council for Higher Education Accreditation. (2002). Accreditation and assuring quality in distance learning. *CHEA Monograph Series*, 1(Whole issue).

Craddock, G. (2002). Partnership and assistive technology in Ireland. In M. J. Scherer (Ed.), *Assistive technology: Matching device and consumer for successful rehabilitation* (pp. 253–266). Washington, DC: American Psychological Association.

Craddock, G., & McCormack, L. (2002). Delivering an AT service: A client-focused, social and participatory service delivery model in assistive technology in Ireland. *Disability and Rehabilitation*, 24, 160–170.

Craddock, G., & Scherer, M. J. (2002). Assessing individual needs for assistive technology. In C. L. Sax & C. A. Thoma (Eds.), *Transition assessment: Wise practices for quality lives* (pp. 87–101). Baltimore: Brookes Publishing.

Craig, A., Michaels, C. A., Prezant, F. P., & Morabito, S. M. (2002). Assistive and instructional technology for college students with disabilities: A national snapshot of postsecondary service providers. *Journal of Special Education Technology*, 17(1). Retrieved January 10, 2003, from http://jset.unlv.edu/17.1/michaels/first.html

Cravener, P. A. (1999). Faculty experiences with providing online courses. Thorns among the roses. *Computers in Nursing*, 17, 42–47.

Cunningham, C., & Coombs, N. (1997). *Information access and adaptive technology*. Phoenix, AZ: Oryx Press.

Cushman, L. A., & Scherer, M. J. (1996). Measuring the relationship of assistive technology use, functional status over time, and consumer–therapist perceptions of ATs. *Assistive Technology*, 8, 103–109.

Davis, H. (1997). *Hearing and deafness: A guide for laymen*. New York: Murray Hill Books.

de Graaf, R., & Bijl, R. (1998). Geestelijke gezondheid van doven. Psychische problematiek en zorggebruik van dove en ernstig slechthorende volwassenen [Psychological well-being of deaf and severe hard-of-hearing adults]. Utrecht, the Netherlands: Trimbos-instituut.

de Jonge, D., Rodger, S., & Fitzgibbon, H. (2001). Putting technology to work: Users' perspective on integrating assistive technology into the workplace. *Work, 16*, 77–89.

Demers, L., Weiss-Lambrou, R., & Ska, B. (1996). Development of the Quebec User Evaluation of Satisfaction With Assistive Technology (QUEST). *Assistive Technology, 8*, 3–13.

Demers, L., Weiss-Lambrou, R., & Ska, B. (2002). The Quebec User Evaluation of Satisfaction With Assistive Technology (QUEST 2.0): An overview and recent progress. *Technology & Disability, 14*, 101–105.

Denham, A., Bennett, D. E., Edyburn, D. L., Lahm, E. A., & Kleinert, H. L. (2001). Implementing technology to demonstrate higher levels of learning. In H. L. Kleinert & J. F. Kearns (Eds.), *Alternative assessment: Measuring outcomes and supports for students with disabilities* (pp. 148–154). Baltimore: Brookes Publishing.

Dew, D. W., & Alan, G. M. (Eds.). (2002). *Distance education: Opportunities and issues for public vocational rehabilitation programs* (28th Institute on Rehabilitation Issues). Washington, DC: George Washington University.

Dugan, M. B. (1997). *Keys to living with hearing loss (Barron's keys to retirement planning)*. Hauppauge, NY: Barron's Educational Series.

Easterbrooks, S. (1999). Improving practices for students with hearing impairments. *Exceptional Children, 65*, 537–554.

Edyburn, D. L. (2000a). Assistive technology and mild disabilities. *Focus on Exceptional Children, 32*(9), 1–24.

Edyburn, D. L. (2000b). 1999 in review: A synthesis of the special education technology literature. *Journal of Special Education Technology, 15*(1), 7–18. Retrieved April 28, 2003, from http://jset.unlv.edu/15.1/edyburn/first.html

Edyburn, D. L. (2001). Critical issues in special education technology research: What do we know? What do we need to know? In M. Mastropieri & T. Scruggs (Eds.), *Advances in learning and behavioral disabilities* (Vol. 15, pp. 95–118). New York: JAI Press.

Edyburn, D. L. (2002). 2001 in review: A synthesis of the special education technology literature. *JSET E Journal, 17*(2). Retrieved April 28, 2003, from http://jset.unlv.edu/17.2T/tedyburn/first.html

Edyburn, D. L., & Gardner, J. E. (1999). Integrating technology into special education teacher preparation programs: Creating shared visions. *Journal of Special Education Technology, 14*(2), 3–20.

Edyburn, D. L., Higgins, K., & Boone, R. (in press). *Handbook of special education technology research and practice*. Whitefish Bay, WI: Knowledge by Design, Inc.

Eggen, P., & Kauchak, D. (2001). *Educational psychology: Windows on classrooms* (5th ed.). Upper Saddle River, NJ: Prentice Hall.

Eldredge, G. M., McNamara, S., Stensrud, R., Gilbride, D., Hendren, G., Siegfried, T., & McFarlane, F. (1999). Distance education: A look at five programs. *Rehabilitation Education, 13*, 231–248.

Equal Access to Software and Information. (2002). *All about EASI: EASI mission.* Retrieved November 20, 2002, from http://www.rit.edu/~easi/

ERIC Clearinghouse on Disabilities and Gifted Education. (2002). *What is universal design for learning?* Arlington, VA: Author. Retrieved November 22, 2002, from http://ericec.org/digests/e586.html

Erikson, E. (1963). *Childhood and society* (2nd ed.). New York: Norton.

Federici, S., Scherer, M. J., Micangeli, A., Lombardo, C., & Belardinelli, M. (in press). A cross-cultural analysis of relationships between disability self-evaluation and individual predisposition to use assistive technology. In *Proceedings of the Association for the Advancement of Assistive Technology in Europe, Denmark.*

Fisher, D., Frey, N., & Sax, C. (1999). *Inclusive elementary schools: Recipes for success.* Colorado Springs, CO: PEAK Parent Center.

Fisher, D., Sax, C., & Pumpian, I. (1999). *Inclusive high schools: Learning from contemporary classrooms.* Baltimore: Brookes Publishing.

Flemming, J. E., & Flemming, J. P. (1995). RESNA 1995 Proceedings: Multimedia for Assistive training and recruitment: Two CD-ROM Training Programs (Available http://www.resna.org). Retrieved April 28, 2003

Flippo, K. F., Inge, K. J., & Barcus, J. M. (Eds.). (1997). *Assistive technology: A resource for school, work, and community.* Baltimore: Brookes Publishing.

Fradd, S. H., Kramer, L. R., Marquez-Chisolm, I., Morsink, C. V., Algozzine, K., & Yarbrough, J. (1986). Teacher competencies in the mainstreaming process. *Journal of Classroom Interaction, 22*(1), 31–40.

Francis, H. W., Koch, M. E., Wyatt, J. R., & Niparko, J. K. (1999). Trends in educational placement and cost–benefit considerations in children with cochlear implants. *Archives of Otolaryngology and Head and Neck Surgery, 125,* 499–505.

Gardner, H. (1983). *Frames of mind: The theory of multiple intelligences.* New York: Basic Books.

Gelderblom, G. J., & de Witte, L. (2002). The assessment of assistive technology outcomes, effects and costs. *Technology & Disability, 14,* 91–94.

Gilden, D. (2002). Using MS Office features as low vision accessibility tools. In K. Miesenberger, J. Klaus, & W. Zagler (Eds.), *Computer helping people with special needs: Proceedings of the Eighth International Conference of the ICCHP* (pp. 469–470). Heidelberg, Germany: Springer.

Goldberg, L. (2000). *From A(nalog) to D(igital): Access to new and emerging media. 2000 Conference Proceedings: Center on Disabilities Technology and Persons with Disabilities Conference 2000.* Retrieved April 28, 2003, from http://www.csun.edu/cod/conf/2000/proceedings/0085Goldberg.htm

Golden, D. (1998). *Assistive technology in special education: Policy and practice.* Albuquerque, NM: Council of Administrators of Special Education/Technology and Media Division of the Council for Exceptional Children.

Goodman, G., Tiene, D., & Luft, P. (2002). Adoption of assistive technology for computer access among college students with disabilities. *Disability and Rehabilitation, 24,* 80–92.

Gregory, G. H., & Chapman, C. (2001). *Differentiated instructional strategies: One size doesn't fit all.* Thousand Oaks, CA: Corwin Press.

Hansell, N. (1974). *The person-in-distress: On the biosocial mechanisms of adaptation.* New York: Behavioral Sciences Press.

Hasselbring, T. S., & Glaser, C. H. (2000/Fall–Winter). Use of computer technology to help students with special needs. *Future Child, 10,* 102–122.

HEATH Resource Center. (1999). *College freshmen with disabilities: A biennial statistical profile.* Washington, DC: American Council on Education.

Heerkens, W. D., Briggs, J., & Weider, T. G. (1997). Using peer mentors to facilitate the match of person & technology. In S. Sprigle (Ed.), *Proceedings of the 1997 RESNA annual conference* (pp. 484–486). Arlington, VA: RESNA Press.

Heine, C., & Browning, C. J. (2002). Communication and psychosocial consequences of sensory loss in older adults: Overview and rehabilitation directions. *Disability and Rehabilitation, 24,* 763–773.

Hetu, R., Jones, L., & Getty, L. (1993). The impact of acquired hearing impairment on intimate relationships: Implications for rehabilitation. *Audiology, 32,* 363–381.

Holloway, S. (2001). The experience of higher education from the perspective of disabled students. *Disability and Society, 16,* 597–615.

Hooper, S., & Hannafin, M. J. (1991). Psychological perspectives on emerging instructional technologies: A critical analysis. *Educational Psychologist, 26*(1), 69–95.

Hourcade, J. J., Parette, H. P., & Huer, M. B. (1997). Family and cultural alert! Considerations in assistive technology assessment. *Teaching Exceptional Children, 30,* 40–44.

Hutinger, P. (1987). Computer-based learning for young children. In J. L. Roopnarine & J. E. Johnson (Eds.), *Approaches to early childhood education* (pp. 213–234). Columbus, OH: Charles E. Merrill.

Hutinger, P., Johanson, J., & Stoneburner, R. (1996). Assistive technology applications in educational programs of children with multiple disabilities: A case study report on the state of the practice. *Journal of Special Education Technology, 13,* 16–35.

Individuals With Disabilities Education Act, Amendments of 1997, Pub. L. No. 105-17, § 602, U.S.C. 1401.

Internet TV for Assistive Technology. (2003). *Corda's software enhance career opportunities for people with disabilities.* Retrieved April 28, 2003, from http://www.at508.com/articles/jw_010.asp

Jary, D., & Jary, J. (1995). *Collins dictionary of sociology.* New York: Harper Collins.

Jensema, C., & Rovins, M. (1997). Instant reading incentive: Understanding TV captions. In *Perspectives in education and deafness* (No. 16/1). Retrieved November 15, 2002, from http://clerccenter.gallaudet.edu/products/perspectives/sep-oct97/instant.html

Johnstone, S. M. (1991). Research on telecommunicated learning: Past, present, and future. *Annals of the American Academy of Political and Social Science, 514*, 49–57.

Judge, S. L., & Parette, H. P. (1998). *Assistive technology for young children with disabilities: A guide to family-centered services.* Cambridge, MA: Brookline Books.

Jutai, J., & Day, H. (2002). Psychosocial Impact of Assistive Devices Scale (PIADS). *Technology & Disability, 14*, 107–111.

Kanigel, R. (1986). Computers will help—someday. *Johns Hopkins Magazine, 38*(2), 38–44.

Kanigel, R. (1997). *The one best way: Frederick Winslow Taylor and the enigma of efficiency* (Sloan Technology Series). New York: Viking Press.

Katsiyannis, A., & Conderman, G. (1994). Section 504 policies and procedures: An established necessity. *NASSP Bulletin, 78*, 6–10.

Kay, R. (1992). An analysis of methods used to examine gender differences in computer-related behavior. *Journal of Educational Computing Research, 8*, 277–290.

Kearsley, G. (2000). *Online education: Learning and teaching in cyberspace.* Belmont, CA: Wadsworth.

Keefe, B. (1994). As Maine goes . . . American Sign Language at a distance. *Technology & Disability, 3*, 72–76.

Keefe, B., Scherer, M. J., & McKee, B. G. (1996). MainePOINT: Outcomes of teaching American Sign Language via distance learning. *Technology & Disability, 5*, 319–326.

Kelker, K. A., Holt, R., & Sullivan, J. (2000). *Family guide to assistive technology.* Cambridge, MA: Brookline Books.

Keller, B. K., Morton, J. L., Thomas, V. S., & Potter, J. F. (1999). The effect of visual and hearing impairments on functional status. *Journal of the American Geriatrics Society, 47*, 1319–1325.

Kemp, C. E., Hourcade, J. J., & Parette, H. P. (2000). Assistive technology funding resources for school-aged students with disabilities. *Journal of Special Education Technology, 15*(4), 15–24.

Kilgore, K. L., Scherer, M., Bobblitt, R., Dettloff, J., Dombrowski, D. M., Godbold, N., et al. (2001). Neuroprosthesis consumers' forum: Consumer priorities for research directions. *Journal of Rehabilitation Research and Development, 38*, 655–660.

Knutson, J. F., & Lansing, C. R. (1990). The relationship between communication problems and psychological difficulties in persons with profound acquired hearing loss. *Journal of Hearing and Speech Disorders. 55*, 656–674.

Koskinen, P. S., Gambrell, L. B., & Neuman, S. B. (1993). Captioned video and vocabulary learning: An innovative practice in literacy instruction. *The Reading Teacher, 47*(1), 36–43.

Kraut, R., Patterson, M., Lundmark, V., Kiesler, S., Mukopadhyay, T., & Scherlis, W. (1998). Internet paradox: A social technology that reduces social involvement and psychological well-being? *American Psychologist, 53,* 1017–1031.

Krendl, K. A., & Broihier, M. (1992). Student responses to computers: A longitudinal study. *Journal of Educational Computing Research, 8,* 215–227.

Kristina, M. (1995). *Educational audiology across the lifespan: Serving all learners with hearing impairment.* Baltimore: Paul H. Brookes.

Krueger, M. W., & Gilden, D. (2002). Going places with "KnowWare": Virtual reality maps for blind people. In K. Miesenberger, J. Klaus, & W. Zagler (Eds.), *Computer helping people with special needs: Proceedings of the Eighth International Conference of the ICCHP* (pp. 565–567). Heidelberg, Germany: Springer.

Lahm, E. A., & Sizemore, L. (2002). Factors that influence assistive technology decision-making. *Journal of Special Education Technology, 17,* 15–25.

Lang, H. G. (1994). *Silence of the spheres: The deaf experience in the history of science.* Westport, CT: Bergin & Garvey.

Lang, H. G. (1996). What makes effective teaching? *NTID Research News, 1*(1), 1–3.

LaPlante, M. P., (1995, September). *Disability demographics: Technology and people with disabilities* (Draft report prepared for U.S. Congress Office of Technology Assessment). Retrieved April 28, 2003, from http://www.empowermentzone. com/tech_dsb.txt

LaPlante, M. P., & Carlson, D. (1996). *The Disability Statistics Report 7: Disability in the United States: Prevalence and Causes, 1992.* Washington, DC: National Institute on Disability and Rehabilitation Research. Retrieved April 28, 2003, from http://dsc.ucsf.edu/UCSF/pub.taf?UserReference=7D1869AE4027EA32 BBB5731E&_function=search&recid=65&grow=1

Leung, P., Owens, J., Lamb, G., Smith, K., Shaw, J., & Hauff, R. (1999, November). *Assistive technology meeting the technology needs of students with disabilities in post-secondary education.* Melbourne, Australia: Deakin University, Institute of Disability Studies.

Leventhal, J. D. (1996). Assistive devices for people who are blind or have a visual impairment. In J. Galvin & M. Scherer (Eds.), *Evaluating, selecting and using appropriate assistive technology* (pp. 125–143). Gaithersburg, MD: Aspen.

Lockwood, R. (1983). The influence of animals on social perception. In A. H. Katcher & A. M. Beck (Eds.), *New perspectives on our lives with companion animals* (pp. 64–71). Philadelphia: University of Pennsylvania.

Maki, D. R., & Riggar, T. F. (Eds.). (1997). *Rehabilitation counseling: Profession and practice.* New York: Springer.

Maki, W. S., & Maki, R. H. (2002). Multimedia comprehension skill predicts differential outcomes of web-based and lecture courses. *Journal of Experimental Psychology: Applied, 8,* 85–98.

Margolis, E. (Ed.). (2001). *The hidden curriculum in higher education.* New York: Routledge.

Marullo, S. (2002, Winter). Innovations expand alternatives to computer access and communication. *RESNA News, 3,* 6.

Maslow, A. (1954). *Motivation and personality.* New York: Harper.

McFadyen, G. M. (1996). Aids for hearing impairment and deafness. In J. Galvin & M. J. Scherer (Eds.), *Evaluating, selecting and using appropriate assistive technology* (pp. 144–161). Gaithersburg, MD: Aspen.

McKee, B. G., & Scherer, M. J. (1987). Winston Smith – there is yet hope: Review of high technology and human freedom. Invited book review for *The Review of Education, 13,* 11–16.

McKee, B. G., & Scherer, M. J. (1994, April). *A formative evaluation of two Gallaudet University/Rochester Institute of Technology courses offered by teleconferencing.* Paper presented at the annual meeting of the American Educational Research Association, New Orleans, LA. (ERIC Document Reproduction No. ED 377 213)

Mencher, G. T., Gerber, S. E., & McCombe, A. (1997). *Audiology and auditory dysfunction.* Boston: Allyn & Bacon.

Messent, P. (1984). Correlates and effects of pet ownership. In R. K. Anderson, B. L. Hart, & L. A. Hart (Eds.), *The Pet Connection: Its influence on our health and quality of life* (pp. 331–341). Minneapolis: CENSHARE, University of Minnesota.

Morris, N., Buck-Rolland, C., & Gagne, M. (2002). From bricks to bytes: Faculty and student perspectives of online graduate nursing courses. *Computers, Informatics, Nursing, 20,* 108–114.

Mulrow, C. D., Aguilar, C., Endicott, J. E., Tuley, M. R., Velez, R., Charlip, W. S., et al. (1990). Quality of life changes and hearing impairment. *Annals of Internal Medicine, 113,* 188–194.

Munk, D. (2003). *Solving the grading puzzle for students with disabilities.* Whitefish Bay, WI: Knowledge by Design, Inc.

Myers, D. G. (2000). *A quiet world: Living with hearing loss.* New Haven, CT: Yale University Press.

National Center for Education Statistics. (1997). *Digest of education statistics.* Washington, DC: U.S. Department of Education.

National Center for Education Statistics. (1999). *An institutional perspective on students with disabilities in postsecondary education.* Washington, DC: U.S. Department of Education, Office of Educational Research and Improvement.

National Council on Disability. (2000). *Transition and post-school outcomes for youth with disabilities: Closing the gaps to post-secondary education and employment.* Retrieved April 28, 2003, from http://www.ncd.gov/newsroom/publications/transition_11-1-00.html

National Council on Disability. (2002, August 13). *People with disabilities need assistive technology.* Retrieved April 28, 2003, from http://www.ncd.gov/newsroom/news/f02–380.html

National Federation of the Blind. (2002, April). *What is braille and what does it mean to the blind?* Baltimore, MD: Author. Retrieved April 28, 2003, from http://www.nfb.org/books/books1/ifblnd03.htm

National Health Interview Survey. (1995). *Current estimates from the National Health Interview Survey: Vital and health statistics* (Series 10, No. 199). Hyattsville, MD: National Center for Health Statistics.

National Information Center for Children and Youth With Disabilities. (2001a). *General information about deafness and hearing loss: Fact Sheet No. 3.* Washington, DC: Author.

National Information Center for Children and Youth With Disabilities. (2001b). *General information about visual impairments: Fact Sheet No. 13.* Washington, DC: Author.

Noreau, L., Fougeyrollas, P., & Vincent, C. (2002). The LIFE-H: Assessment of the quality of social participation. *Technology & Disability, 14,* 113–118.

Ohler, J. (1991). Why distance education? *Annals of the American Academy of Political and Social Science, 514,* 22–34.

Ormrod, J. E. (2000). *Educational psychology: Developing learners* (3rd ed.). Upper Saddle River, NJ: Prentice-Hall.

Overbrook School for the Blind. (2001). *Technology for all: Assistive technology in the classroom.* Philadelphia: Towers Press.

Palloff, R. M., & Pratt, K. (2001). *Lessons from the cyberspace classroom: The realities of online teaching* (Jossey-Bass Higher and Adult Education Series). San Francisco: Jossey-Bass.

Pape, T. L-B., Kim, J., & Weiner, B. (2002). The shaping of individual meanings assigned to assistive technology: A review of personal factors. *Disability and Rehabilitation, 24,* 5–20.

Pardeck, J. T. (1996, June). Advocacy and parents of special needs children. *Early Child Development and Care, 120,* 45–53.

Parette, H. P. (1991). Use of technological assistance and families of young children with disabilities. *Psychological Reports, 68*(3, Pt. 1), 773–774.

Parette, H. P. (1998). Cultural issues and family-centered assistive technology decision-making. In S. L. Judge & H. P. Parette (Eds.), *Assistive technology for young children with disabilities: A guide to providing family-centered services* (pp. 184–210). Cambridge, MA: Brookline.

Parette, H.P., & Van Biervliet, A. (1991). Rehabilitation technology issues for infants and young children with disabilities: A preliminary examination. *Journal of Rehabilitation, 57,* 27–36.

Persson, J., Andrich, R., VanBeekum, T., Brodin, H., Lorentsen, O., Wessels, R., & deWitte, L. (2002). Preference based assessment of the quality of life of disabled persons. *Technology & Disability, 14,* 119–124.

Pillemer, K., & Suitor, J. J. (1996). It takes one to help one: Effects of status similarity on well-being. *Journal of Gerontology, 51B,* S250–S257.

Pollard, R. Q. (1996). Professional psychology and deaf people: The emergence of a discipline. *American Psychologist, 51,* 389–396.

President's Commission on Excellence in Special Education. (2002, July). A new era: Revitalizing special education for children and their families. Retrieved April 28, 2003, from http://www.ed.gov/inits/commissionsboards/whspecial education/reports.html

QIAT Consortium. (2003) *Quality indicators for assistive technology.* Hosted by the Department of Special Education and Rehabilitation Counseling, University of Kentucky (Lexington). Retrieved April 28, 2003 from http://www.qiat.org

Ramsey, C. L. (1997). *Deaf children in public schools: Placement, context, and consequences.* Washington, DC: Gallaudet University Press.

Reed, P., & Walser, P. (2000). *Assistive Technology Checklist.* Wisconsin Assistive Technology Initiative. Retrieved April 28, 2003, from http://www.wati.org/pdf/atcheck1.pdf

Rehabilitation Act of 1973, 29 U.S.C. § 794.

Rochester Hearing and Speech Center. (2001). *Hear better now: Participants handbook.* Rochester, NY: Author.

Rochester Institute of Technology. (2002, Spring). Presidential award a first for RIT. *RIT: The University Magazine.* Retrieved December 12, 2002, from http://www.rit.edu/~umagwww/spring2002/presAward.html

Roulstone, A. (1998). *Enabling technology: Disabled people, work and new technology.* Buckingham, England: Open University Press.

Rubin, D. C., Rahhal, T. E., & Poon, L. W. (1998). Things learned in early adulthood are remembered best. *Memory & Cognition, 26,* 3–19.

Sachs-Ericsson, N., Hansen, N., & Fitzgerald, S. (2002). Benefits of assistance dogs: A review. *Rehabilitation Psychology, 47,* 251–277.

Sacks, S. Z., Wolfe, K. E., & Tierney, D. (1998). Lifestyles of students with visual impairments: Preliminary studies of social networks. *Exceptional Children, 64,* 463–478.

Sax, C. (2002a). Assistive technology education: An online model for rehabilitation professionals. *Disability and Rehabilitation, 24*(1–3), 144–151.

Sax, C. (2002b). Assistive technology online instruction: Expanding the dimensions of learning communities. In M. J. Scherer (Ed.), *Assistive technology: Matching device and consumer for successful rehabilitation* (pp. 213–227). Washington, DC: American Psychological Association.

Sax, C., & Duke, S. (2002). Integration of AT education by rehabilitation professionals. In R. Simpson (Ed.), *Proceedings of the RESNA 25th International Conference on Technology and Disability: Research, design, practice, and policy* (pp. 189–191). Arlington, VA: RESNA Press.

Sax, C. L., & Thoma, C. A. (2002). *Transition assessment: Wise practices for quality lives.* Baltimore: Paul H. Brookes.

Scheetz, N. A. (2001). *Orientation to deafness* (2nd ed.). Boston: Allyn & Bacon.

Scherer, M. J. (1982). Sandpaper-like tickles. *Advocacy News, 2*(3), 4.

Scherer, M. J. (1990a). *Creating quality instructional materials* (NTID Working Paper). Rochester, NY: National Technical Institute for the Deaf.

Scherer, M. J. (1990b). *Interviews with RIT students with disabilities: Summary of findings and needs* (Working paper). Rochester, NY: Rochester Institute of Technology, Office of Special Services.

Scherer, M. J. (1991). Technology and mainstreamed students with physical disabilities: Perspectives toward the end of the 20th century. In M. Foster (Ed.), *Readings on Equal Education, 11,* (pp. 95–112). New York, AMS Press.

Scherer, M. J. (1992a). *The Assistive Technology Device Predisposition Assessment (ATD PA) consumer form.* Rochester, NY: Author.

Scherer, M. J. (1992b, August). *Psychosocial factors associated with the use of technological assistance.* Paper presented at the 100th Annual Convention of the American Psychological Association, Washington, DC. (ERIC Document Reproduction Service No. ED 350 795)

Scherer, M. J. (1994a). *Learning strategies: A program of individualized instruction to improve study skills* (Working paper). Rochester, NY: National Technical Institute for the Deaf.

Scherer, M. J. (1994b). [Recommendations to the Department of Education that emerged from the national symposium on educational applications of technology for persons with sensory disabilities]. *Smithsonian 1995 ComputerWorld Awards.* Retrieved April 28, 2003, from http://www.cwheroes.org/his_4a_detail. asp?id=2094

Scherer, M. J. (1995a, March). *Assessing the outcomes of teaching to students' learning styles.* Invited presentation for the Design for Excellence Conference, San Diego, CA.

Scherer, M. J. (1995b, March). *Fitting technology to your students' learning styles.* Invited presentation for the Design for Excellence Conference, San Diego, CA.

Scherer, M. J. (1995c, March). *How educational technology enhances learning for the deaf.* Invited presentation for Project Needs, San Diego Public Schools, San Diego, CA.

Scherer, M. J. (1995d). A model of rehabilitation assessment. In L. Cushman & M. Scherer (Eds.), *Psychological assessment in medical rehabilitation* (pp. 3–23). Washington, DC: American Psychological Association.

Scherer, M. J. (1996a). Influences on the use of assistive technology. In *Primary care for persons with disabilities: Access to assistive technology: Guidelines for the use of assistive technology: Evaluation, referral, prescription* (p. 23). Chicago: American Medical Association.

Scherer, M. J. (1996b). Outcomes of assistive technology use on quality of life. *Disability and Rehabilitation, 18,* 439–448.

Scherer, M. J. (1998). *The Matching Person and Technology (MPT) model manual and accompanying assessment instruments* (3rd ed.). Webster, NY: Institute for Matching Person & Technology, Inc.

Scherer, M. J. (1999). Matching students and teachers with the most appropriate instructional and educational technologies. In B. Rittenhouse & D. Spillers (Eds.), *The electronic classroom: Using technology to create a 21st century curriculum* (pp. 143–164). Wellington, New Zealand: Omega.

Scherer, M. J. (2000). *Living in the state of stuck: How technology impacts the lives of people with disabilities* (3rd ed.). Cambridge, MA: Brookline Books.

Scherer, M. J. (2001). Matching consumers with appropriate assistive technologies. In D. A. Olson & F. DeRuyter (Eds.), *Clinician's guide to assistive technology* (pp. 3–13). St. Louis, MO: Mosby.

Scherer, M. J. (Ed.). (2002a). *Assistive technology: Matching device and consumer for successful rehabilitation*. Washington, DC: American Psychological Association.

Scherer, M. J. (2002b). The change in emphasis from people to person: Introduction to the special issue on assistive technology. *Disability and Rehabilitation, 24*, 1–4.

Scherer, M. J., & Binder, G. E. (1992). *The Department of Science and Engineering Support (DSES): A phase three report of student perceptions* (NTID Working Paper). Rochester, NY: National Technical Institute for the Deaf.

Scherer, M. J., & Craddock, G. (2001, January/February). Applying the Matching Person and Technology evaluation process. *Library Hi Tech News, 18*(1), 40–42.

Scherer, M. J., & Craddock, G. (2002). Matching Person and Technology (MPT) assessment process [Special issue: The assessment of assistive technology outcomes, effects and costs]. *Technology & Disability, 14*, 125–131.

Scherer, M. J., & Cushman, L. C. (2001). Measuring subjective quality of life following spinal cord injury: A validation study of the assistive technology device predisposition assessment. *Disability and Rehabilitation, 23*, 387–393.

Scherer, M. J., & Cushman, L. A. (2002). Determining the content for an interactive training programme and interpretive guidelines for the assistive technology device predisposition assessment. *Disability and Rehabilitation, 24*, 126–130.

Scherer, M. J., & Frisina, D. R. (1994). Applying the Matching People With Technologies Model to individuals with hearing loss: What people say they want—and need—from assistive technologies. *Technology & Disability: Deafness and Hearing Impairments, 3*(1), 62–68.

Scherer, M. J., & Frisina, D. R. (1998). Characteristics associated with marginal hearing loss and subjective well-being among a sample of older adults. *Journal of Rehabilitation Research and Development, 35*, 420–426.

Scherer, M., & McKee, B. (1991, April). *The development of two instruments assessing the predispositions people have toward technology use: The value of integrating quantitative and qualitative methods*. Paper presented at the annual meeting of the American Educational Research Association, Chicago. (ERIC Document Reproduction Service No. TM 016 608).

Scherer, M., & McKee, B. (1992, April). *Early validity and reliability data for two instruments assessing the predispositions people have toward technology use: Continued integration of quantitative and qualitative methods*. Paper presented at the annual meeting of the American Educational Research Association, San Francisco. (ERIC Document Reproduction Service No. ED 346 124).

Scherer, M. J., & McKee, B. G. (1994a). Assessing predispositions to technology use in special education: Music education majors score with the "Survey of Technology Use." In M. Binion (Ed.), *Proceedings of the RESNA '94 annual conference* (pp. 194–196). Arlington, VA: RESNA Press.

Scherer, M. J., & McKee, B. G. (1994b). *The views of adult deaf learners and institutions serving deaf learners regarding distance learning cooperative arrangements with NTID/RIT: The results of two surveys.* Paper presented at the annual meeting of the American Educational Research Association, New Orleans, LA. (ERIC Document Reproduction No. ED 377 214)

Scherer, M. J., McKee, B. G., & Keefe, B. (1994, April). *Distance learning, interactive technologies, and student learning: Which students blossom and which wilt?* Paper presented at the annual meeting of the American Educational Research Association, New Orleans, LA.

Scherer, M. J., McKee, B. G., & Young, M. A. (1990). *The Educational Technology Predisposition Assessment (ET PA).* Rochester, NY: Institute for Matching Person & Technology.

Scherer, M. J., & Sax, C. (in press). Technology in rehabilitation counseling. In T. F. Riggar & D. R. Maki (Eds.), *Rehabilitation counseling: Professional and practical issues.* New York: Springer.

Schiller, J. (1997). The role of primary school leaders in integrating information technology: A longitudinal study. In B. Conners & T. d'Arbon (Eds.). *Change, Challenge and Creative Leadership: International Perspective on Research and Practice.* Hawthorn: Australian Council for Educational Research.

Schirmer, B. R. (2001). *Psychological, social, and educational dimensions of deafness.* Boston: Allyn & Bacon.

Seppa, N. (1997, July). Hard-of-hearing clients often hide their disability. *APA Monitor,* p. 28.

Simonson, M., Sweeney, J., & Kemis, M. (1993). The Iowa distance education alliance. *Tech Trends, 38*(1), 25–28.

Smart, J. (1999). Issues in rehabilitation distance education. *Rehabilitation Education, 13,* 187–206.

Smith, R. O. (2002). OTFACT: Multi-level performance-oriented software with an assistive technology outcomes assessment protocol. *Technology & Disability, 14,* 133–139.

SRI International. (1993). *The transition experiences of young people with disabilities.* Palo Alto, CA: Author.

STATEMENT Pilot Programme. (2000). *Evaluation report.* Dublin, Republic of Ireland: Author.

Sternberg, R. (1998). Principles of teaching for successful intelligence. *Educational Psychologist, 33*(2/3), 65–72.

Stinson, M., & McKee, B. (2000). *Speech recognition as a support service for deaf and hard-of-hearing students: Adaptation and evaluation* (Year 2 annual progress report to the Spencer Foundation). Rochester, NY: National Technical Institute for the Deaf.

Stinson, M. S., Scherer, M. J., & Walter, G. G. (1988). Factors affecting persistence of deaf college students. *Research in Higher Education, 27,* 244–258.

Strassler, B. (1999). *Deafdigest Gold, 3*(32). Retrieved July 20, 2000, from http://www.deafdigest.com/Gold/index.html

Technology-Related Assistance for Individuals With Disabilities Act of 1988, Pub. L. 100-407, 29 U.S.C. 2201 et seq.

Tehama County Department of Education. (2002). *Learning pyramid.* Bethel, MA: National Training Laboratories. Retrieved December 12, 2002, from http://www.tcde.tehama.k12.ca.us/pyramid.pdf

Telecommunications Act of 1996, Pub. A. No. 104-104, 110 Stat. 56 (1996).

Thomas, A. J. (1985). *Acquired hearing loss: Psychological and psychosocial implications.* San Diego, CA: Academic Press.

Tobias, C. U. (1996). *The way they learn.* Wheaton, IL: Tyndale House.

Tomlinson, C. A. (1999). *The differential classroom: Responding to the needs of all learners.* Alexandria, VA: Association for Supervision & Curriculum Development.

Tuttle, D. W., & Tuttle, N. R. (1996). *Self-esteem and adjusting with blindness: The process of responding to life's demands.* New York: Charles C Thomas.

Tyler, R. S., & Schum, D. J. (1995). *Assistive devices for persons with hearing impairment.* Boston: Allyn & Bacon.

University of Illinois at Urbana-Champaign, Graduate School of Library and Information Science. (May, 2002). *Library services to patrons with blindness and visual impairments: Adaptive and assistive equipment.* Champaign, IL: Author. Retrieved May 7, 2003, from http://alexia.lis.uiuc.edu/~lis405/special/blind.htm

U.S. Department of Education, National Center for Education Statistics. (2000). *Digest of education statistics.* Retrieved April 28, 2003, from http://nces.ed.gov/pubs2001/digest/

U.S. Department of Education, Office of Special Education and Rehabilitative Services. (1998a). *Twentieth report to Congress on the implementation of the Individuals with Disabilities Education Act.* Washington, DC: Author.

U.S. Department of Education, Office of Special Education and Rehabilitative Services. (1998b). *To assure the free appropriate public education of all children with disabilities: Twentieth annual report to Congress on the implementation of the Individuals With Disabilities Education Act* (Code of Federal Regulations, Title 34, Section 300.7, 1995). Washington, DC: Author.

U.S. Department of Education, Office of Special Education and Rehabilitative Services. (2001). *Annual report to Congress on the implementation of the Individuals With Disabilities Education Act.* Washington, DC: Author.

Vanderheiden, G. (1994, July). *Technologies for access to information and instruction.* Plenary presentation for the conference, "National Symposium on Educational Applications of Technology for Persons With Sensory Disabilities," Rochester, NY.

Vanderheiden, G. (2001a, August). *Development of generic accessibility/ability usability design guidelines for electronic and information technology products.* Paper presented at the First International Conference on Universal Access in Human–Computer Interaction, New Orleans, LA.

Vanderheiden, G. (2001b). Fundamentals and priorities for design of information and telecommunication technologies. In W. F. E. Preiser & E. Ostroff (Eds.), *Universal design handbook* (pp. 65.3–65.15). New York: McGraw Hill.

Vanderheiden, G., & Tobias, J. (2002). *Universal design of consumer products: Current industry practice and perceptions.* Retrieved December 17, 2002, from http://trace.wisc.edu/docs/ud_consumer_products_hfes2000/

VandeVusse L., & Hanson, L. (2000). Evaluation of online course discussions: Faculty facilitation of active student learning. *Computers in Nursing, 18,* 181–188.

Vernon, M., & Andrews, J. F. (1995). *The psychology of deafness: Understanding deaf and hard-of-hearing people.* Washington, DC: Gallaudet University Press.

Vincent, C., & Morin, G. (1999). L'Utilisation ou non des aides techniques: Comparaison d'un modele americain aux besoins de la realite quebecoise [The use of technical aids: Comparison of the American model with the needs and realities of Quebec]. *Canadian Journal of Occupational Therapy, 66,* 92–101.

Wallhagen, M. I., Strawbridge, W. J., Shema, S. J., Kurata, J., & Kaplan, G. A. (2001). Comparative impact of hearing and vision impairment on subsequent functioning. *Journal of the American Geriatrics Society, 49,* 1086–1092.

Wessels, R., Persson, J., Lorentsen, O., Andrich, R., Ferrario, M., Oortwijn, W., et al. (2002). IPPA: Individually Prioritized Problem Assessment. *Technology & Disability, 14,* 141–145.

Withrow, F. B. (1991, August 4). *Stars schools: The cutting edge* (Working paper). Washington, DC: U.S. Department of Education.

World Health Organization. (2001). *International Classification of Functioning, Disability, and Health.* Geneva: World Health Organization.

Wormsley, D. P. (2000). *Braille literacy curriculum.* Philadelphia: Towers Press, Overbrook School for the Blind.

Yalom, I. (1995). *The theory and practice of group psychotherapy* (4th ed.). New York: Basic Books.

Zabala, J. S. (1995). *The SETT framework: Critical areas to consider when making informed assistive technology decisions.* Houston, TX: Region IV Education Service Center. (ERIC Document Reproduction Service No. ED 381 962)

Zapf, S. A., & Rough, R. B. (2002). The development of an instrument to match individuals with disabilities and service animals. *Disability and Rehabilitation, 24,* 47–58.

SUBJECT INDEX

Braille 'n Speak notetaker
    BrailleNote comparison with, 36–39
    description by a user, *37, 38, 39*
    invention and description of, 36–39
    levels of, 38–39
Bravin, P., *23–24, 147–148*
    on flexibility in captioning, *112–113*
    research findings from National Captioning Institute, *113–114*

Captioning
    audible but unspoken information and, 113
    closed, 110, 111
    color-coding of speakers and, 112
    decoders for, 111, 122
    live-display, 111
    open, 111
    real-time, 111
    use of, 116
Caregivers
    involvement in Individualized Education Programs, 93
Central hearing loss, 25
Charlie
    experience of
        at New York State School for the Blind, 71
    user and instructor of Braille 'n Speak, 37
Children
    assistive technology use by, 99
    computer use by
        ability by age levels, 129
        freedom and experimentation in, 128
        programs that are fun, 127–128
        success for, 128–139
    with disabilities
        U.S. organizations sites focused on, 253
    hearing loss in, 26, 28–29
        range and effects of, 27
        technologies and accommodations for, 26, 27
    Matching Assistive Technology and CHild (MATCH), 187
    school-age
        disabilities in, 9

    transfer from one school to another, 100, 101
    vision loss in, 26, 29–30
Chong, C., *219*
Closed captioning
    decoding of, 111, 112–113
    glossaries and, 113
    versus open captioning, 111
    Telecommunications Act of 1996 and, 110
Cochlear implants
    description of, 95–96
    Section 504, 1998 amendments to Rehabilitation Act of 1973, 96
College/university
    assistive devices in
        Statement of Need for, 215, 235–236
        transition to work/lifelong learning, 218–220
    disability support offices in, 216
    factors in success of, 217
    faculty advisory committee for, 217–218
    AT training of, 217
Communication
    by persons with hearing loss and their communicators, 28–29
Communication competence, 6
Computer
    in deaf students' classroom discussion, 152
    interaction between blind or deaf teachers and deaf students, 136, 137
    software for, 154
Computer access technology(ies), 193–194
    for college students
        assistive technology device predictive assessment of, 193–194
    computer display and output, 115–116
    keyboards, 116–117
    matching user with, 118–119
    mice, 117
    pointers, 117
    switch access, 117
    voice input with speech recognition software, 116

for success, 170–180
personal goals of, 171
transitioning to post-secondary
school or employment, 198
use of technology and, 158
with vision loss and hearing loss
characteristics of, 83
Support
for computer access technologies,
119
hearing loss and, 66
of peers, 50, 54
Support groups
for persons with hearing loss, 50, 52
Survey of Technology Use (SOTU)
in Matching Person and Technology, 189
reliability and validity of, 194
Synthesized voice output (screen readers), 34–35
Systematic Template for Assessing Technology Enabling Mainstream Education (STATEMENT) Pilot
Programme. *See* STATEMENT
(Systematic Template Enabling
Mainstream Education) Program

Teachers
attitudes toward technology and,
174
of disabled persons
preparation and screening of, *100*
expectations of students, 172–173
Teaching
learning relationship with, 212, 213
Technology
barriers to use of, 105–106
in curriculum design, 154
delivery systems
in instruction design, 154
explosion of, effect of, 55
instructional
for children and adults, 152
strategies for, 155
teacher education for, 152–153
intrinsic factors and in use of, 158
for leaner with vision or hearing
loss, 156
as marker of disability and difference, 129–130

matching with student, 156, 172–
173, 175, 178. *See also* Matching Person and Technology
(MPT)
selection of, 178
subject content of, 155
use by students, 147–157
influence on, 158
instructional design for, 154
needs and preferences and,
148–149
usefulness for individual user, 153,
156
Telecommunication
devices for persons with hearing loss,
13, 14
speech recognition in, 151
Telecommunications Act of 1996
manufacturers and, 110
service providers and, 110–111
Telephone devices (TT or TTY)
conversation abbreviations for, 12
description of, *12*
for persons with hearing loss, 11–13,
14
relay services for, 13
Television
captioned
uses of, 114
Touch cane (Hoover) technique, 77
Transitions
from college/university
to work/lifelong learning,
218–220
from secondary education
to college/university, 214–218

Universal design
for accessibility and usability, 105
advantages and disadvantages of,
114–115
of information and educational systems, 153
in learning, movement for, 114
of products and systems, 114
U.S. Department of Education
Office of Special Education and
Rehabilitative Services
change from exclusive to inclusive environment, *78–79*

U.S. Department of Education, *continued*
Office of Special Education Programs
educational environment definitions, 61–63
service statistics, ages 6–21, 60–62
service to hearing and visually impaired students, 64–65
Usability, technology selection for, 178

Validity
of Matching Person and Technology assessments
concurrent, 192
construct, 192
criterion related, 192–193
predictive, 193
Vincent, C., *193*
Virtual reality systems
applications of, 149–150
for people who are blind, 149–150
Vision loss
accommodations for, 30–32
Braille 'n Speak notetaker, 36–39
categories of, 13–14
in children, 26, 29–30
communication strategies for persons and communicators with, 31–32
educational implications of, 6, *16*
Erikson's stages of psychosocial development and, 43–44
experience as employee, 219, 220
experience of blind person, *4, 5*
incidence of, 6–9, *7*
independent reading and writing and, 4, 30–31

Janet, 44–45
negative impact of, 54
prevalence of, 6–9, *7*
psychosocial learning and behavioral changes in, 48
self-esteem and, 48
in students
accommodations for, 211
technologies for, 14–15, 32–40
braille, 32–34
optical character recognition, 34
Opticon (Optical to Tactile Conversion), 34
refreshable braille keyboard, 35–36
screen readers, 34–35
Visual impairment. *See also* Blind people/students
increase in students served, 60–61
as Individuals With Disabilities Education Act (disability type, 81
service for
educational environments for, 65
Voice input, 116

Web sites
access to, 125–126, 142
World Health Organization Disability Assessment Schedule revised (WHODAS II)
concurrent validity with Survey of Technology Use, 194
Writing
vision loss and, 4, 30–31

ABOUT THE AUTHOR

Marcia J. Scherer is director of the Institute for Matching Persons and Technology in Webster, New York. She is also associate professor of physical medicine and rehabilitation at the University of Rochester Medical Center and senior research associate at the International Center for Hearing and Speech Research (a joint program of the University of Rochester and the National Technical Institute for the Deaf/Rochester Institute of Technology). She received a PhD and an MPH from the University of Rochester.

Dr. Scherer is author of *Living in the State of Stuck: How Assistive Technology Impacts the Lives of People With Disabilities* (3rd ed., 2000) and editor of *Assistive Technology: Matching Device and Consumer for Successful Rehabilitation* (American Psychological Association, 2002). She is coeditor (with Jan Galvin) of *Evaluating, Selecting, and Using Appropriate Assistive Technology* (1996) and coeditor (with Laura Cushman) of *Psychological Assessment in Medical Rehabilitation* (American Psychological Association, 1995), which is Volume 1 in the American Psychological Association (APA) Measurement and Instrumentation in Psychology series.

Dr. Scherer has written widely on technology, is currently on the editorial board of the journal *Disability and Rehabilitation*, and has served on the editorial boards of *Assistive Technology* and *Technology and Disability*. She is a fellow of the APA in Division 22 (Rehabilitation Psychology) and Division 21 (Applied Experimental and Engineering Psychology). She is also a fellow of the American Congress of Rehabilitation Medicine and is a member of the American Association of Spinal Cord Injury Psychologists and Social Workers, the American Educational Research Association, the Rehabilitation Engineering and Assistive Technology Society of North America, the Council for Exceptional Children, and the New York Academy of Sciences.